DEATH IN ROCKY MOUNTAIN NATIONAL PARK

DEATH IN ROCKY MOUNTAIN NATIONAL PARK

*Accidents and Foolhardiness
on the Continental Divide*

RANDI MINETOR

Guilford, Connecticut

An imprint of The Rowman & Littlefield Publishing Group, Inc.
4501 Forbes Blvd., Ste. 200
Lanham, MD 20706
www.rowman.com

Distributed by NATIONAL BOOK NETWORK

British Library Cataloguing in Publication Information available

Library of Congress Cataloging-in-Publication Data

Names: Minetor, Randi, author.
Title: Death in Rocky Mountain National Park : accidents and foolhardiness on the Continental Divide / Randi Minetor.
Description: Guilford, Connecticut : Lyons Press, 2020. | Series: Death in the parks series | Includes bibliographical references and index. | Summary: "A collection of stories about park visitors who have died in Rocky Mountain National Park."— Provided by publisher.
Identifiers: LCCN 2019041592 (print) | LCCN 2019041593 (ebook) | ISBN 9781493038787 (paperback) | ISBN 9781493038794 (epub)
Subjects: LCSH: Rocky Mountain National Park (Colo.)—History—Anecdotes. | Accidents—Colorado—Rocky Mountain National Park—Anecdotes. | Violent deaths—Colorado—Rocky Mountain National Park—Anecdotes. | Missing persons—Colorado—Rocky Mountain National Park)—Anecdotes.
Classification: LCC F782.R59 M556 2020 (print) | LCC F782.R59 (ebook) | DDC 978.8/69—dc23
LC record available at https://lccn.loc.gov/2019041592
LC ebook record available at https://lccn.loc.gov/2019041593

CONTENTS

ACKNOWLEDGMENTS

A BOOK OF THIS LENGTH, SCOPE, AND MAGNITUDE CAN'T COME TO be on its own, so I am grateful once again to everyone at Lyons Press for their participation in bringing it to fruition, especially my editor, Holly Rubino; production editor Meredith Dias; copy editor Melissa Hayes; layout artist Kerry Handel; and proofreader Shana Jones.

Don Hunter, science director at the Rocky Mountain Cat Conservancy, met with me during my site visit to Rocky Mountain and provided terrific insights about the mountain lion population in and around the park. I have relied on Craig Fuller at Aviation Archaeological Investigation and Research for information about plane crashes in national parks, and he came through once again for this book.

Most of all, I thank Regina Ryan, my agent of fourteen years, who keeps me from bankrupting myself for love of writing by helping me land projects like this one. And to all of the friends who support and encourage my writing and who are still there to forgive my long absences from the land of the living, I give my undying gratitude: Ken Horowitz and Rose-Anne Moore, Martin Winer, Paula and Rich Landis, Martha and Peter Schermerhorn, Ruth Watson and John King, Cindy Blair, Lorraine Woerner-MacGowan, Lisa Jaccoma, Bil Walters and Christine Tattersall, and all the people on the periphery who still seem happy to see me when these projects come to their logical end.

Finally, to my husband Nic, who puts up with the creepiest dinner-table conversations of any household we know, who does my laundry and makes sure I eat and get enough sleep, and who still loves me after thirty-five years together . . . I could not do what I do without you, my love.

INTRODUCTION

WE ARRIVED AT THE LONGS PEAK RANGER STATION ON THE LAST day of August 2018, and instantly noted the tension in the air.

This was my husband's and my first visit to Rocky Mountain National Park, our third day of a reconnaissance trip so I could familiarize myself with the park, its most concentrated areas of activity, and its rich history. I was in the process of writing *Historic Rocky Mountain National Park* for Lyons Press, and would soon begin, for the same publisher, my sixth book in the series that details the real-life accounts of deaths in the national parks. Already I found myself a bit overwhelmed by the frequency with which people went missing, sustained injuries serious enough to require rescue, and lost their lives in Rocky Mountain.

Such activity appeared to be happening on Longs Peak at that very moment. I spotted a man with a radio in his hand, sitting at a picnic table outside of the ranger station, and casually made my way over to him just as his radio finished crackling and went still.

"Would you be a good person to ask about some basic safety stuff on Longs Peak?" I asked him.

He glanced at the radio, sighed heavily, and then smiled at me. "This is a good day to ask that," he said. "I'd be happy to tell you about safety up there."

I sat down, introduced myself, and we chatted. He told me he was a volunteer in the park, and had worked search-and-rescue operations for many years. He explained the things everyone needs to know about taking on a climb to the top of the highest mountain in the park—the information you'll find in the epilogue of this book.

People often arrive at the park with the sole purpose of climbing the park's only "fourteener," the one peak over fourteen thousand feet, without the slightest idea of what they might be getting themselves into before they go.

The affable volunteer told me some of the stories found in the first three chapters of this book—about people who took on more than they could handle, ignored warnings from rangers and other climbers, underestimated the difficulty of this climb, forgot to check the weather forecast, or blithely wandered off into the wilderness without so much as a bottle of water to sustain them.

Then the radio crackled again. He inclined his head toward it briefly.

"There's one up there now," he said.

"Someone injured?"

"We hope he's just injured," the volunteer said, and let it go at that.

The following day, Nic and I drove into the park from the Fall River entrance, and as we approached Beaver Meadows, we saw a contingent of rangers and vehicles parked on a paved pad in the middle of the clearing. As we watched, a helicopter circled and landed on the pad. The pilot and others got out and spoke to the rangers, and stood waiting for . . . something.

Not until much later did I determine that they were waiting for the coroner's vehicle. Search-and-rescue teams had located the body of Jens "Jay" Yambert, a 62-year-old man who had been missing for several days, and this was the meeting point to transport his remains out of the park.

I found myself shaken by the immediacy of this. While working on the other five books I'd written in this series, I had never encountered an accident in progress, though some of the stories I've retold to readers have truly moved me to tears. None of the other parks in my books, however, have the sheer volume of search-and-rescue operations in a year that Rocky Mountain National Park must initiate. The park with the highest mountains and some of the most volatile weather in the national park system, and the third-most-visited national park in the United States, gets more than its fair share of injuries and fatalities.

What kind of numbers are we talking about? My research turned up 333 deaths, though I have seen quotes in newspapers that suggest there might be even more. Seventy-three people have died on Longs Peak alone, in mishaps ranging from heart attacks to long tumbles down thousand-foot cliffs. A whopping 104 people have died in falls—some of these on Longs Peak, but many on other mountains throughout the park. In fact, so many people have died from falls in this park that I had to respect my publisher's limits on word count (which I had already exceeded rather significantly), and leave the twenty-eight deaths from motor vehicle accidents out of the narrative in order to fit all the falling victims into the manuscript. One day there will be a second edition of this book, and I will detail the auto and motorcycle accidents then.

Fifteen people perished from hypothermia—what medical science used to call "exposure"—on Longs Peak, as well as Flattop Mountain, Mount Alice, and deep in the forest. Thirteen died from lightning strikes, many of these along Trail Ridge Road in the highest elevations a visitor can reach by car. And seventeen people have drowned in the park, three of them in the Lawn Lake Flood disaster in 1982, an event so dramatic that I gave it its own chapter.

The rest are a miscellany of avalanches (6), plane crashes (11 people in 7 incidents), rockslides (3), accidents involving winter sports (5), a bizarre moment when a tree fell on a visitor, horses throwing their riders (3), 2 homicides, and a single mountain lion attack that killed a ten-year-old boy, the only animal-attack death in the park's history.

More than eighty people died of heart attacks and other medical issues, and while these are listed in the book's appendix, they are not detailed in the text because such deaths usually escape the media's attention, so their backstories are largely lost to history. In addition, a startling twenty-nine people have chosen Rocky Mountain as the last place they would see before taking their own lives. People's reasons for suicide are none of my business, and I don't wish to encourage this practice in the parks, so I no longer write about them. You'll find their names in the appendix, as well.

Six people have been lost in the park and never found. One of these, James Pruitt, disappeared while I was writing this book. While the remains of Micah Tice were discovered in July of 2019, James Pruitt was still missing at the time of publication. (You can check our Facebook page, @minetorbooks, for articles that bring together all of the new information since this book's publication.)

Now, on a personal note, I want to be sure that you understand that while I have written many hiking books, I am not a climber—and for good reason. I have an inherited heart defect known as hypertrophic cardiomyopathy, the same condition that causes sudden-death heart attack in otherwise-healthy high school athletes. Exertion at high elevations could pop my heart like a balloon, so climbing is not an option for me. For this reason, I have left the highly technical explanations of climbs gone wrong to experts who can speak to these errors on discussion boards and websites, like the American Alpine Club's accident reports, and simplified the descriptions so that non-climbers like me can understand what happened.

In a nutshell, this is a book of stories about people going to a magnificent place expecting to have the time of their lives, and coming home dead. There is no kinder way to say this, and I bring it up now to clarify my motives in writing detailed accounts of such cases in our national parks. Read these stories and take the lessons they provide to heart, with the understanding that in each case there is a misstep, a moment at which the result could go the safe way or another way. Mindfulness of the potential for these miscalculations will help you to avoid such consequences in your own visit to Rocky Mountain, making your trip to this spectacular wilderness as exciting as you wish—but with just a little less danger, a little more self-awareness, and a great deal more fun. If, while reading this, you find that you know more details about any of these incidents, or if I've left out anyone (the full list of deaths is in this book's appendix), please contact me at author@minetor.com, on Twitter @rminetor, or on Facebook @minetorbooks.

My goal is not to scare you—quite the contrary. I urge you to visit Rocky Mountain National Park and explore to your heart's content, whether you experience it primarily by car and on easy, level trails or climb to the top of the park and venture deep into the backcountry on foot. Just don't give me the opportunity to include your untimely demise in the next edition of this book. Enjoy the park with the Ten Essentials for hiking safely in your backpack (see this book's epilogue for the list), heed the advice of rangers who know this park better than you do, and watch where you step on talus slopes and scree-covered ledges. Have the time of your life. Just be careful out there.

CHAPTER 1

Cold Comfort:
Deaths from Hypothermia

GOING WEST BECAME THE DARING AND FASHIONABLE THING FOR the very wealthy to do in the late 1800s, and Caroline Josephine Welton, known as Carrie to her friends, could not wait to get there. She and several friends undertook a journey in the summer of 1884 that began with a long train ride from the eastern United States, followed by a stagecoach drive and many more miles on horseback. Welton left the rest of her party in Colorado Springs and proceeded alone to Estes Park—the center of alpine-style hospitality—and once she had braved the twenty-mile ride through the Big Thompson River canyon and arrived in Estes Park, she could explore to her heart's content and challenge her own perceptions of her body's strength and resiliency. At the end of her hectic, uncomfortable journey came the reward: the vast, sparkling view of the Rocky Mountains.

The *Boston Globe* described Welton as "an accomplished young lady, who was passionately fond of natural scenery and loved the open air." History remembers her as "a tall, dark-complexioned and striking looking woman," who received a high-priced education and had "a propensity to do uncommon things and achieve a reputation for courage and physical endurance." A woman of considerable wealth and a "brilliant" horsewoman, she spent her summer riding to every point of interest she could reach on horseback.

Open land surrounded her, but one slate-gray mountain captivated her and drew her to it, making her long for the view from its topmost point. Longs Peak rises to 14,259 feet above the land that in 1915 would become Rocky Mountain National Park, the tallest mountain in the park and one of the highest in Colorado. She could see the snow and ice that clung to its peak, and the many steep, jagged walls of rock that stood between her position at roughly 7,500 feet above sea level and its towering apex, but she had climbed mountains before—in fact, she had hiked to the top of Pike's Peak and Gray's Peak earlier in the summer. The *Boston Globe* quoted a gentleman who knew her about the Gray's Peak climb: "She spoke rapturously of the beauty of the scenery she viewed as the reward of these feats, and expressed regret that in her ascent of Gray's Peak she was unable to remain among the clouds longer, because her lady companion had become faint and was obliged to give up the climb."

Welton corresponded with friends at home about her desire to scale Longs Peak, as the *Globe* noted: "From all she had heard and read of the journey, she expected that it would be the roughest mountain trip she had every attempted." She believed that she could acquire this summit if she selected the right guide, however, even though summer had waned and the first autumn chill had turned the evening dew to frost overnight.

On Monday, September 22, she left Estes Park alone to ride seven miles to the base of Longs Peak. Here she met Reverend Elkanah Lamb, proprietor of Longs Peak House, and his family. Lamb had made a name for himself as a mountain guide, a business he began in 1871 when he led a party up Longs Peak—not because he was the first to do this (he wasn't), but because he was the only person in the party to reach the summit. While the rest of the climbers turned around and made their way back down the Keyhole Route, Lamb took a much more difficult and largely untried route down the East Face. When he arrived at a particularly steep, eight-hundred-foot slope, he slipped on the ice and began to slide, whooshing down the mountain until he managed to grab at a rock that jutted out from the 70-degree trough. With no climbing equipment except a pocketknife, Lamb broke through some ice under his feet and made a step that he could stand on to get his bearings—but the knife snapped and broke, so he found himself once again in as precarious a position as he could imagine. Somehow he made his way to the bottom without further mishap, but history immortalized his epic descent by naming this difficult passage Lambs Slide.

Lamb himself declined to guide Welton up Longs Peak, but he offered the services of his son, Carlyle, who at roughly twenty years old had been up the mountain with many parties. They struck a deal, and Carrie spent the night at Longs Peak House with plans to start out early with Carlyle in the morning.

As the sun rose, the two packed their gear and food and headed out on horseback up the Longs Peak trail. They could ride all the way to Chasm Lake, some three and a half miles hence, and on to the Boulderfield, a wide area of large rocks that signals the change in terrain from this point forward. Here, on the upper edge of the tree line, they left their horses and proceeded on foot. Five hours had passed since they had left the trailhead, and now deep snow covered the trail, a major shift from the warm, sunny day that had greeted them at the outset. "The banks of snow would bear the weight of men, while the horses would break through," a lengthy analysis by an unnamed writer in the Sunday *News-Dealer* in Wilkes-Barre, Pennsylvania, explained.

From their vantage point just above the Boulderfield, Welton and Lamb could see low-hanging clouds not far over their heads.

They removed all of their warmest clothing from their packs and put it on over their hiking clothes. Welton "was warmly clad in a black alapaca [*sic*] dress and black broadcloth riding pants, a heavy black alapaca sacque [shapeless robe], an elegant silk dolman [robe], trimmed in astrackan [*sic*] fur; a heavy cashmere shawl and a ladies' waterproof," the writer said. "On her person was a five-shot Smith & Wesson revolver, with two charges remaining. An elegant gold watch was fastened to the dress with a black silk cord, and in her bosom was a chamois skin bag containing three costly rings, one a diamond valued at $1,000."

They still had four miles to go to reach the summit, so they plodded on with determination. "This ascent was made after much tedious delay and hard work, the top of the black peak being reached about 4 o'clock in the afternoon," the writer noted. "Their stay on the peak was not long in duration."

Not only could they see that the clouds would bring darkness early, but they also realized that a storm had begun below them, "the dark clouds being tumbled about in frightful confusion." Carlyle Lamb knew what Welton could only guess: The storm would make an already demanding descent even more problematic, adding wet, icy conditions that would soak their clothing and turn rocks into icy slides. Earlier, he had recommended that they turn around and wait for another day to summit the peak, but Welton would have none of it. She had come this far and was within a few hundred feet of the top; she would not go home without her summit.

After an hour's rest at the top, Welton and Lamb began the route down. Soon they reached the clouds and descended to a point beneath them, and just as they thought their visibility would improve without the moist shroud hanging around their heads, the clouds played yet another trick on the pair. They opened up and dumped a whiteout snowstorm on top of the climbers—"the heaviest, the guide says, he ever saw on the mountain," the *News-Dealer* reported.

Now Welton knew she might have taken on a greater challenge than she could endure. She began to declare that she was too tired to go on, enough so that young Lamb needed to hold and support her to keep her on her feet. After two and a half miles of this, with another mile and a half to go before they reached the horses, Welton collapsed in the snow, too exhausted to go another step. Lamb picked her up and attempted to carry her, but adding the woman's 140 pounds to his own burden in the deep, blowing snow and darkness made progress virtually impossible. "For two hours he plodded with his heavy burden, and was only able to make two-thirds of a mile," the anonymous chronicler said.

Five hours had passed since they had left the summit, and now Lamb knew that his own strength and endurance had reached their limits. At about ten p.m., Lamb sat down on a rock and explained to Welton that they had only one chance for survival: He would have to leave her here, sheltered somewhat behind a rock, while he proceeded alone to their horses and rode back for help. Welton objected, no doubt certain that while she could no longer put one foot in front of the other, staying here alone and immobile could only result in her death. In the end, however, she could not refute his logic, especially with her brain and body depleted by numbing cold.

"After bidding Miss Welton farewell, the guide made the greatest possible speed," the news reporter continued. "The moon had now arose and materially aided [him] on his way. The horses were found as they had been left, and mounting one of these and leading the other, young Lamb hurried to his father's cabin, seven miles away. He made this distance in an hour and informed his father of what had occurred."

There could be no rest for Carlyle Lamb until Carrie Welton was safe at Longs Peak House, so Elkanah Lamb and his son saddled two fresh horses and headed back down the trail and up the mountain. By the time they reached Welton, their watches told them it was past four a.m. Carrie lay stretched out in the snow, quite dead.

"Her features were placid," the newspaper report tells us. "Sleepiness, the result of the cold, had evidently overcome her soon after the departure of her guide, and she had lain down in the snow bank, well knowing the fate which would soon overtake her." Then the reporter felt the need to provide us with an inventory of her belongings: "Beside her was an ivory-handled riding whip, with her name and place of residence engraved thereon, and in her belt was a handsomely mounted revolver. Her heavy kid gloves had been removed, and her diamond-bedecked hands were covered in the snow."

As the dark before the dawn began to lighten, the two men determined the best way to carry the body between them, and they started the long return trip to their cabin. It was nine a.m. before they arrived there, but they immediately sent for the local justice of the peace to be sure that Welton's death was properly recorded. The justice "had the body placed in a box, and then had it conveyed by a wagon to Longmont, a distance of sixty miles, where it arrived on the 27th ult., and was received by friends who had come from Colorado Springs." The friends accompanied Welton's body back to New York.

This is the story as originally told by Carlyle Lamb to the local media. Accounts by others involved on the periphery of the events of September 22 and 23, 1884, however, remember it somewhat differently.

It seems that the owner of the livery stable, H. W. Gilbert, drove Welton up to Longs Peak House personally on the evening of

September 21, and she gave him instructions to return to the house two days later, at precisely eight a.m., to pick her up and bring her back to Estes Park. When Gilbert arrived as promised, Mrs. Lamb told him that Elkanah and Carlyle were up on the mountain bringing Welton down, and that she had died—information she could not know for certain at that point, based on Carlyle's story.

"The liveryman drove up to the timberline and there met the father and son carrying the body of Miss Welton between them," the reporter wrote. "It was then ten o'clock in the morning, and the story that Lamb, the guide, tells about returning immediately after the body will hardly bear investigation, for Miss Welton's body lay, when found, at the further end of a large and barren place on the mountainside, known as Boulderfield, just a mile from where the team had met them. It does not seem probable that it would take two men six hours to carry the body a distance of a mile."

Others who knew Carlyle Lamb did not speak highly of his guiding skills or his bravery, the writer noted. "They think that when he first saw that Miss Welton was taken with a fainting faint at about dark in the evening, he became frightened at the prospect of a night on the mountain, and abandoned her to her fate," he said. "They further say that the father and son did not ascend the peak in search of her until daylight the next morning."

What's more, those involved in transporting the body away from Longs Peak and into Longmont were startled by the number of bruises she had sustained, especially on her face. They speculated that these might indicate that she "had tried to make her way down the trail after being abandoned by the guide, and had repeatedly fallen against the rocks."

No prosecution resulted from these accusations, and the investigation apparently closed without further conclusions. Whatever the facts might be, Carrie Welton got the last laugh on her friends and relatives by doing an extraordinarily good deed as her last bequest. She left her entire fortune—about $300,000, a whopping sum in 1884—to the New York Society for the Prevention of Cruelty to Animals, infuriating her cousins who received pieces of jewelry and other considerations, but no cash. Her mother, who had repeatedly attempted to have Carrie committed to an asylum for the insane because of her strong-willed and independent nature, received nothing in the will at all. Jane Welton and the many cousins contested her daughter's wishes in court and through several appeals, but after a two-year legal battle, the courts ruled in favor of the will and awarded the bequest to the SPCA.

Meanwhile, Carrie's mansion in Waterbury, Connecticut, a property known as Rose Hill, went from being one of the finest homes in town to nearly worthless in the week after her death. Fraught with strife because of Carrie's frequent rows with her mother, the house was abandoned by both women some time before Carrie's trip out west. Rumors abounded among townspeople that the place was haunted, and some claimed manifestations of this: "One of the many freaks of the spirits is the besmirching of the door knob of the best chamber with a substance like coagulated blood, which reappears every morning after being wiped off," the usually sane *St. Louis Post-Dispatch* reprinted from wire reports. "All sorts of stories are in circulation to-day about the old mansion, one of which is that the daughter had been seen in the yard on horseback at midnight. Although the property was put on the market at a low figure, it is impossible to sell it, as it is firmly believed that a curse rests upon it."

Her friends, however, regarded all of this talk of ghosts as nonsense. A week after her death, the *Boston Globe* interviewed a local merchant who knew Welton well. "Miss Welton's adventurous mountain journeys were made simply because she loved to see nature in all its wild grandeur," he said. "She was in love with nature. She shrank instinctively from any notoriety, and would have rebuked anyone who attempted to spread her reputation as a mountain climber. She was fearless and self-reliant, but perfectly refined and unassuming in her character and manners. Her death is a very great blow to her many warm friends."

A LEARNED MAN DISAPPEARS

"The disappearance of Dr. [Thornton R.] Sampson, president of the Texas Presbyterian Seminary and a close personal friend of Woodrow Wilson, then president, inspired the greatest search in the history of Colorado," the *Gaffney Ledger* in South Carolina declared on July 23, 1932.

A story that began in September 1915 had finally reached its conclusion, closing the chapter that had baffled Sampson's family, friends, and many colleagues and associates for nearly seventeen years.

Sampson had served his church and his country well, traveling with his wife to Greece and Turkey as a Presbyterian missionary in 1878 and remaining there until 1892. When he finally returned to the United States, he became synodical secretary of the church's home mission board in North Carolina, living in Greensboro and then Asheville with his family until he was elected president of General Assembly's Home and School in Fredericksburg, Virginia. His upward trajectory did not stop there: He followed his time in Virginia by becoming head of a Presbyterian institution in Sherman, Texas, meanwhile founding a Presbyterian Theological Seminary for the Trans-Mississippi territory. He then made the last move of his career of service, leading the Presbyterian Theological Seminary in Austin.

Throughout his later years, it was Sampson's summer habit to visit the area that in 1915 had just become Rocky Mountain National

Park, going off alone for "a tramp and fishing trip throughout Estes Park," as the *Asheville Gazette-News* described it in September of that year. Sampson, who was 63 years old, kept in touch with his family during a sojourn in Denver while making preparations for his trip, writing to his wife on August 28 that he expected to be back in Denver on September 5.

Cliff Higby, a mountain guide astride a horse, passed Dr. Sampson on September 2 just two miles from Grand Lake on the west side of the park, "attired in heavy underwear, a light cotton suit, wool shirt and without an overcoat," the *Austin American* reported. Dr. Sampson told him he intended to walk twenty-five miles across the park to reach Estes Park by September 5 to attend the dedication exercises for the newly named Rocky Mountain National Park. Higby provided directions to reach Fern Lake, where Dr. Sampson planned to spend the night, and told Sampson that he would tie a red bandana to a cairn—a stack of rocks used as a trail marker—to signal the place to turn. He also said he would leave Sampson a note there with further directions.

At about two p.m. on the same day, Sampson stopped to rest at a shelter and encountered three female travelers and their guide. They stopped briefly and then continued along the way from which Sampson had just come.

Shortly thereafter, the weather changed dramatically, with snow and gale-force winds making further hiking dangerous at best. "The mountain tops are completely enveloped when the clouds become thick and heavy, making it impossible for anyone to see the cairns marking the different routes of trails," Vinson told the Austin paper. "That night it froze, and next day there was a heavy snow and a high wind. The foresters say the snow forms on the mountain tops and with a high wind is swept into the canyons and gulches in terrific gales. The guides told me that the snow is now 40 and 50 feet deep in that region."

He added, "It is believed that the lone traveler [Sampson] either sought safety in a cave, or slipped and fell, later to be covered by snow. Guide Higby's directions were never reached."

Sampson did not emerge from the park on September 5, and the whereabouts of a man known and respected throughout the Southern states quickly became a matter of national concern.

Search parties began to comb the area, and Sampson's wife, Ella Royster Sampson, his son Frank, and two of his three daughters—Mrs. E. T. Drake and Mrs. H. C. Parsons of Orange, Texas—traveled to the Metropole Hotel in Denver from Austin to await news of his discovery. (His third daughter, Mrs. Arthur Woolridge, lived in Toronto, Ontario, Canada.)

"A man has been found who saw the doctor September 3 as he was entering a big gorge," the Asheville paper reported on September 27, three weeks into the search. "The next day there was a severe snow storm accompanied by much lightning. It is the opinion of guides that Dr. Sampson was either killed by lightning or missed his footing in the storm and fell over a precipice."

Frank W. Sampson arrived late on September 15 and joined the search, along with members of the Denver Rotary Club, who had had the pleasure of hearing Dr. Sampson speak at their annual meeting six months earlier. The search now involved hiking and climbing through deep snow to examine the gorge and the surrounding area. "Heavy snow has fallen in the region, and mountaineers believe the chance of finding the aged minister and educator alive is slight," the Associated Press said on September 20, as if beginning to cushion the blow of Sampson's loss for an anxious public. The Denver Rotary made an offer to incent volunteers of all stripes to continue the hunt: The club put up a $500 reward for finding the missing man, dead or alive.

Not everyone believed that Dr. Sampson's disappearance warranted this kind of effort, however. C. B. Kendall of the US Geological Survey told search officials that Dr. Sampson had said something curious on his way out of town. "Dr. Sampson and Mr. Kendall were on a train going to Steamboat Springs at the time and talked together for two hours," the report in the *Austin American* noted. "Dr. Sampson told Kendall he often lost himself in the hills while on hikes as he loved the mountains. 'Dr. Sampson told me that he took this same trip last summer . . . and that twice before he had traversed these routes. He is evidently a good woodsman and could not have lost himself in the forests. I thought him very competent to take care of himself.'" Kendall went so far as to suggest that Dr. Sampson's absence was deliberate, "for the purpose of getting a thorough rest."

This theory did nothing to dampen the resolve of the searchers, who persevered amid continued snow, cold, and wind. A week later, with no new clues coming to light, the *Austin American* again presented all of the theories to date, including some new ones. "George C. Barnard and Morrison Shafroth, members of the Colorado Mountain Club, returned today after a two days' search in the gullies and ravines about Odessa Gorge, with the theory that the aged minister became confused and mistook Mount Otis for Flattop Mountain," the paper reported. "His body may be found at the bottom of some gorge in the vicinity of the first named instead of in any of those at the foot of Flattop, where most of the search has centered."

The two mountaineers had climbed to the summit on the Continental Divide, searching all of the mountain's slides, gorges, and other concealed places as they went, while a second party, including Shep Husted, John Mainburg, and Sam Service, began at the top of the mountain and worked their way down. They completed this search on September 23, but found nothing that could point them in a direction that might lead to Sampson's body.

By this time, the family understood that there was no hope of finding Dr. Sampson alive. They prepared to hold a memorial service at the Austin Presbyterian Theological Seminary, where the beginning of the fall term had been postponed for a week, "in honor of the missing theologian." Seminary president R. E. Vinson traveled to Colorado to assist in the search, returning to assure his colleagues and the community that the effort was being made with "unquestionable thoroughness." Even officials in Washington, DC, gave the search their attention, with Secretary of the Interior Lane and Secretary of Agriculture Houston instructing all of their staff members in Colorado to participate.

Nonetheless, "practically all hope of finding the minister's body is gone," the *Austin American* reported on September 23. Vinson summarized the theories of search officials: "Since the snow will not melt until next August, and then from the inside outward, it is believed the body of the minister will be washed into one of the deep mountain lakes and probably never will be found. The theory that wild beasts attacked him is regarded untenable, since no case is on record of beasts attacking a person in that part of the mountains. The theory that Dr. Sampson was struck by lightning is fallacious, because the body then would be found."

Another "weirdest of many weird stories," noted the *Ottawa Evening Journal* in Kansas, was that Dr. Sampson had taken a "queer companion," a hermit who lived in the hills around Estes Park. Someone posited that this hermit, whom Dr. Sampson mentioned in a letter to his wife, may have murdered the reverend. The fact that those who remembered seeing him on September 2 all said he was alone quickly discredited this idea, however.

Inevitably, as winter set in and nothing indicating a promising new direction came to light, the search came to a close for the time being. Then, on October 2, cattleman Jim Norval of Steamboat Springs discovered the remains of "an aged man, battered by the elements and torn by wild animals," while rounding up his cattle. The skeleton turned up some sixty miles from the place where anyone had last seen Dr. Sampson, a detail explained away by the media as the result of "wild animal attacks," presuming that animals had perhaps dragged the body to its final location.

Forest Service personnel had the body transported to authorities in Yampa, Colorado, for thorough examination. Telegraph messages between these authorities and Ella Sampson flew back and forth, with Mrs. Sampson providing what information she could that might become the telltale clue that this body was what remained of her husband.

Before positive identification could be made, however, the media picked up the story of the body's discovery and ran with it. "Dr. Sampson's Body Found," crowed the *New York Sun*, its story appearing in newspapers throughout the Southern states. This was not the case, however: The identifying markings and other clues Mrs. Sampson provided did not match the body. Sampson's remains still languished somewhere in the mountains.

Vinson did his best to console his constituents in the *Presbyterian of the South* newspaper in early October. "We cannot but bow our heads in humble submission to this mysterious providence of God which has taken from us one of the most useful servants of His Church, as well as an intimate personal friend," he wrote.

Searchers set out once again in the spring when the snow began to melt, but they were no more successful than they had been in September. Slowly, the disappearance of Thornton R. Sampson became one of the park's unsolved mysteries.

That is, until July 1932—seventeen years after Sampson had been given up for lost.

On or around July 13, someone exploring a rocky overhang that formed a cave-like shelter in the park's Fern Valley made the find of a lifetime: the skeletal remains of a man long dead. With the bones were several personal effects that made identification a certainty: Dr. Sampson's pipe, which he had made himself; his diary, "perfectly legible and in good preservation," and his knapsack. Frank Sampson flew from his home in Atlanta, Georgia, to Denver to examine the items and confirm that they did indeed belong to his father.

Frank postulated his own theory of what had happened to Dr. Sampson:

There is no doubt in my mind that [F]ather failed to survive his first night out of Grand Lake. He had been slightly indisposed for a week prior, as his diary records, and while he was a singularly vigorous man for his 63 years, his vitality no doubt was low on this particular day, after a hike of more than seventeen miles and a vertical climb of more than 4,000 feet, passing about midday a point high above the timberline.

My conclusions are these: The weather records show that there were many showers all through that day—evidence substantiated by others who were on the same trail, on horseback. My father's experience led him to this sheltering rock under which nearly everything except his watch and a few coins were found. On the level beneath the jutting rock were found his knapsack, with toilet articles, a can of tobacco, matches and his pipe. I am positive he built a fire, became warm and fell asleep—and that sleep in wet clothing, on a cold September night, at an extremely high altitude, must have proved fatal.

*But for the anxiety his disappearance caused his loved
ones, I cannot imagine my father wishing for a more peaceful
passing—high in the mountains, from which all his life he had
drawn his inspiration.*

THE SNOWS OF AUGUST

Before Doppler radar gave meteorologists the ability to create
detailed forecasts of weather systems as they crossed the country, mountain climbers had to rely on predictions published in
newspapers and their own instincts to keep from being caught in
storms. These rudimentary tools usually provided enough information to keep climbers from venturing out into dangerous thunderstorms or early-season snows. Most mountaineers stayed off
of fourteeners like Longs Peak when winter gales dominated the
landscape, saving their enthusiasm for the late-spring and summer months. Even summer, however, can turn against a climber
on Longs Peak, transforming a sunny day into a freezing torrent
in the space of an hour.

Gerald Clark, 30, encountered just such a day on August 7, 1939.
A commercial photographer from Denver, he had scaled Longs
Peak's East Face five times before this, bringing all the equipment
necessary to do this as safely as possible. He began to scale the wall
with his friends, Eddie Watson, 23, and Edmund Cooper, 32, but
at about 2:20 p.m., he dropped the hammer he used to drive pitons
into the rock. Without the ability to insert more pitons, he could
not go up any farther. Worse, it had begun to rain—hard.

Watson and Cooper both had ample experience climbing
mountains, including Longs Peak, which Cooper had ascended no
less than eight times before this. Watson had made his first climb
of the East Face the previous New Year's Day. They knew enough to
realize that while Clark had reached an overhanging rock before he

dropped his hammer, they couldn't make it to the same place with the sudden change in the weather.

"Cooper was in the lead when we started," Watson told the Grand Junction *Daily Sentinel*. "He tried for an overhanger, but couldn't make it. He came back and he and I agreed it couldn't be made in the rain that was falling then. Cooper and I wanted to turn back, but Clark wanted to try it. He took the lead and made it over the overhanger."

Watson and Cooper called to Clark to come back. "He kept on going up in the Chimney and kept calling back to us for more rope ... He didn't hear us, or pretended not to, and kept on going, calling for more rope until there was only a few feet left."

By this time, they knew that their friend had gone too far, but they had a responsibility to make sure he was safe. "Cooper and I started then to try to get [to] another overhanging ledge to one side," Watson said. "The ledge was nothing less than a waterfall then, with the rain pouring down. It was impossible to get a handhold."

Then Clark dropped his hammer.

"We called up to Clark. He couldn't go any further up and he couldn't start back down because he couldn't drive a petane [*sic*]. We decided Cooper and I should go back for help. All three of us started calling for help but got no answer. There were some people on the peak, but they must have thought we were fooling."

By this time, snow and sleet had started to fall along with the rain. Watson and Cooper managed to get the attention of a guide on the East Face—none other than Walter Kiener, whose legendary climb of the East Face in winter with Agnes Vaille in 1925 is featured in this book, in chapter 3. Kiener was on the mountain with a party from the Colorado Mountain Club, but when the two men conveyed to him that Clark was truly in trouble, he took his party back down the mountain and called for help.

"Cooper and I climbed down," Watson said. "Cooper took a rope and went up to Broadway, the trail above the Chimney."

Taking the easier route up the East Face to connect with Clark seemed like a good idea, but once he reached Broadway Ledge, he knew that he could not get the additional rope Clark needed before dark. A rescue party, including Ranger Ernest Field and two climbing experts from Denver, Bob Boyd and Bob Lewis, started up the north face at about the same time, hoping to reach Clark from above as well. Cooper moved quickly to join them. Chief ranger J. Barton Herschler took charge of the rescue operation, establishing a base camp at Chasm Lake.

"They told me to go to the Boulderfield," said Watson. "I waited there for news."

By this time, the wind had picked up as well, and Clark, clad only in a cotton flannel shirt and denim pants, remained trapped on a ledge as water poured down the mountain and directly over him. As hail mixed with the snow, conditions became too hazardous for Ranger Field and his party to begin to climb down the East Face to reach Clark. A long afternoon of bad weather and biting cold had given way to night, and darkness set in on the mountain. Clark had no choice but to spend the night on the exposed ledge.

Watson went back up the Longs Peak trail at first light and reached Chasm Lake. He found Ranger Field and his party, who had spent the night on a wide ledge, coming down the East Face of the mountain toward Clark as snow and sleet continued to swirl around them. He also met Ranger Paul Hauk at Chasm Lake, on his way to assist. Watson and Hauk started up the East Face from the base.

Where exactly Clark had spent the night, however, was a mystery to the rangers and climbers on their way to help him. "Clark was so much hidden by the storm and the trough that the rescuers could not find him after they started down after dawn," the Associated Press reported. They called to Clark, telling him to throw out his pack so they could see where he was. "He tossed out his pack then," said Cooper. For the moment, at least, he was still alive and conscious.

Finally Field's party reached Clark, and determined in minutes that he was suffering from hypothermia and could not use his muscles to assist in his own rescue. He lost consciousness as they began lowering him down with a rope to Kiener's Route, where Watson and Hauk were waiting. It took a total of five hours to move Clark down 1,500 feet from the ledge to the rescue camp rangers had established at Chasm Lake, working in small increments. Rescuers on the ground had called park headquarters for blankets, stimulants, a stretcher, and an ambulance to wait at Longs Peak campground, and eighteen Civilian Conservation Corps enrollees made their way to the rescue camp to help carry Clark five miles on the stretcher to the campground and ambulance.

In all, Clark had spent twenty hours on the ledge.

"Clark was still alive when we lifted him on down," said Watson, "but he was gashed on the head. He must have been hit by a rock while Field and Boyd and Lewis were letting him down."

By the time he reached Mills Glacier, however, Clark's life had all but ebbed away. Artificial respiration could not save him.

Coroner Orville Miller in Larimer County completed the autopsy and determined that the cause of death was exposure—what we now call hypothermia. The gash on his head was only a scalp wound.

Despite the disastrous outcome, Watson still felt that the day could have ended with a successful climb. "If the weather hadn't turned bad, we all could have made the climb to the top without trouble," he concluded.

THE SNOWS OF APRIL

Taking a break from studies at the end of April, four students from the University of Colorado at Boulder set off into the Rocky Mountain National Park wilderness on Monday, April 18, 1960, with the goal of reaching the summit of Longs Peak.

Prince Willmon, 23, of Fort Smith, Arkansas, was the oldest of the group. James A. Greig, 21, came from Glenview, Illinois, and David Jones, 19, had come from Webster Groves, Missouri. They were joined by their friend Jane Bendixen, 19, of Davenport, Iowa. By Tuesday morning, however, Greig felt he was coming down with something, and he turned back. Willmon, Jones, and Bendixen continued down the Longs Peak trail and began their trek up the mountain.

Somehow, all four students had missed seeing the signs at the trailhead and elsewhere along the trail to the mountain, telling them that these trails were closed to all but technical climbers at this time of year. Late April is still snow season on mountains in the Front Range, so the hiking party could expect to find ice and snow at higher elevations that would make climbing without equipment and proper footwear a hazardous endeavor.

The three climbers, all of whom had substantial experience on mountain trails, made their way up Longs Peak without incident until they had nearly reached the summit. Then, in what seemed like minutes, the weather changed from a generally overcast but comfortable day into a raging blizzard. Ice coated the rocky trails, and snow gathered in deep drifts. None of the climbers were dressed for this kind of weather, so they soon began to feel the effects of exposure. Bendixen and Willmon knew that their hands, feet, and faces were starting to freeze.

By Wednesday morning, as they fought their way through the endless blizzard, Willmon felt he could not continue. Jones and Bendixen found an ice cave and left Willmon there, telling him that they would head down the mountain and go for help. Soon Bendixen found herself out in front of Jones, moving quickly in her descent. Suddenly her feet went out from under her. She fell down a rocky cliff, hit her head, and lost consciousness.

When she came to sometime later, she began calling for Jones, but she received no response. She wondered if he had fallen as well, but she didn't see him close by, so she determined that despite her injuries and the sense that frostbite had enveloped her hands and feet, she had better move or forfeit her own life where she lay. She began walking, continuing her descent until she reached the base of the mountain and could see lights far in the distance. She walked toward the lights, finally finding herself at a mountain home in Allenspark.

When the family answered the door, they saw immediately that she was in terrible trouble. Soon Bendixen was in an ambulance on the way to a hospital, while rangers began the search for her friends.

Willmon and Jones were not so lucky. Rangers found Willmon frozen to death in the ice cave, and Jones at the base of a cliff, where he had fallen as much as one thousand feet. He did not survive the fall.

TRAGEDY AT CAMP ST. MALO

At the foot of Mount Meeker, an elevation of about nine thousand feet, Camp St. Malo, a camp for young Catholic boys, opened in 1936 just inside Rocky Mountain National Park. Now known as the Chapel on the Rock, the striking stone buildings served as the camp's facilities until 1984, when the site became a religious retreat and conference center. Today the Archdiocese of Denver has started a major restoration of the buildings and the surrounding area, including the trail that Pope John Paul II walked when he visited here in 1993. Our story begins in 1958 as the camp's summer season drew to a close.

Ten-year-old Bobby Bizup (pronounced BY-zup) attended the camp that summer. The only son of Sergeant and Mrs. Joseph Bizup of Denver, the young camper was hearing-impaired and wore a hearing aid, but the fairly new technology only provided the child with minimal help. Although he spoke with a speech impediment, he could read lips, and his fellow campers treated him much like anyone else, including him in all activities. Nonetheless, Bobby kept to himself most of the time, choosing activities he could do on his own.

On Friday, August 15, 1958, Bobby's parents received a cheerful letter from their son, from camp:

> *I bought an airplane and I paint all over it. The paint is silver and the other is yellow. I pulled two teeth and put them under the pillow. We went to a short hike and came back and went to church. Were going to bed and in the morning we went to church, and I was going to fix the bed and I saw under the pillow 25 cents. I said, wow, how come, for my two teeth? I caught a chipmunk. It's missing. You give me two papers, please.*
> *Love, Bobby*
> *Good luck and lots of kisses*

As it happened, August 15 was the last Friday night before the camp closed for the summer on Sunday, but the day came to an end much the way every day at camp did—with supper served promptly, and bedtime not long after. Bobby had been out fishing at Cabin Creek when a counselor came to let him know it was time for supper. The counselor started down the hill to the pavilion with Bobby behind him, checking over his shoulder several times to make sure the camper was following him.

One moment Bobby was there, but the next time the counselor looked behind him, the boy was gone.

The counselor looked around for Bobby and called to him, but he did not emerge. Running back to the camp for reinforcements, the counselor brought other older boys and Reverend Richard Hiester, camp director, to look for the missing child. They returned to the creek where he had been fishing and began searching the thick brush on either side of the trail. Reverend Hiester called Bobby's parents right away and notified the US Forest Service.

Within hours, a search party of "sheriff's officers, mountain rescue experts and other volunteers" arrived at the camp to begin looking for the boy, according to the Associated Press, and Meeker Park deputy sheriff Frank Burke sent Undersheriff Wray Andrews to the area as well. Soon they were joined by six members of the Rocky Mountain Rescue Group, made up of forest rangers and members of a rescue unit from Longmont. They searched through the night and into Saturday as Joseph and Constance Bizup, Bobby's parents, arrived at the camp from their home in Denver. Sergeant Bizup joined in the search, but Mrs. Bizup, stricken to the point of panic, stayed behind in a camp cabin under the care of a doctor.

"Sgt. Bizup, 38, said his son is a good swimmer," the Associated Press reported on Sunday, August 17. "The stream where he was last seen is narrow enough for a child to step across."

Bloodhounds and their handler from the Calo Rescue Unit near Oakland, California, arrived by helicopter and joined the search on Sunday, as the operation swelled to more than one hundred people—including thirty camp staff, forty Civil Air Patrol members, and twenty-five volunteers—and covered an area of more than sixty square miles. The helicopter stayed and assisted with the aerial search, and two skin divers from Longmont searched beaver ponds and other deep water in the area.

A whoop went up when the dogs discovered Bobby's bait box and fishing pole about a mile from the camp, sparking hope that the boy would soon turn up. That hope fizzled, however, as daylight waned and another night shrouded the mountainside, chilling the air down to 40 degrees. Bobby wore "a sport shirt, light blue summer jacket, blue jeans and sneakers" when he wandered off, according to United Press International (UPI), not enough to keep him warm through a Rocky Mountain night.

At the end of the day Sunday, Camp St. Malo closed for the season as scheduled. Reverend Hiester sent the counselors home as the ranks of the adult searchers swelled, with as many as five hundred people participating in the search since Friday.

On Monday, the fourth day of the effort, the *Greeley Tribune* reported that Commander Lew Kitts of the Colorado wing of the Civil Air Patrol had assigned a contingent of men to assist in the ground search.

Meanwhile, the *Estes Park Trail*, the town's newspaper, printed and distributed handbills with Bobby's picture and description throughout the park's entrance towns and other areas nearby. When a vacationing doctor in Estes Park saw the photos, he approached the local police. He was certain he'd seen a boy who looked like Bobby in the town on Monday. Later in the day, a motorist driving up a mountain road reported that he, too, had seen a boy fitting Bobby's description, standing near large rocks along the roadside.

"Searchers were becoming convinced that the boy is somewhere in the vicinity of the downtown section of [Estes Park], but the wilderness 11 miles south was being combed," UPI reported. "A belief that the boy may be here was raised when the clerk of a hardware store reported seeing a child who answered his description in the place Monday night."

The clerk said that the boy came into the shop, but "left hurriedly when approached." He noted that "the boy failed to answer his questions, pointing to his mouth and ears." A clerk in a clothing store reported the same kind of incident with a boy in his store on Monday night, as well.

"There are growing indications that the boy is hiding from the searchers," Undersheriff Andrews confirmed to the media.

Sergeant Bizup agreed with the theory. He told the Associated Press that he thought Bobby "got scared because he didn't go to supper when he was supposed to, and when he saw the councilors [sic] looking for him, he just ducked into the woods to dodge them."

Despite the continued search and the absence of any further clues, Sergeant and Mrs. Bizup left the park area on Tuesday for their home in Denver. Mrs. Bizup, on the verge of utter collapse, required the care of her own doctor and could no longer bear the barrage of media, the consistently dismal news about the search, and the brisk winds and cold rains that brought an early fall to the mountains. Higher in the Rockies, snow had begun to fall, leaving gleaming white fingers along the peaks. Bobby's mother knew that her son could not withstand one cold night after another in the Colorado wilderness.

The tone of the search began to change on Wednesday, however, as authorities started to wonder if the massive hunt for the boy might actually be scaring him and driving him farther into the woods. "We decided to pull back a bit in the search in the hope the boy might show himself," Estes Park deputy sheriff Everett "Granny" May told the Associated Press.

"I think he just took off," said Reverend Hiester. "We definitely think he's somewhere near the camp."

The Bizups, thinking every piece of information could be vital, had told Hiester that Bobby "had wanted to remain at the camp after its formal seasonal closing date last weekend," and they suggested that he might be hiding so that he could stay in this place where he felt happy and comfortable. He was "probably some place in the immediate vicinity," authorities told UPI, and added that they had redirected their efforts to nearby haylofts in horse stables, garages, and other buildings in the Mount Meeker area.

As if to reinforce this theory, a woman motorist called the police in Estes Park on Friday to report that she had seen a boy about Bobby's age "duck into the brush near the highway" about two miles southwest of town. The police went to the area right away, but they did not find Bobby or any other boy in the vicinity.

The theory that Bobby was in hiding proved fruitless, however, and on Friday, a week after Bobby had vanished, eighty airmen from Lowry Air Force Base refreshed the search effort, examining the edges of Lilly Lake, a body of water between Camp St. Malo and Estes Park, as a heavy rain drenched the area. Authorities ordered six beaver dams in nearby ponds dynamited and broken up, an activity that usually signals a last-ditch effort before an unsuccessful search comes to a close.

Officials even recruited the skills of an "Indian tracker," Richard Drabble, who followed a set of tracks through the woods to a spot where a boy had been seen on Tuesday. "Col. W. A. Coe of the Civil Air Patrol said the tracks turned up by Drabble may have provided the first lead to the boy's whereabouts," the Associated Press reported. "But he added, 'We're not even sure they were his tracks. The feeling is that the boy is alive but is not in this mountain country.'"

Still clinging to the idea that Bobby might be hiding somewhere in the area, the Civil Air Patrol dropped about five thousand handbills from planes on Sunday with a message to Bobby from his parents, asking him to come out of hiding and show himself to authorities.

Bobby did not appear despite all of these efforts. At the end of the tenth day, with no credible clue to Bobby's whereabouts coming to light, the organized search came to an end. "We feel we have exhausted all possibilities in this area," Reverend Hiester told the media.

"Bobby's parents say they have given up hope," the Associated Press reported. Sergeant Bizup told the press, "We don't know what has happened to our boy, but we don't think we will ever see him again."

Hope sprang to life once again at the beginning of September when a hotel manager in Thermopolis, Wyoming, contacted the local sheriff to report that a boy fitting Bobby's description had checked into the hotel with an older man. Sheriff Eddie Todorovich wasted no time in checking out the lead, but it turned out to be false: The boy at the hotel was Billy Reed, staying there with his father, Ed Reed of Pocatello, Idaho, while a local mechanic repaired Reed's car.

With the search called off and the camp closed, the area around Camp St. Malo remained quiet through the fall, winter, and spring. The camp reopened as scheduled the following June, 1959, and campers and counselors soon filled the woods and mountainside, hiking, fishing, canoeing, and exploring as they always had.

On a pleasant June day, counselors Neil Howitt, Jerry Cusack, and Mike Courtney hiked partway up Mount Meeker until they came to a ravine up near the timberline. There they spotted something that made them all stop in their tracks: scraps of blue clothing, and what looked like it might be bones. They scrambled down into the ravine for a closer look, and found the key that told them exactly who these remains had been: a piece of a child's hearing aid.

The counselors rushed back to camp to tell Reverend Hiester what they had discovered. Later that day, the reverend told the Associated Press that Bobby Bizup's remains had been found, and that the boy had "apparently died in the ravine's heavy underbrush at the 11,000-foot level on the mountain, three miles from the camp."

How and why Bobby had strayed so far from camp, how long he had lived beyond the night he had disappeared, and how he came to be concealed in the ravine remain unanswered questions more than six decades later.

OUT OF THEIR ELEMENT

Some visitors to Rocky Mountain arrive with their own ideas, grown from often vast experience, of what a national park will be like. They may believe that their frequent weekend trips into the wilderness of their home state have prepared them in mind and body for the wonders of the Colorado high country, even though they have never hiked or climbed at high altitudes. Given that they intend to visit a park, they expect amenities that are not necessarily present in all parks, like shelters fully stocked with food and firewood, as they are on Mount Washington in New Hampshire, or metal railings and chains to help them cross narrow ledges and scale sheer vertical cliffs, as they found in Acadia National Park in Maine (where the highest elevation is 1,529 feet) or Zion National Park in Utah.

Many of these wilderness enthusiasts have strong skills that serve them well in their home state's parks, but that are hopelessly inadequate for the rigors of the Rockies. Today these visitors can find online all the instructions and caveats they need to keep themselves safe—but in the 1970s, when homes had no computers and the military had the only rudimentary Internet access, they were at the mercy of their own willingness to write to parks for information and to do extensive research before traveling.

This is how Fred Stone, 20, and Joan Jardine, 21, became victims of their own expectations in January 1972. Both natives of Minneapolis–St. Paul and students at Colorado State University (CSU), they had explored Minnesota's north country in winter, cross-country skiing around the many lakes and enjoying the hospitality of state park shelters. Minnesota contains vast plains planted with the nation's agricultural food supply—the Valley of the Jolly Green Giant actually exists there, in and around the community of Le Sueur—and the verdant northern half of the state includes many square miles of forested land, but the state's highest elevation is at Eagle Mountain, just 2,301 feet above sea level. Stone and Jardine could not fully comprehend what skiing at an altitude of nine thousand to eleven thousand feet would be like, especially in harsh winter weather.

They planned to ski up to Chasm Lake and spend the night in the shelter cabin there, setting out at 2:30 p.m. on Friday afternoon for what they expected to be a fairly quick 4.3-mile ski to the lake. Signs at the Longs Peak ranger station informed them that anyone planning an overnight hike in winter had to register their intention with park headquarters, but they either did not see the prominent signs or they chose to ignore them. Elevation is 9,405 feet at the trailhead, an altitude that placed Stone and Jardine well outside their normal comfort zone. How long they may have been in the area before they set out on their weekend trip remains unknown, but we can assume that they had not fully acclimated to the difference in oxygen level between Estes Park and Minneapolis–St. Paul.

They signed the register at the trailhead, but in not speaking to a ranger before they started up the trail, the two Minnesotans did not have the opportunity to discover that they had made assumptions that proved to be incorrect. They expected that the shelter cabin would have a stove and firewood inside, which is not the case. The food they brought required cooking, something that would be very difficult without a stove, and they did not have any kind of a camp stove in their packs. As they expected firewood, they also did not have the means to cut fallen logs into firewood so they could build their own campfire.

"The trail to the Chasm Lake shelter cabin is a long, uphill grind," a detailed article in the *Alpine Rescue Team News* explained in April 1972. "The first half is in timber, and in the winter is mostly in deep snow. The upper half is above timberline: windswept and cold, and near the cabin has a bad traverse across a 60 degree slope, which can be very hazardous in the winter . . . Leaving the ranger station at 2:30, it is doubtful that they reached Jim's Grove at timberline before 5:30."

Stone had hiked in as far as Chasm Lake sometime during the week preceding this ski trip, and while he had not gone all the way to the shelter, he could see it in the distance. He knew the route, but he may not have realized just how rugged a crossing this would be once they got above timberline. When they arrived at the tree line on Friday evening, the sky was already growing dark and they had the most difficult part of the journey still ahead of them—another three to four miles. Snow blew across the open expanse, driven by high winds, the beginnings of a characteristic winter storm. They cached their skis, weighing them down with rocks against the wind, and began hiking to the cabin.

"By the time that they reached the hazardous traverse across the steep slope above Peacock Pool they were undoubtedly cold, tired, and frightened about traveling bad terrain in the dark in the middle of a blizzard," the Alpine Rescue Team (ART) report continued. "If they had not had the misconception that the shelter cabin contained a stove and firewood, they probably would have bivouacked at Jim's Grove or in the shelter of boulders on Mills Moraine. However, they were really not prepared for a comfortable bivouac and forced themselves on to the imagined warmth and comfort of the cabin."

The couple soldiered on into the darkness, blowing snow, and subzero temperatures . . . and disappeared.

On Sunday evening, friends who had expected Stone and Jardine back by Saturday afternoon contacted Rick Perkins, a student at Colorado State University whom they knew had once been involved in the ART. Rick called active team member Dave Moore, who recommended that the friends contact rangers at Rocky Mountain National Park. Jardine's roommate contacted the park on Monday morning, and park personnel began their investigation immediately, finding the couple's car still in the parking lot at the Longs Peak campground. This triggered a full-scale search, activating the Colorado Search and Rescue Board, the Rocky Mountain Rescue Group, and twenty-one ART members. At 6:30 a.m. Tuesday, rangers Steve Hickman and Walt Fricke began to coordinate a search that also involved members of Club 100 of Fort Collins, Snowmobile Rescue Units, the local sheriff's department, two avalanche search dogs and a team of handlers from Seattle, and many park rangers.

The first day's wide-ranging search produced only a few tracks in the valley and to the east of the lake, and given the snow and wind that had continued on and off since Friday evening, these were not given much weight in the overall search. To gather information that might lead to better clues, ART leaders interviewed the couple's friends at CSU, learning that both Stone and Jardine owned lug-soled boots, information that could help in identifying tracks. Their skis and ski boots had been rented, as neither Stone nor Jardine were experienced cross-country skiers, though Jardine had skied downhill on many occasions. The friends also told the rescue team members about the couple's expectation that the shelter would be stocked with a stove and firewood, dramatically narrowing the potential search area to a route that would lead to the shelter.

On Tuesday morning, the search resumed in a more concentrated field, and people with experience in identifying boot tracks worked to carefully brush and study the few tracks they had found. This strategy began to pay dividends, as the tracks toward the valley had been left by lug-soled boots in Jardine's size. The following day, the cached skis turned up just where the couple had left them, at timberline in the Jim's Grove area, where the trail splits—one trail leads toward Chasm Lake and on to the East Face, while the other goes to the north and west. It now became clear that they had not attempted to ski out by a different route; they had proceeded on foot.

"Most of the ground above timberline was bare and windswept, easily searched both from the air and from the ground," the ART report said. Wednesday was the first day that the wind abated enough for a helicopter to join the search, but this served only to help rule out that the couple had headed across the rocky terrain above the tree line. "Everything pointed to the grim conclusion that the couple had gone into the deep, soft snow below timberline on foot."

Bad weather halted the search on Thursday, January 27, but the teams spent Friday focused on Jim's Grove, the Roaring Fork valley, and the area around the shelter cabin. One of the teams, following faint tracks left by lug-soled boots, spotted a stick standing straight up in the snow with something orange on the end of it. They moved quickly to reach it and discovered that it was a pair of underwear, a clear indication that someone had placed it there as a marker flag. Here, near the bottom of the valley, they discovered Joan Jardine's body, mostly buried in snow, about halfway between Chasm Lake and the highway. Fred Stone was nowhere in sight.

On Saturday, another discovery tightened the circumference of the search once again, while personnel in the field numbered more than 120 people, including 40 members of the Army National Guard. "Fred Stone's pack was found under a light snow cover near a large boulder at the base of large, steep snowfield a short distance from the shelter cabin," the ART report said. "The trail to the cabin crosses the upper part of this snowfield, and in the wintertime it is considered a dangerous traverse. He had evidently lost his purchase on the trail above and had gone down the steep slope; his pack was damaged, one strap was torn loose, indicating some pretty rough treatment."

Stone's pack lay on top of his unrolled sleeping bag, and Jardine's pack was attached to it. "His sleeping bag was frozen solid, indicating that he had spent some time in it," the report continued. "The pack contained quite a volume and assortment of food, but no stove. No drinking liquids or container were found. His hat and glove were found beside the pack."

Stone couldn't be far off, so a team of avalanche search dogs and personnel combed the area on Sunday, but their efforts produced no new clues. By the end of the day, with a week's worth of searching behind them, park officials ended the full-scale operation with the understanding that Stone could not have survived the winter conditions. "Park rangers would continue to search on days when weather and changes in the snow cover improved the chances of finding something," the ART report said. Park staff also hoped that the considerable backcountry ski travel in the area throughout the winter would turn up some clues, but the winter passed with no additional discoveries.

Winter gave way to spring and summer on the mountain. One day in early August, park rangers received the first break in the case since January's failed search: the discovery of a pair of ski boots in the Lower Roaring Fork River Valley. Rangers determined that the boots belonged to Fred Stone, and called in a canine squad from the Denver Police Department to track Stone's scent. On Friday, August 4, the dogs led the search team to Stone's body in the river valley, a good two miles from the shelter cabin he had attempted to reach.

Chuck Burdick, ART mission team leader, did his best to reconstruct what had happened to Stone and Jardine in the ART's April 1972 newsletter. "All evidence indicates that Fred Stone slipped down the long, steep snowfield below the difficult traverse on the way in to the cabin Friday evening," he said. "His pack contained a great deal of food, apparently untouched. Indicative of their planning regarding the cabin, his pack contained no stove; and if they carried drinking water or any other liquids, nothing was found with Joan's body or the pack to indicate it. He was likely injured in the fall . . . He may have been able to yell up to Joan on the trail, but it is doubtful that there was enough light remaining for them to see each other. The frozen, unrolled sleeping bag suggested that he tried to remain there for some length of time, and probably left when he could no longer tolerate the cold bag. He was surely in bad shape when he left the pack and bag . . . He evidently left without a hat and missing a glove, and without taking much of anything in the way of food. He either felt he could no longer stay there and wait for help, or simply wandered away in the final, disoriented stage of hypothermia."

Jardine, meanwhile, found herself quite alone in the dark and in the midst of a snowstorm, unable to reach Stone and desperate to try to get help. Burdick believed that she attempted to find a way down into the valley, from which she could reach the highway and maybe some homes in the area, where she could call for a rescue. "After finding that it was a very long way before she could get down, and after what must have been an extremely frightening and exhausting trip down, she probably decided that it would be faster just to keep going down the valley to the highway to get help. She covered a surprising distance considering the conditions, part of it floundering through deep snow."

Exhausted, chilled to the bone, and aware that she would soon succumb to exposure, she emptied her small pack, set up a marker flag using her own underwear, laid down on her back near Roaring Fork Creek, about a mile and a half from the highway, and settled into the final stages of hypothermia. The coroner confirmed that she had probably perished on Friday night or early Saturday morning, just hours after she and Stone had set out from the Longs Peak trailhead.

"Inexperience was the one factor which precipitated all the conditions leading to the tragedy," Burdick summed up. "Ski touring and winter mountaineering are not necessarily the same thing. Inexperience in high-altitude winter mountaineering is what led to the inadequate preparation, the very poor timing of the start of the trip, and the lack of knowledge of how to handle the situation. With each tragedy of this sort, the need for mountain safety education is given stronger emphasis."

BLIZZARDS ON THE GROUND

We tend to think of a blizzard as a snowfall event, dumping so much of the white stuff from clouds gathered above that it occludes vision. Add winds to this kind of storm, and we experience whiteout conditions and arctic cold that stops cars in their tracks, freezes fingers, noses, and toes, and makes it virtually impossible to travel.

The Rocky Mountains have such storms, but the region also experiences a different phenomenon: ground blizzards, in which snow already fallen becomes airborne in high winds and blinds anyone unfortunate enough to be out in such a gale. Forecasts can warn hikers and climbers that powerful winds are on their way, but ground blizzards can be so localized that they do not make it into weather forecasts. Winter climbers simply take their own lives in their hands when they venture up a mountain in Rocky Mountain National Park, especially if they plan to reach a summit, where winds can be much stronger than they are at the trailhead.

Ruth Magnuson, 29, and five other experienced climbers attempted a summit of Mount Alice, which tops out at 13,310 feet, on Saturday, March 8, 1980, a day hike that would require some climbing up to icy ridges. Each climber carried a day pack, fully expecting to reach the summit and make it back down in a single day. They may have been aware that snow was predicted, as it is nearly every winter day somewhere in the park, but they were not prepared for the power of the winds that turned the snowy mantle under their feet into a roiling fog. Soon they could not see their own hands in front of their faces, much less the others in their party. The last they saw of Magnuson was on a ledge about one thousand feet below the summit.

Franz Mohling, a University of Colorado physics professor who led the party up the mountain, turned around to account for all of the climbers and realized that he could not see Magnuson. "Suddenly she was gone," he told the Associated Press (AP) two days later. "I left two climbers there to watch for her, figuring she'd be coming up, and three of us continued on to the summit."

Forty-five minutes later, Mohling and the two climbers with him returned to the spot where he had left the others. Magnuson was not with them. "Then I realized I'd made a bad error," he admitted. "I thought surely she'd turned around and gone back to timberline, but she hadn't."

The party returned to their base camp, fully expecting to find Magnuson comfortably waiting for them there. When they discovered that she had not made it back, three of the climbers turned around and went back up the mountain the way they had come originally, hoping to find that she had taken refuge behind a large boulder. They searched until dark, but nothing revealed her position.

Storm conditions on Sunday prevented searchers from returning to the mountain, perhaps sealing Magnuson's fate. On Monday, two rescue parties set out to find her, one from west of the Continental Divide and one from the east. "They encountered winds of up to 70 miles an hour and ground blizzards that dropped visibility to zero," park spokesperson Joyce Bennett told the AP. Even in these miserable circumstances, however, they managed to spot Magnuson near the summit, which she had apparently attempted to reach alone in hopes of linking back up with her climbing party. Whether she attained the summit can never be known, as she succumbed to the high winds and frigid temperatures and froze to death.

"Conditions have been real bad up there," said Ranger Larry Van Slyke, who coordinated the search.

If March weather can be unpredictable in the Rocky Mountains, December provides a virtual guarantee of winter storms, so it's baffling why two high-rise window washers from Boulder would venture out on a trail usually frequented in midsummer to climb Longs Peak on December 14, 1981. While both of these men had considerable climbing experience—Michael O'Donnell had climbed El Capitan in Yosemite National Park and the Matterhorn in Switzerland—and they taught rock climbing in Boulder, they carried no overnight gear, expecting to be back before sunset on what looked at first to be a mild late-fall day.

It makes even less sense when we take into consideration that one of the climbers, 25-year-old O'Donnell, had been involved in a climbing accident on the same mountain earlier that year on January 12. In the January incident, O'Donnell's climbing partner, Robert Elliott, fell ninety feet off of a ledge, and O'Donnell stayed there and yelled for help until someone heard him and brought rescuers. Elliott did not survive the fall. An investigation determined that O'Donnell had done nothing wrong in that case, so he set out once again for a winter summit, this time with 24-year-old James Duffy III. The two-man party did not register their intended route or gain a permit for their winter climb.

According to O'Donnell's account to the search-and-rescue team, he and Duffy started up Longs Peak early on Sunday, December 13, and reached the summit in continued pleasant weather. But as they started their descent, blizzard winds blowing up to 120 miles per hour nearly buried them in snow and ice. Somewhere along their route down, they stumbled—literally—upon a "foot-locker-sized wooden survival box" where rescue supplies are stored, and climbed inside, clinging together to share their body warmth in a dire effort to keep from freezing to death.

"It was the most desperate thing I'd ever been through anywhere in the world," O'Donnell told the media. "You couldn't look into the wind more than 10 seconds. Your eyelashes would close. You had to take your gloves off and free your eyes of the ice."

On Monday conditions had not improved, but they knew they could not stay at the summit and expect to live through the ordeal. They also realized that while they were already a day late returning from their climb, no one was looking for them. Because they had chosen to ignore the requirement to register their climb with rangers, no one knew they were on the mountain at all. They decided that they could either accept their fate where they were, or make the marginally less risky decision to head down and take their chances on reaching the trailhead. Slowly, struggling to keep from being blown clean off the mountain, they began to creep down in the high winds and swirling snow.

"At one point I had to hold on to the rocks with my hands because the wind was taking my feet like a flag and just flapping them in the air," O'Donnell told the AP. "It sounded like a whole squadron of Phantom jets flying over your head at five feet." He added, "I've never been in winds like that before ... the winds didn't come from one direction—they came from all sides."

Before long, however, their already depleted condition became a dangerous liability. Duffy became "irrational, belligerent and disoriented," the AP reported. O'Donnell had a life-and-death decision to make: He could continue down the mountain, save himself, and send help back up to Duffy, or they could both die where they were in a matter of hours . . . or less. Barely able to see a foot in front of them, the men could not know that they were only a few hundred yards from the Agnes Vaille Shelter, where they could have had relief from the wind and an opportunity to regain some strength.

O'Donnell left Duffy and crawled away on his hands and knees to avoid being tossed about in the high winds, inching his way for two miles down the mountain. Finally he reached a ranger station and told the rangers that Duffy was still on the mountain. Soon O'Donnell was resting in Estes Park's hospital, recovering from second-degree frostbite in his right hand and both feet. Two more days would pass before the blizzard finally subsided enough to allow two mountain-climbing instructors to head up Longs Peak to find the stranded man. By then, no one expected Duffy to have survived.

Duffy had not gone far since O'Donnell had last seen him late Monday. The climbers found him just half a mile from where his partner had left him. "The body was frozen because the temperatures in that area [had] been zero and below the past few nights," said Rocky Mountain National Park spokesman Glen Kaye. "It looked like he died from exposure." Kaye told the media that the two climbers spent the night in the Vaille Shelter on the mountain, where temperatures remained below freezing, and that they would be joined on Thursday by a team of twenty technical climbers who would assist in removing Duffy's body.

Perhaps the prior story can help us to better understand how a pair of climbers departing for the Longs Peak summit on September 12,

1993, did not realize that a winter storm might overtake them. Charles B. "Bo" Judd, 24, and Kelly Thomas, 27, registered their plans with the Longs Peak Ranger Station and started their route up the mountain's East Face on Saturday night, September 11, bivouacking on Mills Glacier to start out fresh on Kiener's Route in the morning. Before they began their climb, however, they decided to hide their bivouac gear on the east side of Chasm Lake—a decision that had a direct impact on their ability to survive.

Because of this relocation of their gear, they started for the summit later in the day on Sunday than they intended, and they missed the opportunity to watch other climbers on Kiener's Route to see where and how they went up the rock face. The hike back to Chasm Lake also used up their morning energy, making their progress up the East Face later and slower than they had planned. That is how they found themselves in near-darkness after sunset, "at the base of the dihedral adjacent to the Diamond step," reported Longs Peak supervisory climbing ranger Jim Detterline. "They did not figure out the simple third-class connection to the summit."

This was enough to prevent them from reaching the summit, but darkness and difficulty in determining the best route were only the beginning of their problems: They had apparently missed the weather forecast that warned of a severe winter storm on the way. "One and a half feet of snow, high winds, low temperatures to near [zero degrees Fahrenheit], and low visibility blew in late that evening as predicted," the report continued.

The climbers waited out the night on a ledge, and in the morning, with the storm still raging, they managed to descend. "Although they heard a rescuer calling to them in the storm, they dismissed his calls as hallucination," the report noted. Their difficult descent became fraught with small mishaps that fell just short of becoming life-threatening: a rappel anchor failed just above Broadway Ledge;

Thomas slipped down Lambs Slide when his crampon came off his "goretex [*sic*] hi-tech sneaker type of footwear (inappropriate with his crampons)," according to Detterline's report.

They finally arrived at Mills Glacier after dark and began making their way to Chasm Lake, where they had cached their bivouac gear, but by this time they were both experiencing the first symptoms of hypothermia, complicated by their general exhaustion. They became separated as they hiked out to the lake's east side, though they stayed in voice contact.

"Judd reached the camp first, probably after midnight, according to his recollection, and collapsed in his sleeping bag," the report said. He did not know how far behind him Thomas was, and it's likely that Judd's own hypothermia and fatigue clouded his ability to reason, enough so that he did not look for Thomas before taking shelter.

"To Judd's credit, it must be mentioned that his survival of this tragedy was an amazing feat of willpower above all odds, and that he made every attempt to push his partner toward the critical stash of survival gear," Detterline noted.

Nonetheless, the day ended in tragedy. "Thomas succumbed to hypothermia on the north side of Chasm Lake in a boulder field," the report said. On Tuesday, when the weather finally improved, searchers in a helicopter found Judd conscious in his camp, and located Thomas about two hours later. Judd was flown to Poudre Valley Hospital in Fort Collins and was treated for frostbite in his toes.

Judd and Thomas had led rock climbs in more temperate weather and were proficient climbers, but "they were not alpinists," the club's report says in its analysis of the incident. "Most of their background was gained in short 'sport routes' at low elevation and in a benign climate. Their training and experience on snow and ice was almost nil. Their route-finding abilities, most critical in an alpine environment, were of the 'tunnel vision' type, where one focuses on the immediate problems of the terrain in the direct line in front of oneself, instead of the overall picture."

Detterline reflected on the change he had seen in the climbers who came to Longs Peak in the early 1990s. "Those of us working rescue in alpine areas have noticed an increasing number of folks with backgrounds in sport or indoor climbing assuming they were automatically fit for the big wall or alpine routes just because they were capable of performing at high standards in the gyms and on the short bolt-protected outdoor walls," he said. "Judd and Thomas attempted to make the transition by doing a lot of reading research, but this unfortunately could not measure up to the experience of learning directly from either a guide or an experienced alpinist."

Thomas was survived by his wife and two young children.

A sudden change in the weather on a September afternoon claimed one more victim in 2004. Sudheer Averineni, a 26-year-old engineer from India employed by Hewlett-Packard, made his third attempt to reach the summit of Longs Peak on Saturday, September 4. This time he made it to the top, but on the way down, a winter storm settled in, with frigid temperatures and blowing snow. Averineni, wearing only a hoodie, sneakers, and jeans, was not prepared for this at all—nor did he have any technical climbing equipment with him. (The mountain had been under "technical conditions" throughout the summer, recommending that only experienced climbers attempt to reach the summit, and that they bring ice axes, crampons, rope, and other gear with them.)

When he did not return on schedule, Averineni's friends notified the park. "Search crews from Rocky Mountain National Park began a late-night search for Averineni but called it off early Sunday morning when conditions near the Keyhole prevented them from going farther," the *Fort Collins Coloradoan* reported. "His body was found about 1 p.m. Sunday."

Ajay Jha, president of the India Association of Northern Colorado, told the media that Averineni had been in Colorado for three years. "He was a very lively guy," he said. "He was pretty friendly with all the people at CSU who belonged to our India group. This is an unfortunate day."

INCIDENT AT ODESSA LAKE

The most recent death from hypothermia came not from winter storms or high mountain summits but from an unusual accident on the Fern Lake Trail, a strenuous trail along the Big Thompson River with a 1,400-foot elevation gain, in the Moraine Park section of the park.

Carol Nicolaidis, 62, of Boulder, chose this trail for a hike with her friend Debra Layne on September 4, 2009. Somehow she tumbled off the trail and down the bank some twenty-five to fifty feet at about 12:30 p.m., landing in Fern Creek. Creeks in the park are mostly fed by snowmelt, so they run especially cold, often just a few degrees above freezing.

"Debra Layne made the first of many frantic 911 calls to summon help," wrote Phyllis J. Perry in her book, *It Happened in Rocky Mountain National Park*. "Her call went unheard because of poor cell phone communication in that area of the park. It was about thirty minutes before anyone else passed by. And it took another thirty minutes for these hikers to make their way to where Carol Nicolaidis lay."

Carol feared that she had broken her back, so moving her became a risky proposition. Debra and the other hikers used rocks to construct a makeshift dam, diverting the water around her as much as they could and wrapping her in a space blanket to conserve body heat.

By one p.m., hikers in the area had contacted park dispatch by cell phone, but the calls were garbled by bad cell service and did not provide complete information about where the accident had occurred. Nevertheless, two rangers set out from the Fern Lake trailhead at 1:56 p.m. and hiked five and a half miles to the area near Odessa Lake. Meanwhile, additional calls came in to Dispatch, so rangers gained a better understanding of where the injured woman was, sending another team of rangers in from the Bear Lake trailhead, which was closer.

Rangers reached Nicolaidis at about 3:40 p.m. and "found her barely conscious and hypothermic," the park's news release said. They got Carol into dry clothes and placed heat packs around her to stave off the effects of the cold water. Soon more rangers and medical personnel arrived—a total of twenty-two in all—with an automated external defibrillator (AED) and other medical equipment, and they performed CPR for more than an hour and used cardiac medications to try to stabilize her. None of these methods had much effect, however, and she continued to fade. She was pronounced dead at 5:56 p.m.

A coroner's examination concluded that Carol had died of "blunt force internal injuries combined with the effects of hypothermia," Perry learned.

CHAPTER 2

The Highest Mountain: Falls on Longs Peak

THE JOLLY PARTY THAT LEFT MICHIGANTOWN, INDIANA, ON JUNE 1, 1921, for an automobile tour of the Western United States included four schoolteachers—Mr. and Mrs. Waldo Wood, Goldie Reigle, and Opal Bostick—and the family of Dr. and Mrs. F. P. Aubuchon, including their two sons and two daughters. *The Catholic Advance*, the newspaper of Wichita, Kansas, reported that the Aubuchons made a stop in Okmulgee, Kansas, where they visited Mrs. Aubuchon's sister and two brothers before continuing on to the Rocky Mountains.

Driving cross-country in 1921 meant traveling on two-lane paved roads that served as the nation's main highways, more than thirty years before the modern interstate highway system became America's main passageway across the continent. Construction of improved roads had barely started in some states, so the party from Indiana most likely encountered gravel-covered roads, dusty streets in small towns, and deeply rutted dirt roads that made their trip to the Western national parks feel quite rugged indeed.

One of the planned stops on this summer-long drive took the travelers to the recently designated Rocky Mountain National Park, a crown jewel among the seventeen national parks in the five-year-old park system. Here, they knew, they could hike across expansive valleys, climb tall mountains and stand in snow in the middle of July, and perhaps encounter moose, black bears, bighorn sheep, elk, yellow-bellied marmots, pikas, black-billed magpies, golden eagles, and other creatures whose names sounded very exotic to Midwestern ears.

The Aubuchons knew Rocky Mountain well, enjoying trips there in previous summers, and their 18-year-old son Gregory had long since developed a deep fondness for the park and its stunning scenery. A native of Macoupin County, Illinois, Gregory had lived in that state until he was eleven, when his parents packed up the family for their move to Michigantown. In the summer of 1921, he had just graduated from the Michigantown high school, an event that no doubt made him feel less like a teenager and more like a grown man with his own mind and independent pursuits.

The happy party set up camp in Estes Park and spent several days there, with a plan to move on to Cheyenne, Wyoming, on July 20. The morning of their scheduled departure, however, Gregory set off before dawn on the kind of solitary all-day hike that young men dream of taking, braving whatever elements may come their way as they conquer a high peak, follow a rushing stream, or traverse a mountain meadow. He left no word of his destination or when he might return, but his parents trusted that he would be back by the time the family intended to leave and that he knew how to watch out for himself in the wilderness.

Day waned, night fell, and the sun rose the following morning, but Gregory did not return. The Aubuchons extended their stay in Estes Park and thought hopeful thoughts: Perhaps he had just gotten turned around on a trail and lost his way. They notified park rangers first thing in the morning and asked for their assistance in locating their son. The family recalled one thing that they thought might be useful: Gregory had often expressed a desire to climb Longs Peak, the 14,259-foot mountain that towers above all others in the park.

As Rocky Mountain's only "fourteener," Longs Peak stands as the thirteenth-highest mountain in Colorado, but it inspires the kind of fascination that encourages climbers to risk their lives to reach its summit. It rises more than nine thousand feet above the Colorado plains, so the unobstructed view from the top provides the ultimate payoff for the labor of reaching it: the glacially sculpted Front Range with peaks that nearly parallel Longs' summit; the Colorado River headwaters to the west; and the stretch of thirteen-thousand-foot peaks that make up the Indian range to the south.

Getting there, however, presents a host of obstacles a teenager from the flat Midwest cannot begin to imagine. What passes for the easiest trail to the summit—what is now known as the Keyhole Route—requires climbing, not hiking, with what the American Alpine Institute describes as "high-consequence scrambling." This is often accompanied by sudden changes in weather, including thunderstorms, snow squalls, hail, fog, and low clouds, robbing climbers of visibility and turning rocky trails into slickened slides. The most popular route through the Keyhole does not officially require ropes and other climbing gear, but for the woefully inexperienced on their first climb, these precautions may result in more deliberate and thoughtful progress.

Just two hikers in recorded history had met their deaths on the mountain by the summer of 1921, however. One of these unfortunate incidents happened barely a month before the Aubuchons arrived in the park; the other—Carrie Welton's death, in 1884—is described in chapter 1.

H. F. Targett, a 50-year-old man from Los Angeles, California, left his room at the Longs Peak Inn on June 21 to hike to Chasm

Lake. Already at 9,405 feet at the trailhead for this hike, Targett intended to hike 3.4 miles along the Longs Peak trail to the lake at an elevation of 11,540 feet—a strenuous hike for a Colorado resident acclimated to changes in altitude, but a breath-stealing exertion for someone accustomed to the air's hearty oxygen content at sea level. Targett brought no food with him and only wore a sweater over his clothing, indicating that he had no idea what kind of challenges he might face along his route. He never returned from this hike; in fact, the search for any trace of him continued even as Gregory Aubuchon set out for Longs Peak on July 20. (A human skull believed to be Targett's turned up at last in September 1940, found in the undergrowth near Chasm Lake by two visitors who had to crawl through the brush to retrieve it.)

To 1921 visitors peering up at the fourteener with a nimble foot and a zest for challenges, this peak appeared to be relatively accessible, a grand day out culminating in a tall mountain summited and won.

Knowing all they knew about the difficulty involved in climbing Longs Peak, especially alone, the rangers realized that Gregory had no clear understanding of the challenges involved. If he had intended to be back at the campsite in time to depart with his family, chances were that he tried to proceed up the mountain too quickly and without the clothing or equipment he would need to reach the summit and return safely.

An extensive search got under way immediately. "Since his disappearance, searching parties have been working night and day in every part of the mountain," the *Lafayette Journal and Courier* reported on August 1, when this local paper first became aware of the effort. The Aubuchons' friends and neighbors at home did not receive word of Gregory's disappearance until that day, when Mrs. Destie Strain of Frankfort, Indiana, received a letter from her sister,

Mrs. Waldo Wood, with the troubling news that Gregory had gone missing in Rocky Mountain National Park.

By this time, Gregory had been absent more than ten days. Authorities told the Aubuchons that "either Gregory had gone on across the mountains into the vast plains on the other side, or that he had met his death in his lonely adventure," the *Journal and Courier* reported. "On the advice of the head of the rangers, the family returned to their home in Michigantown in the hope that the young man might wander into some settlement from which he could communicate with them."

An agonizing five additional weeks passed. "We still have hope," Dr. Aubuchon told the *Advance* on August 27, "that Gregory has not met his death in the climb; but is just lost, and will be heard from before the passing of many more days." He noted that he and his family had cut their trip short and returned home, "believing that [Gregory] has arrived in some western town, and, not knowing where to reach his parents, would send a letter" to their home in Indiana.

Their hope might be well founded, the *Advance* affirmed, because the paper had been in touch with "the Inn on the peak"—perhaps the Longs Peak Inn, which was at the base of the mountain—and had heard that a young man who looked like Gregory had been seen "in company with a party of four two days after he had left the Aubuchon camp in the national park. No further information could be ascertained, nor was it stated in which direction the party was traveling." Why the young man might run away from his family, take up new companions, and strike out across the Continental Divide toward Wyoming—another theory suggested by the *Advance*—without communicating with his parents seemed to be beyond the unnamed reporter's ability to explain.

"In Cheyenne a round-up was in progress and the family, with longing eyes, searched the crowds in vain," the writer continued. Indeed, the Aubuchons did proceed to Cheyenne after leaving Estes Park, in hopes that Gregory had found some way to cross the Rockies and continue to Wyoming, where he knew he could meet up with his family again. When he did not appear there, however, Dr. Aubuchon offered "a liberal reward" for any information that could lead to Gregory's whereabouts, according to the *Salt Lake Telegram* on August 3.

"Rangers, with bloodhounds, have kept up a continuous search for the young man—over crags and cliffs, and through the canyons—with no result," reported the *Advance* in mid-September. "We'll ask you to say a little prayer—that he may be found, though dead—at least, so the mother, in this critical hour, may have the strength to bear the burden. The family, back in the old home in Michigantown, Ind., fervently pray for some word, if he is still alive—or from the searchers that he has been found." It then quoted an apropos poem by William Cullen Bryant, "The Murdered Traveller":

> *But there was weeping far away,*
> *And gentle eyes, for him,*
> *With watching many an anxious day,*
> *Were sorrowful and dim.*

Perhaps this appeal to a higher power had some effect. The same day the Wichita paper offered its encouragement of prayer, murmurs began among the newspapers in Colorado that Rocky Mountain rangers, who had never stopped looking for the young man from Indiana, had located Greg Aubuchon's body. "Confirmation of press dispatches bearing the sad news of the tragic death of Gregory Aubuchon, missing youth of Michigantown, was received Saturday [September 17] when Dr. F. P. Aubuchon, father of the young man, received a telegram from Superintendent L. C. Way of the Rocky Mountain Park," the Lafayette paper reported.

The telegram was dated September 16, but the message had taken a full day to reach the Aubuchons:

BODY OF YOUR SON GREGORY LOCATED TODAY BY PARK RANGERS AT FOOT OF PRECIPICE ON LONGS PEAK. ACCEPT MY SINCERE SYMPATHY. PLEASE WIRE INSTRUCTIONS AS TO DISPOSITION OF BODY.

The rest of the details came to the boy's parents by way of their local newspaper editor, who shared with them the dispatches he received by wire from reporters in Estes Park. They noted that rangers found the "crushed and battered" body at the base of a cliff, where it had landed in a snowbank when Gregory had fallen a staggering 2,800 feet. "It was not discovered until the summer sun and rains had melted the great drifts, leaving it exposed to the keen eyes of the rangers," the Lafayette paper reported. Years later, the American Alpine Club speculated in its annual journal that Gregory had fallen from the Notch Chimney, on Longs Peak's East Face, a climb far too difficult for a young man to attempt alone with little or no climbing gear or experience.

The family decided to honor Gregory's love of the Colorado mountains by burying his body there. Dr. Aubuchon made his way out to Estes Park one more time to see his son laid to rest. *The Catholic Advance*, however, spun the tragedy a little differently, claiming "the body was in such a putrid condition that they were unable to remove it to the family home." The paper, far removed from the facts of the case, added, "It is believed that he had lost his way and starved to death, or had met with foul play," and ended with a mawkish flourish borrowed from Henry Wadsworth Longfellow:

Sweet as the tender fragrance that survives,
When martyred flowers breathe out their lives,
Sweet as a song that once consoled our pain,
But never will be sung to us again,
Is thy remembrance. Now the hour of rest
Hath come to thee. Sleep, dear one; it is best.

THE MOUNTAIN TAKES ITS TOLL

As more people discovered the wonders of America's national parks and highway system construction made the remote Western parks accessible to anyone with a car and the time to travel, Longs Peak's popularity soared with adventurous hikers and climbers. The Keyhole Route became well known as the easiest route to the summit, though calling it "easy" fooled many a hiker into believing it could be accomplished with far less skill than it actually requires. Its round-trip length of 14.5 miles, its 5,100-foot elevation gain, and its traverse of talus slopes, an area known as the Boulderfield, and the appropriately named Narrows ledges make this a strenuous hike for people of every skill level.

"You get to the Boulder Field and everything changes," said Kyle Patterson, Rocky Mountain National Park spokesperson, to Sady Swanson at the *Windsor Beacon*. "Sometimes people are like, 'Oh, there's a mile and a half left until the summit,' but that's by far the most difficult mile and a half."

Hikers find a sign at the base of the Boulderfield, warning them of what's to come:

KEYHOLE ROUTE AHEAD
DO NOT CLIMB IF UNPREPARED
The Keyhole Route is a climb that requires
scrambling on exposed narrow ledges, loose rock and steep slabs.
Sudden changes in weather may create high winds, lightning, rain,

hail, snow, freezing temperatures, and ice-covered rock at any time.
A slip, trip, or fall could be fatal. Rescue is
difficult and may take hours or days.
Self-reliance is essential.
Stay on route and be willing to turn around at any time.
Safety is your responsibility.

Other signs and warnings make it clear that Longs Peak is a climb, not a hike, especially in its last mile: From the Keyhole to the Homestretch, it involves significant scrambling over rocks that may be crusted with ice or slick with water runoff. Coming down this mountain is every bit as rigorous as going up, a detail often lost on less-experienced hikers who find themselves utterly depleted when they reach the smooth, flat summit.

All of this being said, quite a number of Longs Peak enthusiasts find the Keyhole Route insufficiently challenging after completing it more than once. Some of these intrepid climbers have found ways to increase the difficulty to achieve a personal best: climbing the far more treacherous East Face, a technical climb that can include a one-thousand-foot vertical slab of rock known as the Diamond—a route discussed in this book, in chapter 3—or taking on the mountain in the middle of winter, when snow, ice, and wind turn every route into a potential death trap.

The vast majority of climbers who attempt Longs Peak live to tell the tale, coming away footsore but otherwise unharmed. When all of the park's fatalities are calculated, however, nearly 18 percent of them take place on this mountain, according to a story by Swanson in the *Beacon* in November 2018.

In recent years, however, an average of two people die annually on the mountain. Some of these suffer heart attacks, succumbing to the body's inability to sustain prolonged exertion in air that contains substantially less oxygen than they usually breathe. Others fall off of ledges, lose their footing in precarious places, or run into sheer bad luck.

Robert F. Smith fits into the latter category. On July 18, 1932, the 41-year-old general manager of the American Legion Publishing Company in Chicago left Bear Lake Lodge at four a.m. with a party that included his wife, another couple from Peoria, Illinois, and three young women from Chicago. He stopped to rest halfway between the lodge and a ranger station, and managed to sit down in exactly the wrong place as a boulder came rolling down the nearby mountainside. The rock, said to be about the size of a man's fist, struck him in the head and killed him instantly. No one else was injured.

A month later, on August 29, 17-year-old Gray Secor Jr. and his friend Carroll Frantz set out to summit the peak for the first time. They took the Keyhole Route, which eventually led them to the wide notch in the rock from which the trail gets its name. Passing through the Keyhole allows hikers to access the remaining 1.3 miles of the trail to the summit, so approaching this landmark generates excitement among hikers. Secor saw an opening ahead that he believed was the Keyhole, so he quickened his pace, even though Frantz had warned him that this particular notch did not look like the actual Keyhole to him. Secor ignored his friend's warnings and dashed through the notch . . . and found nothing on the other side. He dropped 150 feet and landed on his head on the rocks below. Mountain guides Robert Collier and Paul Cook had the grisly job of retrieving the body, tying it to a two-by-four to carry it over the rocky trail, and then strapping it to a horse to bring it to the Hewes-Kirkwood Inn to Secor's father, a well-known attorney in Longmont, Colorado, for whom young Gray was named.

Not all of the fatalities have been the result of inexperience. Twenty-year-old John Fuller, a student at Iowa State College, had summited Longs Peak no less than thirteen times when he decided to take a particularly difficult route up the left tail of the Dove, a large, permanent snowfield that stretches across the mountain's midsection. He was scaling the steep cliff above the Dove when he fell roughly fifty feet onto the ice, then slid at breakneck speed another four hundred feet across the snow and into a boulder field. The impact ended his life.

On the day that Earl Franklin Harvey, 19, of Gretna, Virginia, and his friend Joseph Burrell, 20, chose to summit Longs Peak by the Keyhole Route, the young men did not expect the wide snow-fields, drifted snow, and frozen conditions they found on June 5, 1954. The two Denver University students reached the summit and began to descend, but they soon realized that going down the same drifts they had climbed earlier could result in a serious accident. Instead, they decided to take the Cable Route down the mountain's north face.

The Cable Route served as one of the more popular routes up the mountain beginning in 1925, because the park had installed steel cables that made the route somewhat easier than others. Over time, it became clear that the cables attracted lightning, so the park removed them in 1973 but left the eyebolts in place, turning this into a favorite technical climbing route. In 1954, the cables were still in place, and there seemed to be less snow on the north face, so Harvey and Burrell may have believed that they would have an easier way down if they worked their way over to them. What they did not realize, however, is that no cable system could minimize the danger of the amount of snow and ice on the way to the cables. With no climbing gear and no crampons or other ice-gripping footwear, the two young men were at the mercy of the elements.

They had reached a precipice known as Zumie's Chimney on the way to the Cable Route, with Harvey about fifty feet ahead, when he lost his footing on the ice. "He started sliding, and despite one lunge at a rock could not stop his fall," the Associated Press reported. "After sliding about 40 feet, Harvey plunged over the precipice. His body bounced several times against the face of the cliff before landing on the snowfield, which also sloped. His body came to a stop about 1,000 feet down the peak from where his fall started."

Rangers later said that Harvey most likely died on first impact.

As quickly as he could, Burrell crept to the edge and looked over. When he saw the distance Harvey had fallen and his battered body at the bottom, he knew that there was nothing he could do for his friend. He managed to gather his wits and make his way to the Cable Route, descending as fast as he dared and hurrying to the Hewes-Kirkwood Inn to notify rangers of Harvey's death. By this time, however, the sun had descended, and chief ranger J. Barton Herschler knew that any attempt to retrieve the body would not go well. He waited until Sunday morning—which dawned bright and windless—to climb back up with Burrell, District Ranger Edward J. Kirk, and three other rangers to the snowfield at 12,500 feet, where Harvey had breathed his last.

As it turned out, it was good that the rangers had made the trek up the mountain as expeditiously as they did. That afternoon, a massive late-spring blizzard raced through the area, dumping two to three feet of snow on the Front Range and stranding dozens of cars at the 12,100-foot level of Trail Ridge Road on a busy near-summer Sunday. Rangers including Kirk, who had just come down from bringing Harvey off of Longs Peak, worked with snowplow crews to make their way up the road and rescue the stranded motorists. The operation extended well into the evening and finally wrapped up around midnight, with visitors forced to abandon some of the cars and ride in others' vehicles until crews could dig their cars out of the drifting snow.

"It was blowing so hard," Kirk said, "that often the snowplows would progress only 5 to 10 feet, have to stop for maybe 15 minutes, then get another 100 yards."

Had they waited until afternoon or another day before heading up Longs Peak, Harvey's body may well have been buried in deep snow until August or September.

ANYONE CAN MAKE BAD DECISIONS

Camp counselors at the National YMCA camp in Estes Park need days off just like everyone else, so when a Monday in late August of 1962 looked like a great day to climb Longs Peak, Kem Arnold Murphy, 21, of Kingfisher, Oklahoma, and his fellow counselors Wayne McCormick, 20, from Normal, Illinois, and Scott Shaw, 19, from Kettering, Ohio, set off early in the morning to make their way to the summit.

Murphy had finished his sophomore year at Oklahoma State University in Stillwater the previous spring, where he was a member of the Wesley Foundation, the United Methodist campus ministry, and the Army Reserve Officers' Training Corps (ROTC). He majored in Russian and planned to continue his studies after college with the intention of becoming a minister, and had already preached at small churches in his neighborhood and elsewhere in Oklahoma. Despite growing up in the Great Plains, he loved climbing and knew his way around a mountain, so he soon took the lead and moved faster than his friends, reaching the summit well before they did.

When McCormick and Shaw got to the top, however, Murphy was nowhere to be found. They guessed that he had grown bored with waiting for them and started down a different route, so they, too, began their descent and returned to camp. When they got there, however, no one had seen Murphy. The young men soon realized that he had not come down from the mountain.

The counselors notified authorities in the park immediately, and a search party departed late Monday and worked through the night in freezing temperatures to locate Murphy, with hopes that he would be found alive. At daybreak Tuesday morning, they discovered him not far from the summit, at about 13,400 feet.

"A preliminary investigation indicated he had fallen 100 feet straight down and rolled another 100 feet over rocks," the *Daily Oklahoman*, the newspaper of Oklahoma City, reported. "Rangers said he had strayed from a safe trail on the north face of the mountain and had taken a route to a rock formation on the edge of a cliff."

Murphy's father and brother-in-law arrived in Estes Park Monday night to await news, and were there to join the YMCA camp's staff, park rangers, and Estes Park personnel for a memorial service for Kem. After the service, they flew home with his body for burial in Kingfisher Cemetery.

Good climbers like Kem Murphy can make questionable decisions on an impulse, but those with the least experience often are more prone to the spontaneous choices that lead to the most devastating consequences. Such was the case on June 12, 1972, when 24-year-old Paul Russell and his friend Bob Doettel, 21, both from Lincoln Park, Michigan, decided to extend their hike to Chasm Lake by making a try for the Longs Peak summit.

The night before their climb, the two men had discussed their plans with a ranger, who told them that there was still plenty of ice and snow near the top of the mountain, making it very treacherous for climbers who did not have the necessary crampons, ice axes, and other equipment to keep themselves safe. The ranger told them not to attempt the summit, especially because they had no experience in the kind of conditions they would find as they approached the top.

Russell and Doettel decided to just hike as far as Chasm Lake. Once they reached the lake, however, they looked at the conditions ahead and decided to ignore the ranger's warnings and make a try for the summit anyway. They chose the Keyhole Route, even though only technical climbing is allowed on this route in June because of the lingering snow cover. Russell wore tennis shoes, and the men carried no rope with them.

Once they got as far as the Keyhole, Doettel determined that he had gone far enough and told Russell it was time to turn back. Russell looked ahead and saw that only half a mile of trail remained between him and the summit. He decided to go for it alone.

Whether Doettel saw what happened next is not clear from the news reports, but Russell never made it to the summit. He fell 150 feet from "near the summit of the peak's west side," and died on impact.

A search-and-rescue team reached Russell's body at about 8:30 p.m. that evening, but it was already too dark to risk bringing the body down from the peak. In the morning, the Rocky Mountain Rescue Group from Boulder joined the National Park Service team in bringing the body to a place where a helicopter could transport it out of the park.

Making it to the Homestretch only to perish in a fall brings a sense of futility to the planned climb, affecting other people as well as the deceased. Perhaps Corbin Mabon, 22, of Colorado Springs, felt a kind of deflation of the triumph of summiting Longs Peak when he came across the lifeless body of 29-year-old Jeffrey Rosinski in the vicinity of the Homestretch at about 5:30 a.m. on Friday morning, July 16, 2010.

Rosinski, a pastor from New Hampshire with a wife and two young children, had been camping with his brother and two others when he decided to set out on a solo hike at about 4:15 p.m. the day before. Perhaps he did not fully understand the dramatic difference between the mountains that top out at 6,800 feet in New Hampshire and the elevation of a Colorado fourteener, but he made his way nearly to the top of Longs Peak before something—fatigue, dizziness, darkness, or a simple misstep—made him fall. He plunged 250 to 300 feet before striking the ground.

Mabon found himself in the difficult position of having to tell Rosinski's brother what had happened to him. "I felt really, really, really sorry for his brother," he told 9news.com. He added that when he had been on the summit, shortly before finding Rosinski, the winds were so strong that he'd stayed prone on the ground, fearing that if he'd stood up, he'd have been blown off.

Not all accidents are the result of a split-second's questionable decision. Some come at the end of a cascade of events that seem destined to lead to disaster.

A group of twelve Boy Scouts led by Gary Quinn, an employee of the Tahosa High Adventure Base Boy Scout camp in Ward, Colorado, chose June 26, 1980, as a good day to climb Longs Peak via the Keyhole Route.

"People seem to have difficulty comprehending that conditions at 14,000 feet in June can be, and often are, much, much different than at lower elevations, including those found at the Longs Peak Ranger Station at 9,500 feet," noted Larry Van Slyke, an employee of Rocky Mountain National Park, in his report of the incident to the American Alpine Club. "Many people take a chance on those conditions and survive. Some people do not."

On this particular day, there was no snow at the ranger station, but plenty of snow and ice remained at fourteen thousand feet and above. When the group reached the Keyhole at about 13,600 feet, four of the Scouts looked up at the snow-covered Homestretch half a mile above them and announced that they were going no farther, leaving seven to continue to the top.

At the base of the Homestretch, two others stopped and watched as Robert Silver, 16, struggled to reach the summit. Silver had moved to the north of the normal route to avoid the snow and continue on dry rock, but the rock that he had moved to jutted upward at a high angle. He turned to a nearby companion and told him that he was stuck; he could not move upward or downward.

Meanwhile, Quinn had reached the summit with four of the Scouts, and watched from there as Silver wavered on the rock. He called instructions to the waylaid Scout about where to place his hands and feet, but Silver moved only a short distance before he determined that he was stuck once again.

Seeing that the situation might be insurmountable, Quinn made his way down from the summit to assist Silver. The boy, however, decided he needed to move more quickly. He started to adjust his feet, but he lost his hold and slipped down on the angled rock. In another second he was gone, falling through the air for three hundred feet before landing on the rocks below.

Jim Bast, one of the Scouts who had stopped at the base of the Homestretch, made his way to Silver and checked his pulse. He found none. Quinn arrived a few minutes later and checked as well, but Silver had no heartbeat. The fall had killed him.

Quinn quickly rounded up the Scouts and sent all but Bast and another boy, Greene, down the mountain to get help. He, Bast, and Greene waited with Silver's body until a rescue party arrived hours later and airlifted the boy's body from the peak.

"After a winter of very heavy snowfall, the Keyhole Route still had sufficient snow on it so that it was considered a technical climb by Ranger personnel," said Van Slyke. "Numerous warnings as to the hazards of the route were posted at the Longs Peak Ranger Station where the Scouts began their hike to the summit. Had they read and then given credence to the posted information concerning conditions on the peak, they surely would not have continued their trip."

Young people rely on guides and other adults to make good decisions that are in the best interests of the group. Either the organizers of this climb did not see the park's signs that warned of icy conditions, or they chose to believe that the warnings were overcautious and took their chances—not only with their own lives, but with the lives of twelve children in their care.

A LOSS TO A COMMUNITY

The terse news release from Rocky Mountain National Park offered but the briefest details about the death of Scott Alan Corliss:

A 61-year-old man from Greeley, Colorado, died yesterday, Saturday, October 1, [2016,] on Longs Peak in Rocky Mountain National Park. He fell approximately 100 to 150 feet, apparently slipping on ice, along the Narrows section on the Keyhole Route. Park rangers were notified of the accident around 10 a.m. via cell phone by visitors who were in the area when the fall occurred. Park rangers were flown to the summit of Longs Peak via helicopter and reached the man's body at approximately 4 p.m. His body was recovered by a long-line helicopter operation at 5:40 p.m., and transferred to the Boulder County Coroner's Office. His name will be released after next of kin are notified.

News stories about this accident barely mentioned Corliss's name, including it as an afterthought in a busy season of search-and-rescue operations in which another man died of hypothermia on the Loft, one was located alive on the Clark's Arrow route, and a third wandered off the North Longs Peak Trail and spent a cold night out among the elements. Scott Corliss became one more fatality among sixty-four on the mountain to that date, since Rocky Mountain became a national park in 1915.

His family, however, would not let that be Corliss's legacy. They wrote a tribute to him that tells us much more about the man who lost his life on a cold October day, on a mountain he had summited many times before.

Born in Hebron, Nebraska, Scott Corliss moved to Greeley, Colorado, as a child and graduated from Greeley West High School in 1973. He went on to graduate from Colorado University Medical School in 1985, choosing family medicine as his specialty. "He brought so many new lives into the world that he had long since lost count," the writer tells us.

He then chose a new path, moving into preventive health care as a life coach for Take Shape for Life. "[A]s a life coach he had many people say that he brought hope into their lives at times when they had none," the tribute says. At the same time, he began work on a master's degree in aerospace biomedical engineering, at the tender age of 59. He visited elementary schools to talk to children about space, becoming known as "Rocket Man" to young students. The nickname was particularly apt, because he had achieved his Level 3 certification from the National Association of Rocketry, and had designed and built by hand a ten-foot-tall rocket he called "The Spirit of Colorado."

His day out on Longs Peak in October 2016 actually was one of many he spent on high mountains, climbing most of Colorado's other fourteeners, as well as Mount Rainier in Washington State, Mount Kilimanjaro in Tanzania, and Longs Peak on many occasions. "He loved being outdoors and sharing the experience with anyone who felt like coming along with him," the tribute notes.

His parents, brother, and sister and their families all outlived him, as did his wife Peggy, sons Ben and Luke, as well as their spouses and children, and his daughter Kelsey.

"Despite the incredible loss of someone who meant so much to so many, Scott's family takes great solace in knowing that Scott passed doing what he loved most in one of his very favorite places," the tribute concludes. "Scott was always full of vibrancy, and he truly lived life to its fullest, even unto his last moments."

The same, it seems, can be said of John Bramley of Littleton, Colorado, who met his end on Longs Peak on September 11, 2009, in a "significant fall" on the north side of the mountain. A passionate runner who once trained for the Olympics, Bramley held the record for the fastest running ascent of Mount Evans, an achievement he accomplished thirty-one years before. He was a graduate of Colorado State University and an employee of Frontier Airlines, and he raised three daughters, Stephanie, Stacey, and Rebecca. When he was discovered lying below the False Keyhole at 10:15 a.m. by an off-duty park employee, he was 55 years old.

Media coverage would lead us to believe that the most interesting thing about the death of Paul G. Nahon III, who fell from the Narrows on the Keyhole Route on August 15, 2013, was that his body's removal from the mountain had to be delayed while the recovery teams rescued a fallen climber elsewhere on Longs Peak. Twenty-year-old Nahon's memorial tells us much more about him: His trek up Longs Peak should have added one more fourteener to the list of those he had already summited in Colorado. He had a number of achievements for a man so young, including the title of Missouri State Tennis Champion in 2010 and 2011, with the most tennis wins in Missouri history—an overall record of 117 wins and 7 losses. This earned him a place in the National High School Tennis All-American Foundation, and he netted several awards for sportsmanship at the state and national levels.

Nahon also served as media chair of his high school's Student Council Cabinet, and he held positions in student government, the World Language Club, and the National Honor Society. Academically, he ranked in the top 3 percent statewide, which earned him a place on the school's Wall of Honor. A student at the University of Richmond at the time of his death, he became the first tennis team member since 2005 to be named to the All-Academic Honors Team. He also had the highest grade point average in his class in his freshman and sophomore years. In short, his life had been full of promise until a misplaced footfall on a slippery trail sent him over the edge one mid-August day.

So many of those whose missteps resulted in the end of their lives on Longs Peak become little more than names, dates, and accident reports in the mountain's history. It's comforting to take the opportunity to learn more about them as people, and what their lives meant to those who experience their loss long after their names have been entered into national park databases.

WHEN THE CLIMB ISN'T OVER

The culmination of a demanding climb can seem like an end in itself, especially if the climb takes place on a particularly treacherous rock wall. Even the most skilled climbers can experience mental fatigue after reaching the top of their climb, enjoying the sense that the most difficult part is over and all that's left to do is head down. "Down" may require no more than a trail hike, or it may involve a descent on a simpler course than the one the climbers conquered on the way up. The comparative ease of the way down can be deceiving, however, especially on a mountain like Longs Peak.

It took the better part of three days for Jay Van Stavern, 19, a sophomore at the University of Colorado, and his climbing partner, Peter Kopetsky, 22, of Denver, to reach the Longs Peak summit using Kiener's Route on the East Face. This is the route followed by Walter Kiener and Agnes Vaille in 1925, when they tried several times to climb the east side of the mountain in winter (their story appears in chapter 3 of this book). While it's considered the easiest route up this side of Longs Peak, a winter's worth of snow and ice can make it an arduous technical climb.

Van Stavern and Kopetsky reached the summit on Monday morning, April 2, 1973, and clearly felt that they could now relax some of their safeguards. After enjoying their accomplishment, they began their descent on the north face, proceeding down the much easier route unroped.

Suddenly, Van Stavern's feet went out from under him. He slid on the icy surface and headed for the nearest cliff at top speed. Before he or Kopetsky could react, Van Stavern disappeared over the edge, free-falling one thousand feet to the rocks below.

Alone on the north face, Kopetsky completed his descent as quickly as he could manage without becoming a casualty as well. He finally reached the timberline, where he ran into two hikers and had the first opportunity to tell someone what had happened. Together the three made for the nearest ranger station, seven miles off down the trail, to notify officials about the accident. Search teams found Van Stavern's body the following day and removed it from the park before day's end.

Even the most skilled climbers can make a small mistake that turns into tragedy. Carl Siegel, 30, and Tim Cumbo, 35, spent five days on the peak beginning at the end of January 1993, scaling the sheer wall on the east side of the mountain known as the Diamond. (I'll go into more detail about the East Face and the Diamond in chapter 3.) Siegel "was an outstanding and experienced climber, with major climbs on several continents," reported Jim Detterline, Longs Peak supervisory climbing ranger, to the American Alpine Club.

They completed the climb on February 3 using the D7 route, described on the Mountain Project website as "the unquestioned favorite for those few demented souls who climb the Diamond in winter." With this supreme challenge behind them, they chose to descend via the Cable Route, a hiking trail also covered with snow and ice that made it a technical climb in winter. Siegel began to make his way down to the highest of the eyebolts, and he had descended to within one hundred feet of it when something happened. Later, investigators would find a crampon stab mark on his left gaiter, indicating that a second's misstep may have resulted in him tripping over his own foot. He fell on the snow patch and began to slide. Instantly he employed his ice ax to try to slow himself, but he had neglected to wrap the strap around his wrist. "The ax ripped out of his hands and remained planted in the snow," the report noted.

With no other way to self-arrest, Siegel lost control of his descent. He slid five hundred feet, tumbling over rock cliffs and plummeting down snowfields until he finally came to rest downhill of the point known as Chasm View. No doubt as a result of the belief that the hardest part of the climb was over, Siegel was not wearing his helmet.

Cumbo moved quickly to descend to Siegel's position, shouting to another climber, Derek Hersey, for assistance. The two climbers reached Siegel and checked for life signs, but there was no heartbeat.

Larimer County coroner Charles Lavato examined Siegel and determined that he had died from "cerebral contusions due to multiple blunt trauma to the head and face." Siegel had no other serious injuries, leading Lavato to speculate that if Siegel had worn his helmet, he might have survived the fall.

OVER THE LEDGES

While the Keyhole Route has been labeled the "easiest" route to the summit, this trail can exact the ultimate price when hikers become overwhelmed by its most challenging features. For example, many hikers thrill at the prospect of traversing the Ledges, a thirty-foot-long series of narrow lips of rock extending just eighteen inches or less from the vertical rock face above and below. Hikers need to hug the rock wall as they cross this short section even in the driest and warmest weather; when the Ledges gain their ice rime or collect deep snow any month of the year, they can become a formidable test of skill and courage.

Jun Kamimura, a 33-year-old man from Boston, chose August 25, 1995, as the day that he would solo-hike the Keyhole Route to the summit. He spoke with rangers at the mountain's base before departing, and they told him that he'd picked a tough day: A snowfield 130 feet across had formed three-quarters of a mile from the summit, making the way much tougher than usual for late August. This didn't stop him, however, and he made his way up as far as the Ledges, at an elevation of 13,160 feet, taking no technical equipment with him that might help him cross the snowfield.

At the Ledges, he encountered two rangers and told them that he was feeling the effects of the altitude, so he had decided not to proceed any further to the summit. The rangers thought this was a wise idea and invited him to follow them down the trail.

Whether the lack of oxygen impaired Kamimura's judgment or he had a natural inclination to take chances, he did not take the commonsense precautions to keep himself safe. He followed the rangers but ignored their frequent pleas to stop hopping from rock to rock. Finally, he made one leap too many, missing his mark and plunging four hundred feet down the side of the mountain, in full view of the two rangers and several other hikers.

The rangers worked their way down the mountainside and reached Kamimura in less than half an hour, but he had already perished from the impact. A helicopter crew and recovery team removed his body from the mountain the following morning.

Another August day, this one in 1999, led to the death of Gregory J. Koczanski, a 42-year-old Washington lobbyist and co-director for federal government relations at Citigroup. Koczanski was in the midst of a brilliant career that began with his degree from the School of Foreign Service at Georgetown University, and more recently, with him receiving professional credit for spearheading passage of a bank modernization bill in Congress. He served as co-chairman of the Christmas in April home rehabilitation group in Washington and as a member of the John Quincy Adams Society and the McLean Bible Church. Healthy and well-off, he and his family visited Colorado regularly and engaged in a number of outdoor activities.

On August 14, Koczanski and his wife, Kathryn, set out on a long-planned hike to the top of Longs Peak. They made it through the Keyhole and crossed the Ledges, but the winds this close to the summit were so strong that they decided not to continue. They had turned around and started back, with Kathy in the lead as they traversed the narrow ledges once again, but this time a powerful wind gust knocked Gregory off his feet. He fell straight down, hitting the rocks some 450 feet below.

John Regan's death on the Ledges received little attention from the media in late September 2010, but the 57-year-old hiker from Wichita, Kansas, created an indelible memory for the three hikers who saw him fall. Regan lost his footing on the narrow rock at about 12:30 p.m. and fell three hundred feet, dying on contact. Remarkably, at least one of the hikers who witnessed the event soon found cellular service and called the park's rangers to trigger recovery efforts. Rangers reached Regan at 3:17 p.m., according to park records, and remained with the body until the following morning, when it could be transported off the mountain and to the Boulder County coroner.

No one saw what happened on June 9, 2014, however, when a 25-year-old hiker from Fort Collins did not return from his trek up Longs Peak.

Matthew D. Burklow had literally thousands of miles of hiking experience, including an Appalachian Trail through-hike he completed in 2012 in a scant ninety-nine days—something most other through-hikers take five to six months to accomplish. He and his wife, Haley, married at nineteen and had moved from their home in Murfreesboro, Tennessee, to Fort Collins in October 2013, with plans to enroll in Colorado State University. They drove to Yellowstone and the Grand Canyon in their spare time, but the Colorado mountains became Burklow's first love.

Twice before he had attempted to reach the summit of Longs Peak, but he had had to turn back because of weather and trail conditions. This time, he prepared meticulously for a successful journey. The day before, a foot of new snow had fallen on Longs Peak and in other areas of the park, enough that rangers closed sections of Trail Ridge Road as sheets of ice formed over the pavement. Burklow knew that the way would be dangerously slippery, but he proceeded with his plan, trusting his skills to get him to the top.

He left the Longs Peak trailhead at two a.m. on Monday, June 9, wearing mountaineering boots and warm clothing, and carrying crampons and an ice ax. He told Haley he intended to return in time for his four p.m. shift as a pharmacy technician at King Soopers Pharmacy.

Later, rangers looking through the images on his digital camera would find photos of Burklow at the summit, grinning into the lens. His attempt to reach the top had been successful, and he had begun his return hike in triumph.

"He'd already traversed the steep Homestretch and the snowy Narrows and had nearly reached the Keyhole, the final hurdle before the simple scramble down the Boulder Field, and was on the easy but long trail back to his vehicle, his pharmacy job and Fort Collins home," wrote outdoor recreation reporter Stephen Meyers in the *Fort Collins Coloradoan* several weeks later. "Perhaps euphoric from reaching the summit and maybe feeling a time-crunch to return to Fort Collins, Burklow fell from the Ledges section of the mountain."

Whatever momentary lapse took place—an icy patch, a sudden sense of fatigue, a piece of loose scree, a buckling knee—was enough to send him over the edge and tumbling down the mountain for more than six hundred feet. Reports noted that he was not wearing a helmet, though a fall of that length on solid rock would not be survivable even if he'd had a hard hat, according to Meyers's interview of Rocky Mountain National Park chief ranger Mark Pita.

When he didn't arrive at work, Haley notified park rangers, who mobilized quickly to begin scouring the Keyhole Route with the hope of finding him alive. Knowing which route he had taken helped lead them to the right place: His body had come to rest in the Trough area of the mountain, "in a rocky outcropping below the marked section of the Trough," Meyers clarified.

Rangers worked to remove the body from the mountain as quickly as possible and had it flown by helicopter to the coroner for an autopsy.

"Matt is one of those guys, he's so determined, the conditions he encountered on that mountain wouldn't have mattered," said Kent Burklow, Matthew's father, in an interview with the *Fort Collins Coloradoan*. "He had the kind of determination and spirit about him, and it didn't matter what the obstacle was, he was going through it. He was like a bull in the woods with that kind of stuff . . . I do believe Matt was one who was fully prepared for everything he came into contact with, but I think in this case, he underestimated what he was going to run into."

This may also have been the case for Peter Jeffris, a 25-year-old hiker from Oregon, Wisconsin, whose personal quest involved hiking all of the Colorado fourteeners. A University of Colorado–Boulder graduate with a bachelor's degree in mechanical engineering, he had a long history of athletic pursuits, including cross-country running, swimming, and lacrosse, and he honed his love of the outdoors as an Eagle Scout. A technology company in the Boulder area hired Jeffris after college and put him to work in his chosen field, creating a robotic component for future use on the International Space Station. He had settled in Broomfield, a location that gave him access to Colorado's highest mountains.

All of this came to an abrupt halt on November 16, 2014, when Jeffris set out on Sunday morning to climb Longs Peak. He told friends he was considering the Cable Route, which would take him up the north face in frigid winter weather. Sunday came and went and Monday morning arrived, but Jeffris did not come into work as scheduled. His friends and family notified the park that he might be lost on the mountain.

A search began immediately on Monday afternoon, but dark comes early in November, so teams had to wait until Tuesday morning to expand their efforts beyond a small segment of the mountain. "Teams are facing extremely high winds, blowing snow, and gusts up to 85 mph at 14,000 feet," the park's news release said about the Monday search. "Aerial search efforts are not possible due to extreme winds."

With such volatile winds, teams had no choice on Tuesday but to restrict their continued work to areas below the tree line. "Teams will focus on drainages leading to the north and east from Longs Peak," the park said in a statement. "Teams will also use spotting scopes from a distance to search areas including the Ledges and Trough along the Keyhole Route, Kiener's Route and Lambs Slide." A dog team was dispatched to begin searching from Jeffris's car, which was parked at the Longs Peak trailhead. Thirty-two people in all participated in the effort, with teams from every rescue organization in the area.

On Wednesday, the winds finally calmed and aerial searches by helicopter began, taking advantage of a forecast that didn't call for snow until Thursday afternoon. The helicopter crew surveyed an area of nearly twenty square miles, much of it heavily forested, with alpine and subalpine areas above the tree line. As they followed the Keyhole Route from the air, the crew found what they were looking for: a man's body some two hundred feet below the Ledges.

The chopper crew flew four members of the Rocky Mountain National Park Search and Rescue Team to a landing spot in the Glacier Gorge drainage, from which they could access the area below the Ledges. They climbed up about 1,800 feet on the snow-covered mountain wall to reach the body, preparing it for helicopter transport. By four p.m. Wednesday, Jeffris's body had arrived at Upper Beaver Meadows, where it was transferred to a vehicle to bring it to the coroner's office.

As we have seen, some of the most perplexing cases are the ones in which no one sees the accident, leaving friends, loved ones, and even the park staff with more questions than answers.

Thirty-nine-year-old Pawel Abramczyk left the Longs Peak trailhead at 2:30 a.m. with two other winter mountaineers on March 18, 2017, intending to climb to the summit. Once they had reached the top of the Loft at 9:30 a.m., however, Abramczyk decided that he had gone far enough, so he told his friends that he would return to the trailhead at that point. He began a solo descent through the icy conditions they had all just traversed.

It was nearly 6:00 p.m. when the two others in the party made it back to the trailhead, and they discovered with alarm that Abramczyk's car was still in the parking lot. They notified rangers at 6:15 p.m., and the search that began early the following morning came to a fairly rapid close at about noon, when the park's search-and-rescue team found Abramczyk's body halfway down the Loft. No cause of death has been reported publicly, but it seems likely that Abramczyk took a fall fairly soon after he'd left the other two climbers.

One more death on Longs Peak has a direct connection to the Ledges—and chances are that it's very fresh in the minds of readers, as it was resolved just a few days before I wrote this.

Ryan Albert decided to make Longs Peak his first fourteener and determined that Thursday, October 4, 2018, was the right time to do this. The 30-year-old Rowan University senior, majoring in computer science, set out early that morning from Denver wearing dark clothing and carrying a backpack. He drove a rental car to the park and left it at the Longs Peak trailhead. Later that morning, at about 10:30 a.m., a park visitor saw Albert on the trail in the area of Granite Pass, on his way to the Keyhole.

This, in essence, is all we know about Albert and his plans.

The thing about climbing Longs Peak in October, however, is that the weather can change in an instant, and generally not for the better. Temperatures can drop from the 50s into the 30s and below, in the space of just a few minutes. Clouds can dump a foot or more of snow, ice, or sleet on already slick surfaces and fill couloirs and gullies with heavy, wet snow. Winds can blow hard enough to knock a hiker right off a ledge.

Accounts of Albert's intentions say nothing about his previous hiking experience or his reasons for taking on such a difficult climb at a time when weather can spiral into such extremes. The weather lived up to its promise, as noted in the park's records: "Inclement weather that started on October 4 was the beginning of a multiday weather pattern of extreme conditions including low visibility and fog, thunderstorms and snow showers and freezing temperatures in the 20s and 30s."

When he had not emerged from his hike by Friday afternoon, Albert's family contacted the Denver police, who in turn notified the park. Rangers went to the Longs Peak trailhead and found the rental car, and began to mobilize a search effort on the chance that they might find the young man alive. They had one significant obstacle from the start, however: Albert had not shared with anyone which trail he planned to take.

"That puts us on our heels right at the beginning," said spokesperson Kyle Patterson to the *Windsor Beacon* later in the search effort. "It just makes the search area expand exponentially." Luckily, on Saturday the park received information that indicated Albert had chosen the Keyhole Route to the summit, narrowing the field for the search.

Teams began at higher elevations, covering the entire Keyhole Route as well as the Boulderfield, the Loft, Chasm Cirque, North Longs Peak, and Boulder Brook, but soon the ice buildup at this altitude became insurmountable. "Search teams faced pockets of deep snow as well as verglas ice," the park's news release said, referring to the kind of ice that leaves a thin coating on every exposed surface, making each rock and ledge a falling risk. As they worked on Saturday and Sunday, October 6 and 7, temperatures dropped into the 20s, and ice fog, snow showers, and even thunderstorms hampered their ability to see long distances or venture into rock-strewn areas at the base of cliffs. "Up to three inches of snow is predicted tonight in the search area, and the extended forecast includes cold temperatures and snow throughout next week," the park reported.

Nonetheless, they moved lower on the mountain and continued their efforts, with members of Larimer County Search and Rescue, Rocky Mountain Rescue from Boulder County, and Colorado Search and Rescue Board joining park rangers to cover more ground. Dog teams from Larimer County Search and Rescue, Rocky Mountain Rescue, and Front Range Search and Rescue Dogs also participated when they could be effective during breaks in the snowstorms.

On Tuesday, October 9, more of the promised brutal weather arrived, featuring "waist-deep snow drifts, decreased visibility, cold temperatures, ice-covered rock, avalanche hazards, wind and falling snow throughout the day," according to a park news release. "This caused slow-moving travel with slips along the way." Park spokesperson Lindsey Lewis told the *Fort Collins Coloradoan* that four teams of technical rescuers used "ropes and climbing equipment for fall protection in order to mitigate those hazards." She also noted that they had not found a single clue that might point to Albert's location on the mountain.

The weather forecast called for three additional inches of snow overnight and seven more in the morning, forcing the search teams to take a break on Wednesday. "The safety of the search teams continues to be the priority for those managing the search," the park's statement said.

They renewed search efforts on Thursday, October 11, with five teams totaling twenty-seven people returning to the mountain and focusing on "high-probability areas below tree line." The complement of searchers grew to include members of the Alpine Interagency Hotshot Crew, Rocky Mountain National Park Search and Rescue, and Larimer County Search and Rescue. They found more than a foot of snow at the Longs Peak trailhead, with drifted snow piled deeper in many places, a challenging environment for Larimer County's dog team.

The missing element in the search, its supervisors knew, was aerial reconnaissance. Helicopters could not fly in the series of gales and snowstorms, so eight days passed without this critical tool in the search effort. Finally, on October 12, a helicopter from Northern Colorado Interagency Helitack flew over the search areas, and observers took video footage of the most likely areas where Albert might have fallen or become lost. "Rocky Mountain National Park Search and Rescue team members spent the next three days reviewing the extensive footage," the park records said.

Despite all of these efforts, not a single clue revealed itself. Any sign of whatever became of Ryan Albert had been buried in the snow within a day of his disappearance.

Late on Saturday, October 13, another major winter storm put an end to further searches. Five days passed before teams could once again venture out to the upper portion of the mountain, but they found waist- and chest-deep snow that slowed their activities to a crawl. Icy slopes made close examination of areas where Albert might have fallen virtually impossible. They proceeded as far as the Ledges before turning back from the peak, ending three days of searching for a scrap of clothing, a discarded pack, or any other evidence of Albert's resting place.

Another team set out for Chasm Cirque on Sunday, October 21, a vantage point from which they could scan areas of the mountain with binoculars and spotting scopes in case Albert had diverted from the Keyhole Route and taken a different trail toward the peak. They examined Lambs Slide, Mills Glacier, Camel Gully, and the Chasm View fall line, but nothing of substance revealed itself.

The park officially called a halt to the October effort on November 2, 2018. "In the absence of additional clues combined with extreme winter conditions at higher elevations that will exist until late spring, we will have no active search operations during the winter months," the park's statement said. "We plan for search efforts to resume when the snow melts and conditions improve. Ryan Albert is still a missing person and our investigation will continue in hopes of gaining further information as to his plans on the day of his disappearance."

The long winter passed with no further search efforts or clues. Then, on May 25, 2019, two rangers conducting a routine climbing patrol of the Trough section of the mountain, about one thousand feet below the Ledges, made the first meaningful discovery of the search effort: They found a single glove that matched the brand Albert was wearing on the day he began his hike to the summit. Chief ranger Mark Pita told the media that the rangers had a detailed list of the clothing Albert was wearing when he went missing, so they knew immediately that this glove had to be his. They marked the area where they had found it, but a weather system moved in and parked itself over the mountain, so four days passed before they could return to search the area.

On May 30, a team of "four highly skilled park climbing rangers," according to the park's news release, searched the deep snow in the Trough for several hours. "The team was ready to call it a day when the unbelievable happened about 200 feet below where the glove was found, at an elevation of 12,300 feet," wrote Miles Blumhardt in the *Fort Collins Coloradoan*. "One of the rangers skied to an opening in the snow that Pita described as 12 to 18 inches wide. The cavity was dark. The ranger peered into it and noticed what appeared to be a human body, about 3 feet under the snow."

The rangers dug until they reached the body and removed it from the snow. "They wrapped up the body and marked with GPS the location—about 1,000 feet below the Ledges," the *Coloradoan* said.

The rangers completed their investigation of the site on May 31, and a helicopter flew the body off the mountain for transfer to the Boulder County Coroner's Office. On June 5, the coroner confirmed that the body was Ryan Albert.

Did Albert fall from the Ledges and land more than one thousand feet below? The cause of death, released by the Boulder County Coroner's Office at the end of July, was twofold: blunt force trauma, followed by hypothermia. "It appeared Albert fell into the Trough area or purposefully went into it when severe weather moved into the area shortly after he went missing," the *Fort Collins Coloradoan* reported on July 28.

"When we notified the family that we [had] found him, they were very appreciative, extremely gracious and thankful, and told us that they didn't want anyone involved in the search to get hurt," Pita told Blumhardt. "Finding him was a huge relief. We care a lot and put a lot of time into these searches. We hope this brings closure for the family so they can move forward with their lives."

Shortly after rangers halted the search for Ryan Albert in November 2018, another young man went missing on Longs Peak. Micah Tice was last seen on November 24, 2018.

The US Air Force Academy in Colorado Springs contacted the park on Monday, November 26. Tice, 20, was a cadet candidate at the academy, and he had mentioned to friends on the previous Saturday that he planned to hike on Longs Peak. That night, however, Longs Peak experienced a major snowstorm with heavy snow and subzero cold. Park rangers found Tice's car at the Longs Peak trailhead at 3:30 p.m. on Monday afternoon and initiated a search beginning at dawn the following day.

Over the next few days, rangers pieced together a tentative time-line for Tice's hike up the mountain. Two park visitors said they had met him on the trail and chatted with him for twenty minutes or so, during which they learned that he had started his hike at about 6:30 that morning. They encountered him between 7:30 and 8:00 a.m. in the Battle Mountain area, about two and a half miles up the trail from the Longs Peak trailhead. "The visitors indicated the weather was terrible at the Longs Peak trailhead, and that visibility and weather conditions continued to worsen," the park's news release said. A later release recapping the search noted, "Conditions on November 24 in the area were severe, including significant snow accumulation, extremely high winds, blizzard conditions, and bitter cold temperatures."

"Tice was wearing a black sweatshirt, black sweatpants, black lightweight gloves, tennis shoes and a light blue backpack," the hikers told park rangers. "The visitors discouraged Tice to continue to the summit due to his clothing, footwear and weather conditions."

They had no information about Tice's planned route, however, so search teams focused first on sections of the Longs Peak trail on the Keyhole Route. Dog teams from Summit County Search and Rescue, Alpine Rescue Team, and a Colorado National Guard helicopter all joined in the search on Tuesday, November 27, braving heavy snow and high winds that became too violent for safe aerial reconnaissance. The search proceeded as far as the Ledges section of the Keyhole Route, but ice encrusted the mountain above this level, so they went no farther.

"In the third day of the search for Tice, crews continued to face extreme weather, including chest-deep snow, a high avalanche danger, strong wind gusts, and bitter wind chill," Sady Swanson of the *Fort Collins Coloradoan* reported. The park's own news release on the search noted that winds hurled gusts of more than 90 miles per hour, grounding a Colorado Air National Guard Blackhawk helicopter.

The search area expanded on Wednesday in spite of the weather, to include East Longs Peak Trail, Granite Pass, Jim's Grove, the Estes Cone area, the Boulder Brook Trail area, Storm Pass, and the Roaring Fork drainage, the paper said. Rocky Mountain Rescue, the Air Force Academy Mountaineering Club, Diamond Peaks Ski Patrol, Colorado Avalanche Information Center, Grand County Search and Rescue, Douglas County Search and Rescue, Colorado Search and Rescue Board, Front Range Rescue Dogs, FLIR Systems, and Larimer County Search and Rescue all joined the search.

Meanwhile, the park requested assistance from the military in forensic analysis of cell phone data to see if the data could help them narrow down Tice's whereabouts. "Cell phone data provided broad areas of potential transactions but was vague information given the limitations of the signal in that area," the park's statement said. "These transactions were not 'pings,' nor texts nor phone calls. This information indicated Tice's cell phone was picking up a signal early Sunday morning, November 25." The park continued its search efforts in the "large, broad area" where the analysis suggested that Tice might be, but this did not lead them to Tice.

The teams finally got a break in the weather on Sunday, December 2, so Colorado Air National Guard helicopters from Buckley Air Force Base circled the mountain, looking for any sign of the young man. Nothing new came to light, and on December 4, after a week of searching in weather that seemed to fight their efforts at every juncture, the park suspended its efforts until weather improved.

"Micah Tice is still a missing person and our investigation will continue in hopes of gaining further information as to his plans on the day of his disappearance," the park's news release said.

Three days later, on December 7, the park resumed its search from Granite Pass to the lower northern slopes of Longs Peak, including the Wind River and Boulder Brook drainages. When the weather improved further, teams climbed the Keyhole Route to the summit and covered the Chasm Lake area, Clark's Arrow, and the Loft. Snow stood in chest-deep drifts, and some passages were blocked by dead and downed trees that had fallen during the high winds the week before. "At higher elevations, winds scour the landscape leaving it bare or depositing deep drifted snow," the park said in a statement. "These conditions have existed since the first day of search operations and can cover or erase clues."

The US Air Force Academy worked closely with the park throughout the search, which finally had to end for the winter after a last attempt to find Tice in the Wind River drainage area on December 11. The Academy provided "investigative and operational assistance," and a team from the Air Force Academy Mountaineering Club assisted with the first few days of search efforts. Parents of other cadets headed up the process of keeping the searchers fed throughout the effort, coordinating the many individuals and organizations that donated meals through the Air Force Academy Colorado Parents' Club.

On December 10, when the park informed Tice's parents that the search would be on hiatus until snow melted in spring, the Tice family announced to the media in a news conference that they were offering a $10,000 reward for "information leading to the location of their son" to volunteers that would continue the search in the park. They asked specifically for "skilled hikers with appropriate winter gear," but the park's spokesperson cautioned that a search of Longs Peak in winter conditions could pose a life-threatening danger level for inexperienced hikers and climbers.

"We have significant concerns that offering a reward to find Micah may encourage individuals to take additional risks and potentially lead to further tragedy in the Longs Peak area," park spokesperson Kyle Patterson told the media. "Rocky Mountain National Park is the fourth most-visited national park, and last year was the third busiest park for search and rescue operations in the country. We have some of the most experienced and trained search and rescue professionals in the country."

Whether or not volunteer searchers went up the mountain over the winter is not clear; if they did, their findings did not rise to the level of a media story. The following summer, however, a group of "private searchers affiliated with the Tice family," according to the *Fort Collins Coloradoan*, discovered the first solid clue to the young man's whereabouts: On July 4 in the Boulder Brook drainage area, they discovered "items" that matched what Tice was known to be wearing or carrying when he disappeared.

The private search party notified the park's search-and-rescue officials, and a team searched the area on July 5. "The Boulder Brook drainage was an area where initial search efforts were heavily focused," the *Coloradoan* reported the following day, "but the area was covered in deep snow throughout the winter and spring." Here, at last, the searchers discovered the remains of a body, 238 days after Tice had disappeared.

Three days later, the Larimer County Coroner's Office confirmed that the skeletal remains were indeed Micah Tice, and that he had died from "hypothermia and exposure."

"We never stopped looking for you," Omar Khalek, one of the searchers affiliated with the Tice family, wrote on his Facebook page when Tice had been found and identified. "I am thankful that we are able to bring closure to your family in a way. May your soul rest in peace."

One other man who went missing in 2018 remains on the mountain: James Pruitt, whose story as we know it to date appears in chapter 11 of this book.

OTHER ROUTES TO THE TOP

Not everyone wants to join the crowd climbing Longs Peak via the Keyhole Route on a summer day. Climbers describe bottlenecks at the Ledges and at the Narrows, another slim passage farther up the mountain, as well as lines of hikers waiting at the bottom of the Homestretch for the opportunity to scramble up the last three hundred feet to the top. Knowing that this congestion can be frustrating, some hardy hikers choose other routes—some longer and more difficult, but with rewards of their own, like the chance to bag an additional summit on the way to the desired fourteener.

The Loft Route takes hikers past the Chasm Lake turnoff, where most people turn toward the lake to begin the Keyhole Route, and up past a formation known as the Ship's Prow to a steep section of what the Yosemite Decimal System ranks as Class 3 terrain—requiring the use of hands as well as feet to scramble up the slope. This leads into the area known as the Loft, a boulder field that puts hikers on a direct course to summit Mount Meeker at 13,911 feet.

From here, the route leads back down through the Loft and then down again, a tricky change-up that leads to Keplinger's Couloir—a narrow gully with a steep pitch on the side of Longs Peak opposite the Homestretch. The trail continues around to the Homestretch, where hikers queue up with everyone else for their last push to the summit.

The Loft Route can be tougher than the Keyhole on the most temperate summer days, but in winter, it becomes as perilous as any other route to the peak. That may be why Erin Colby Sharp, a 27-year-old, highly experienced climber from Marlin, Texas, chose it as part of his training for taking on North America's highest mountain, on March 3, 2000. Climbing the 20,310-foot mountain now known as Denali—still Mount McKinley at the time— would require significant skill in scaling ice-crusted granite walls in year-round winter conditions, breathing air containing minimal oxygen. Sharp outfitted himself for a technical climb and clearly had the gear he needed for the challenge, knowing that the mountains in early March would be covered in deep snow and ice. It's hard to guess what specifically might have gone wrong to result in his three-hundred-foot fall on the Loft between Longs Peak and Mount Meeker. The only known detail is that Sharp was not roped when he fell.

Six years passed before another hiker lost his life on the Loft Route. Two park rangers on climbing patrol had the shocking experience of seeing this one happen. On September 3, 2006, 58-year-old Clayton Smith of Louisville, Colorado, lost his footing and plummeted eight hundred feet from the Loft to the jagged rocks far below. Knowing how to descend swiftly without personal injury, the rangers made their way to the man and reached him in less than half an hour, but Smith could not have survived such a fall. Smith and his hiking partner had reached the summit of Mount Meeker that morning and were on their way back down when he slipped.

Ronald Graham Webber, however, vanished unobserved on January 19, 2016, while making his first solo winter trek in the Longs Peak area. When his family notified the park on January 21 that he had not returned from his hike, rangers checked parking areas and found his car at the Longs Peak trailhead.

Webber, 58, had been a teacher and coach at Bishop Kenny High School in Jacksonville, Florida, and had more recently started a landscaping business. His wife and three children did not know his intended hiking route, but his family thought that he was not carrying supplies for an overnight stay in the wilderness. The January weather brought high winds and freezing temperatures shortly after he set out.

Search teams began right away to cover the Roaring Fork drainage and the east cirque of Longs Peak in the Chasm Lake area, both on land and by air. No clues turned up on the first day, but on Friday, January 22, about a half mile east of Chasm Lake, search teams spotted his body at the base of a broken cliff band at Peacock Pool. "He apparently fell 200 feet," the *Fort Collins Coloradoan* reported. The aerial team airlifted his body from the area to their accustomed landing spot at Upper Beaver Meadows in the park, where he was transferred to the coroner's office.

Lost and Found, and Lost Again

The story of Jens "Jay" Yambert, a hiker from Champaign, Illinois, begins when he was 58 years old and is one of twists and turns, false starts, and bad ends, with a disquieting sense of déjà vu. It starts on Sunday, July 27, 2014, when Yambert left the Longs Peak trailhead to take the Loft Route to the summit. Despite the midsummer date, weather changed abruptly on the peak as fog moved in by midmorning, and he soon lost sight of trail markings and became confused about direction. At 4:30 p.m., he called his family from the mountain—remarkably, he hit a patch of cellular service, which is not always possible in the area—and told them that he would be late getting back to the trailhead.

Evening extended into nightfall, and Yambert did not emerge from the wilderness. Meanwhile, temperatures dropped overnight into the 40s, and wind picked up, gusting to 47 miles per hour. In the morning, Yambert's family contacted the park and told rangers that they had not heard from him since the previous afternoon. The park mobilized a search effort by 8:45 a.m., beginning at the Loft trailhead and retracing what his family believed had been his route up the mountain.

Three hours later, Yambert called his family again. They were thrilled to hear that he was not injured, and that he had spent the night on the mountain unexpectedly when nightfall and severe weather made him decide to stay put until morning. The family immediately notified the rangers, telling them that Yambert believed he was somewhere on Mount Meeker. The rangers tried to reconnect with the lost man by phone, but they could not reach him, so they asked the family to tell him to call 911 if he contacted them again, so they could get his GPS coordinates and pinpoint his location.

With no further clue about Yambert's current whereabouts, the park requested help from Northern Colorado Interagency Helitack in finding him from the air. The helicopter crew had to wait for the high winds to dissipate before they could begin aerial surveillance, so it was well into the afternoon before they were airborne and searching the mountainside for any sign of the missing man.

Finally, at about four p.m., the helicopter crew spotted Yambert below Peacock Pool in the Roaring Fork drainage east of Chasm Lake, somewhat south of the trail but only a quarter mile or so from it. Nearby rangers reached him in fifteen minutes, and he was only too happy to accept food and water from them before insisting that he could walk out on his own, refusing a helicopter evacuation or medical examination. In fact, he did not even want a ranger escort to the trailhead; he simply requested directions. The rangers walked him back to the trail anyway and pointed him in the right direction, and he returned to the trailhead shortly thereafter.

Perhaps it isn't surprising, then, that Yambert returned to Longs Peak in August 2018 to make a second attempt at reaching the summit. This time he began his hike on August 26 at two p.m.—an odd time to set out for the peak, as the round-trip usually takes even experienced hikers as much as twelve hours.

He spent the night on the mountain, and park visitors later told rangers that they had seen him the following morning, August 27, on the Keyhole Route. The pleasant weather of the day before had taken a turn on the mountain, however, with rain, sleet, early-season ice, and high winds. His family did not expect him back until the following afternoon, but by nightfall, Yambert had not arrived at the trailhead. They contacted park rangers late in the day on August 28 to initiate a search, and rangers went to the trailhead immediately to see if Yambert had returned. They found his rental car in the parking lot, untouched since two days earlier.

The next morning, search-and-rescue teams fanned out along the Keyhole and Loft Routes, as well as in the Clark's Arrow, Boulderfield, North Face, Lambs Slide, and Peacock Pool areas. Northern Colorado Interagency Helitack added their efforts to the search. When they found no sign of Yambert by day's end, they began fresh on August 30, adding the Chasm Lake and Roaring Fork areas and Keplinger's Couloir to their coverage. Members of Rocky Mountain Rescue in Boulder and Larimer County Rescue joined the search, including a dog team.

On Friday morning, August 31, the search ended in the rugged, rocky terrain west of the couloir. Yambert's body lay where it appeared to have come to rest after a tumbling fall, some two hundred feet below the Homestretch in a particularly steep area. Weather prevented an immediate recovery of the body, but rangers lowered it to a less precarious point fifty feet below its original position and out of an area of "extremely loose terrain covered in loose scree," according to the park, where it could be removed safely using a long line from the helicopter. The rangers camped there overnight and assisted with the evacuation early the following morning.

The medical examination on site indicated that he had died instantly. Whether Yambert had made it to the summit and had fallen on the way down, or never made it at all, remains unknown.

What do so many of these stories have in common?

In nearly all cases, the hiker chose to make this difficult and potentially dangerous climb to the summit alone. Hiking or climbing alone is not in itself a harbinger of certain death, but if bad judgment or bad luck do overtake a lone hiker, he or she can be lost forever at the bottom of a couloir or under several feet of snow.

Today, one such hiker—70-year-old James Pruitt—has been lost on the mountain for months, with the formal search suspended since March 15, 2019. Pruitt set out from the Longs Peak trailhead in winter conditions on February 28, 2019. An additional search in October 2019 produced no new clues.

With no hiking or climbing partner, solo hikers who fall or suffer an injury have no one to tell searchers where the accident took place and no one who can go for help. A partner may not be an absolute guarantee of survival, but having someone who knows exactly where they are can mean the difference between closure for families and days, weeks, or months of anguish until a loved one's remains can be found. In some cases, a lone hiker can vanish forever, leaving family members and friends to wonder what happened to their parent, spouse, or child for the rest of their lives.

CHAPTER 3

The East Face:
Death at the Diamond

It takes a certain kind of person to look up at the tallest mountain in Rocky Mountain National Park, sort out the various routes to the summit, and decide to take on one of the most difficult—the East Face. More than ten thousand people summit Longs Peaks annually these days, the vast majority of whom follow the non-technical Keyhole Route in July and August, when climbers are least likely to encounter snow. The East Face, however, presents its own set of challenges, enough to earn it a Yosemite Decimal System rating of Class 4, Grade II, with ratings as high as 5.9 for specific rock climbs—making it a very challenging, gear-intensive technical climb.

Beginning with a hike around Chasm Lake, the route gets progressively steeper as climbers pass over Mills Glacier and into the Lambs Slide couloir, a rocky route with pockets of ice even in July. This leads to a series of narrow ledges known, with characteristic irony, as Broadway. Snow on the Broadway ledges never melts away completely, so climbers encounter ice here along an eight-hundred-foot drop-off, followed by a crossing to the landmark known as the Notch Couloir (not to be confused with the Keyhole, which early climbers sometimes called the Notch). From here the climb becomes technical, requiring ropes and the use of pitons established by previous climbers. The last ice-covered section before the summit requires climbers to carve steps in the snow, or to use the steps carved by other parties that may have passed through recently. It's a hard day's climb that begins before dawn, and the descent may be every bit as challenging as reaching the top.

If you have managed to assemble a picture in your mind of this route up the East Face, let's add another level of difficulty: Imagine climbing it in a blizzard.

Walter Kiener and Agnes Vaille spent the better part of the winter of 1924–1925 attempting to master this climb, leaving enough of an impression on history that this trek is now known as Kiener's Route. A native of Switzerland who had considerable experience climbing in the Alps, Kiener moved to Denver around 1923, worked as a butcher, and became a member of the Colorado Mountain Club, often climbing with Vaille, who served as the club's outing chairperson.

Agnes was no ordinary young woman, especially by 1925's standards. At 34 years old, she had a well-established business career as appointed secretary to the Denver Chamber of Commerce, a Smith College education, and a record of travel to Paris during World War I to volunteer for the Red Cross there. She earned her reputation as a mountaineer by taking on a number of peaks around her home in Boulder and elsewhere in Colorado, and according to Janet Robertson's book, *The Magnificent Mountain Women*, she was "one of the state's earliest female technical climbers."

Longs Peak's Keyhole and other routes to the summit had become popular climbs for visitors to Rocky Mountain National Park, but only one woman—Elmira Buhl—had traversed the East Face to reach the summit, in September 1922. Vaille had strong rock-climbing capabilities and at least one "first" to her own credit, a summit of James Peak in winter. She and Kiener joined a climbing party in early fall 1924 with Herman and Elmira Buhl, and together they summited Mount Evans at 14,265 feet, just a few feet higher than Longs (at 14,259 feet). Elmira must have described her climb up the East Face that day, because Vaille and Kiener became intrigued by the prospect of duplicating her achievement. As snow and cold arrived in the fall of 1924, they decided to attempt their own precedent-setting climb: the East Face in winter, a feat that even the most skilled climbers among the club's members had not attempted.

Their first try took place in October, before the winter's heaviest snowfall, but they encountered plenty of ice as they made their way up. Then Kiener dropped his ice ax, an error that could easily have led to a deadly fall from the ice if he'd had no way of arresting a slide. He informed Vaille that they had to turn back, and she did not question his judgment, following her Colorado Mountain Club training to obey the leader in all cases. By this time, they had to make their way down the ice in darkness, giving them a good idea of what the process would be like if they chose to pursue this goal later in the winter.

Undaunted, they planned another ascent in November, apparently unconcerned about the difference between weather in October and the potential gales, blizzards, and precipitous drops in temperature they could encounter on the exposed rock faces in late fall. Vaille got in touch with her friend Carl Blaurock, one of the most respected mountain climbers in the region, and asked to borrow his ice ax.

"He was horrified to hear that she was going to try the climb in a season when storms could come up quickly and temperatures plunge dangerously without warning," Robertson wrote in her book, based on an unpublished manuscript dictated by Walter Kiener to friend Charles Edwin Hewes. When Blaurock could not convince Vaille that she was taking her life in her hands, he offered to come with her and Kiener, because he was most familiar with the mountain.

This time, they nearly made it to the summit, but the route they chose slowed down their progress enough that they would have to complete the climb and descend in pitch darkness. The descent took so long that they had to rush back to Denver just to get to work on time on Monday, making their failure to reach the summit even more frustrating. Vaille and Kiener were ready to plan another attempt, but Blaurock declined to accompany them if they planned to do so in winter.

In December, with winter well established, Vaille and Kiener planned their third try, but weather kept them from getting very far at all. "By now Agnes's friends and relatives regarded her desire to climb the East Face in winter as an 'obsession,'" Robertson noted. So many of these people insisted to her that the climb was too dangerous that Vaille dug in her heels, becoming even more determined to proceed, regardless of the admonishments. Even Kiener claimed in his account to Hewes that he attempted to talk Vaille out of another climb.

Nonetheless, the afternoon of January 10, 1925, found them driving through ice and snowdrifts toward Longs Peak with their friend Elinor Eppich, their vehicle sliding on the ice and finally stopping altogether when the snow on the road became too deep to navigate. Here they donned skis, loaded up their supplies, and skied the rest of the way to the Longs Peak Inn and Timberline Cabin, where they arrived in the wee hours of the morning. They spent a chilly night with wind and snow coming through the cracks in the walls.

In the morning, gale-force winds made the party certain that there would be no climb that day—but suddenly the wind died, the clouds parted, and Longs Peak stood out clearly against the crystal-blue sky. Kiener would later tell Hewes that Vaille was "enthusiastic" about starting their ascent, while Eppich wrote that Kiener not only insisted that they make the climb, but tried hard to persuade Eppich, who had no boots or climbing gear with her, to join them for the trek. In an unpublished manuscript discovered by Robertson, Eppich did her best to set the record straight as rumors and suppositions circulated that "it was all Agnes's stubbornness and poor judgment that were responsible for the whole tragedy. That simply is not so."

It was already nine a.m., too late in the morning for a successful summit before dark. Normally the climbing party would have left well before dawn, but their late arrival at Timberline Cabin—one account says they got there at three a.m.—gave them little time to sleep before they started out.

Kiener and Vaille headed for Chasm Lake and began the climb, making the most of the bright, sunny conditions, but when the early sunset found them only partway up the mountain, they had a critical decision to make. Continuing upward could take them many hours, and they could not stay at the summit and wait for daylight to come down, because temperatures had already plunged with the fading light. Turning around and heading down meant admitting defeat once again, although that would have been preferable to risking their lives with the cold and fatigue. Kiener already recognized that Vaille had lost much of her energy; her strength was "about spent."

"We decided we'd just as well go up, as we would have to make the descent in the dark," Kiener told the media two days later. He noted later that they achieved the summit at about four a.m. Monday morning. "Arrived at the top we didn't tarry—we started downward immediately." He checked his thermometer at the summit, and found that the mercury had sunk to 14 degrees below zero. They had a long way to go, and the weather was getting worse.

Rather than go back the precarious way they had come, Kiener got his bearings during a break in the cloudbank that swirled around them and led them down what is now the Cable Route, a well-established and somewhat shorter route that had led many climbers to a successful summit. (Later that year, the park installed steel cables to assist climbers in navigating to the top, but when Kiener chose it as his return route, it had no such guide wires.) He and Vaille stumbled down the route as best they could, but by this time, Vaille's strength had flagged to the point where she had difficulty continuing to move. Her feet and hands were numb with frostbite. "We were coming down a slope when Miss Vaille slipped," Kiener went on. "She slid and rolled 150 feet down before she stopped. She wasn't hurt physically, but after the hardships, it unnerved her. We continued . . . 'I can't go on,' she declared."

It's interesting to note at this point that in the account Kiener told to Charles Hewes, he said that he asked Vaille if she could go on, and "she nodded in the affirmative."

He tried to carry her, but his own endurance had limits, and soon they were both prostrate in the snow. Kiener dragged Vaille to the shelter of a large boulder and left her there while he descended the rest of the way. He fell, and fell again, but eventually, through blowing snow, he could see the outline of Timberline Cabin, and he called out to whoever might be nearby.

"Just as I managed to get within calling distance, I went down," he said.

He'd gone far enough to save his own life, however. By this time it was one p.m. on Monday afternoon, and Eppich, knowing that the pair had to be in trouble on the mountain, had assembled a rescue party who were ready to start a search. Hearing of Vaille's precarious condition, they left immediately, "fighting every inch of the way through a blinding snowstorm," the *Nebraska State Journal* reported.

Herbert Sortland, who was twenty-three, was one of the members of the rescue party. Caretaker of the Longs Peak Inn, he had joined the group, which included Hugh Brown, his son Oscar Brown, and Jacob Christen, and was ready to head out into the gale to find Kiener, had he not reappeared, and the suffering Agnes Vaille.

By sheer force of will, Kiener gathered his last strength and began to lead the party to the Boulderfield, where he had left Vaille. Oscar Brown stayed behind, and soon Sortland and Hugh Brown realized that they did not have the proper clothing and equipment to negotiate their way through the weather or up the icy mountain. Brown left first, following his own trail back to Timberline, and soon Sortland followed him. Christen and Kiener continued on to the Boulderfield.

When they arrived at the boulder where Kiener had left Vaille, they found that she had frozen to death. They attempted to lift her to bring her down with them, but Kiener had no strength to spare, and Christen had exhausted himself just getting to this place in the snow and wind. In the end, they knew that since the time for rescue had passed, there was no urgency requiring them to risk their own lives to bring Vaille down now. Instead, they made their way back down to the cabin. Christen took the lead and assisted Kiener, who by this time could barely stand; his hands and feet were frozen nearly solid. They fought blindly through whiteout conditions, using wind direction like a compass point until they managed to reach Timberline Cabin at about 7:30 p.m.

When they arrived, they found the Browns, but no Sortland. A search party went out the following day, but they could find no sign of him, and by the end of the day they knew that any further effort would be to find the young man's body.

"Then at intervals struggled in men whom the drifts and gale and flying snow and bitter cold of the winter night could not keep back," said an account by John Dickinson Sherman, editor of the *Chicago Herald* and the Western Newspaper Union, which appeared in dozens of papers across the country.

Each had started as the news reached him that Agnes Vaille was in danger on Longs Peak. By 10 o'clock had arrived Tom Allen, assistant superintendent of the park, and Jack Moomaw and Walter Finn, park rangers. At 4:30 Tuesday morning Superintendent Roger W. Toll (cousin of Agnes Vaille) arrived from Denver, with Edmund Rogers, George C. Barnard, William F. Ervin and Carl Blaurock, veteran mountaineers of the Colorado Mountain Club. Daylight found them all trying to keep from freezing about a fire kept burning on top of the cabin stove. To recover Agnes Vaille's body was impossible. At 9:30 all descended to the valley . . . Not until Thursday could Agnes Vaille's body be reached. It lay at an elevation of about 13,300 feet on the north slope, 200 feet back of the edge of the East Face, and about 50 feet above the perpetual snowdrift on the edge of Boulderfield [sic] . . . Two skis were placed end to end and a third lashed across the joint. The body was strapped to these skis and carried with the aid of ski poles. Eight men carried the body across Boulderfield, relays taking part at frequent intervals. Further down a toboggan could be used.

Six weeks would pass before the body of Herbert Sortland finally came to light, just about three hundred yards from the Longs Peak Inn, where he had fallen and apparently dislocated a hip. Unable to walk, he succumbed to the elements on the edge of a frozen swamp near the inn's garbage dump, where Oscar Brown happened upon him while bringing a load to the dump on February 25, 1925.

Kiener's survival of the incident did not bring him comfort for some time after the ordeal that took his friend's life. He himself lost several fingers and most of his toes, leaving him unable to continue his career as a butcher, the only trade he had learned when he left school at fifteen to apprentice with his father as a sausage maker in Bern. The Vaille family, who were well-off enough to assist the young man, paid all of his medical expenses as well as his tuition to attend the University of Nebraska. He majored in botany and eventually earned a doctorate, leading the university to hire him as an assistant in botany, a position he held for ten years. He then became a biologist with the Nebraska Game, Forestation, and Parks Commission, where he rose to the position of chief biologist, and established the commission's Fisheries Research Department. He died of pancreatic cancer in 1959, leaving an extensive library of more than fifty thousand plant samples that are now in the Charles E. Bessey Herbarium at the University of Nebraska.

In 1927, Vaille's family also made a donation to the park to construct a monument to Agnes on Longs Peak. The Agnes Vaille Memorial Shelter stands at 13,400 feet, with a fireplace, wood, and food inside for anyone who may be stranded on the mountain. "It's used all the time," Karen Waddell, cultural resources specialist at the park, told the *Daily Camera* in 2013. If it has saved even one life, the Vailles' well-placed generosity did its job for adventurers who choose to take themselves to the limits of their own endurance on one of the most challenging mountains in Colorado.

"Longs Peak Exacts Its Penalty"

Fascination with Longs Peak's East Face long predates the ill-fated Vaille-Kiener expedition, but for the most part, those who have attempted it have managed to survive to tell the tale. "The fatalities caused by the East Face have only spurred the interest of men of sporting instinct," an editorial in the *St. Louis Post-Dispatch* in Missouri pontificated in 1926. "The east face still repels all but the hardiest or the most experienced climbers ... The east face is a sheer, snow-streaked granite precipice of almost architectural symmetry and grace, but whose hardness and massiveness impart a dour and threatening aspect ... Each year, as hundreds take the easier trail, a few hardy souls begin the grueling and uncertain grind up Longs cathedral-like facade."

The next to lose his life in the attempt was young Forrest Ketring, a 19-year-old man from Denver. Rather than making a winter attempt, Ketring and his climbing partner, 21-year-old James Real, chose July 23, 1926, for their climb of the East Face. Ketring had taken the lead, but his foot slipped and he went over a cliff.

"The sinister east face of Longs Peak has claimed another victim," the *Post-Dispatch* lamented. "When Ketring's footing failed, he fell 1,000 feet, hit a snowbank and slid 300 feet more. His body was found crushed against the rocks on that wild slope at whose base lies lonely Chasm Lake ... Ketring's death is unfortunate, but as a youth living in the mountains, he understood the east face with the full knowledge of the terrible penalty that the mountain has exacted of those who fail to conquer it."

Three years later, the American Alpine Club's accident report chided Charles W. Thiemeyer, a 28-year-old man from Denver, for lacking the skill required to scale the East Face on August 18, 1929. Thiemeyer "fell while ascending the Notch Chimney," the report noted. "The fall of over 1,000 feet was of course fatal ... Thiemeyer's companions were forced to spend the night on the Chimney and were rescued the next day by guides with the aid of ropes. This party of three were members of the Swiss Alpine Club and were using a rope, although all of the party were not tied to the rope at the time of the accident." The writer added, "The east face has, as usual, proved too difficult for inexperienced climbers."

The club may have been a bit unfair in its criticism. Thiemeyer, it turns out, was "an expert Swiss mountain climber," according to news reports, and had two equally experienced companions with him, dentist Arthur Stacher of Boulder and his wife, Rosie. Together they had taken on a number of Colorado's highest mountains, but this was their first time attempting to scale the East Face of Longs Peak.

They "set out early Sunday to match their skill against the treachery of the East Face," noted the Associated Press. At about two p.m., as they reached Chimney Notch, Thiemeyer held a position about one hundred feet ahead of the Stachers, and he began to climb a precipice above them, looking for a stable rock to which to tie the rope so the Stachers could pull themselves up. He had tied the rope firmly around his waist, and Arthur held a section of the rope in his hands.

As the Stachers watched, Thiemeyer suddenly slipped on a loose stone and began to fall. Arthur braced himself to take the weight of the fall on the rope with his arms and hands, but the rope whipped through his palms and away, burning and ripping his flesh and leaving a sizable gash in each hand. Thiemeyer plummeted to earth, landing far below them.

The Stachers found themselves essentially stranded as fog and darkness set in on the mountain. They shouted to others in the area for help, but no one could reach them before nightfall, so they spent a frigid August night huddled together at high altitude on the narrow ledge at Chimney Notch with no food, afraid that they, too, might slip and fall to the jagged rocks below.

In the morning, park rangers heard their cries and sent a rescue party to the top of the mountain to help them. The rangers dropped ropes down to the couple and helped them climb up the remaining seven hundred feet to the summit, from which they could hike down with the rangers to the shelter at the Boulderfield.

Later the same day, rangers made the trek to the boulder-strewn area on the East Face just above Chasm Lake to locate and retrieve Thiemeyer's body.

Little is known of R. B. Key, 45, who fell from the East Face on September 13, 1931, except that he had lived in Lynchburg, Kentucky, worked for the Jefferson Coal Company in Piney Forks, Ohio, and originally hailed from Mississippi. "He was accompanied here by Vernon Woodlee, who left at the same time," mining officials told the media, adding that they believed he was single.

The six rangers who retrieved his body, led by park superintendent Edmund Rogers, located Key on Mills Glacier. They made the connection between the body and Jefferson Coal Company because Key had a time slip from the mining operation in his pocket.

"Rogers said he believed the man had attempted to climb or descend the treacherous east face of the mountain and had slipped on the icy footholds, probably falling about 100 feet," the Associated Press reported on September 14. "When Rogers and his party reached the body last night, it was just before dark, and attempts to carry the body down the mountainside were abandoned until today."

After Key's death, however, rangers received reports that something looking like another body remained on a ledge on the East Face. Results of that investigation were not significant enough to make it into park records or to gain additional media attention.

Fifteen years passed before the East Face claimed another falling victim, one that reminds us that anyone, including the most experienced of climbers, can place a foot in the wrong spot or grab for an unstable handhold. The *Chicago Tribune* carried the coverage of the death of Charles Grant, 19, a former child actor on Chicago radio until he was 14, and a recently discharged merchant marine with service in North Africa, Italy, and Spain. Grant planned to complete his bachelor's degree in the arts and philosophy at the University of Chicago in the fall. The only child of Charles and Blanche Grant, he had spent the previous three summers at the Cheley camp for boys in Estes Park, where he had developed his climbing skills. "[He] was considered the most accomplished climber at the camp," the newspaper noted. "Chuck" had made more than thirty ascents of Longs Peak, including two in the last week of August 1946, days before the one that would be his last.

On September 2, 1946, Grant and his companions, John Purvis and Walter Gray of Estes Park, chose the Stettner's Ledges route for their climb up the mountain, a route the Mountain Project website describes as a "classic, mountaineering-style climb." As they made their way up the rock face, a fog settled in around them, leaving them visually separated from one another. Grant took the lead and was not roped, though Purvis and Gray remained roped together. "All three were in difficulty, but Chuck had found the safety of a ledge, and seemed to be out of a tight place," his obituary tells us.

One of the men behind Grant threw him a rope, but in the fog Grant thought that this was an appeal for help in reaching the ledge. Grant grabbed the rope and held it firmly, pulling the man behind him to a foothold—but in doing so, Grant lost his own balance. He fell off the ledge and down, dropping four hundred feet.

Purvis and Gray made their way down the mountain as quickly as they could and used a forest service phone to call rangers for help. Rain and fog prevented the rangers from approaching the peak until the following day, delaying retrieval of Grant's body until Monday.

FATHER AND SON

It had been six years since Denver attorney C. Blake Heister Jr., 48, attempted a climb of Longs Peak's East Face when he led his son, Richard, who was 18, and two friends, Pete DiLeo and Nelson Gieseke, up Kiener's Route on August 27, 1966. The route proved particularly challenging for the group on this day, with a difficult crossing of Lambs Slide, taking them five hours instead of the expected three to reach Broadway Ledges, but they proceeded to Notch Chimney with all due haste. In the distance, they could see an approaching thunderstorm, so they quickened their pace as they started up toward the Notch, deciding to proceed unroped in what appeared to the American Alpine Club reporter to be an effort to save time.

Blake knew that there were several routes up the Chimney, and he chose one that was slightly off the route used by most climbers, probably because he expected it to be a little easier. As he began, Richard offered him a belay rope, but Blake rejected it.

A few moments later, he fell from the Chimney. Richard saw his father lose his balance and reached out to break his fall, hoping beyond hope to catch him and pull him onto Broadway. His attempt was futile, however; momentum carried Blake off the 5-foot ledge and down the mountain, rolling another 1,250 feet down a rock face nearly perfectly perpendicular to the ground. He came to rest on Mills Glacier far below.

It's hard to imagine a son recovering from the shock of seeing his father killed, but Richard had little choice but to put aside his grief and get himself and his friends off the mountain. Together they realized that they could not descend safely from this point, as few climbers used the East Face as their exit route from Longs Peak; instead, most climb to the top and take the easier Keyhole or Cable

Route back to the trailhead. With admirable resolution, they roped up and continued to the top, arriving there at about 6:30 p.m., then descended as quickly as they could via the Cable Route.

When they reached Chasm View, a patrol ranger met them, and they finally had the opportunity to tell someone in authority about Blake's death. The ranger proceeded with them to the Longs Peak ranger station and put efforts in motion to recover the man's body.

The retrieval operation took place the following day, with rangers using a rubber raft to transport Blake's body off the glacier and across Chasm Lake. "The rest of the trip was made on horseback," United Press International reported.

American Alpine Club reporters guessed that fatigue had set in by the time Blake had reached the Notch Chimney, given the party's delays in crossing Lambs Slide and making it to Kiener's Route. "To continue up on any route or variation from this point while unroped is folly," their report notes, adding that the route is rated a "stiff 4th Class" in climbing circles. "The easiest (regular) route is around the corner from the approximate location of the fall."

Little information remains about 21-year-old Michael Neri of Pascoag, Rhode Island, who fell off of Broadway Ledges on June 2, 1977. Neri was climbing a sheer rock face—probably the Diamond—with Jim Johnson of Estes Park when he fell eight hundred feet to his death. Even the American Alpine Club had only this to say about the season: "Late spring and early summer in Rocky Mountain National Park was plagued with several fatalities from unroped accidents." (The others took place on Mount McGregor, and are discussed in chapter 4.)

In the case of 36-year-old Colorado state patrolman Charlie Nesbit's death in 1979, however, Ranger Chris Reveley left us a detailed report of the accident.

"While on patrol on October 6, I was contacted at the Chasm Meadow Shelter Cabin by William Barber at 12:40 p.m.," he began. "He reported that Charles O. Nesbit (31), a member of their three-man climbing team, had fallen down the feature known as Lambs Slide on the East Face of Longs Peak."

Barber told him that at around 10:30 a.m., when the party had made it about two-thirds of the way up Lambs Slide, Nesbit had begun sliding down an icy patch and could not stop himself with his ice ax.

Barber descended as quickly as he could to reach Nesbit where he lay on the talus at the base of Lambs Slide. It took him a good forty minutes, but he found Nesbit "conscious but not coherent," according to the report. "Nesbit lost consciousness two minutes later."

Barber began CPR immediately and continued for an hour, when he was joined by Dr. Bert Honea, another climber who had been working his way up the Stettner's Ledges route. The Denver physician apparently saw the lifesaving activity below him and retreated from the route to help. He performed an examination, and it quickly became clear to Honea that CPR would have no effect at this point. He gently advised Barber to cease his efforts.

Realizing that the inevitable had occurred, Barber left his friend with Honea and Peter Bradley, the third member of Nesbit's climbing party, and walked down past Chasm Lake to the Shelter Cabin, where he found Ranger Reveley.

"I collected information from Barber, then suggested that he continue down the trail to the Longs Peak Ranger Station," the ranger reported. "I arrived at the scene of the accident at 1:05 p.m. . . . A brief examination of Nesbit confirmed that he showed no vital signs. He had expired quite some time before my arrival."

What had made Nesbit lose control? Park ranger Larry Van Slyke offered his analysis: "It appears that the accident was a direct result of Nesbit's catching the front point of his crampons on the hard snow while in a facedown, ice-ax-arrest position, which caused him to be flipped over backwards. Out of control, he fell some 700 feet to the base of the snowfield. The climbing helmet he was wearing undoubtedly saved his head from massive trauma, although it did not prevent the basal skull fracture."

THE TROUBLESOME CRAMPON

Eleven years passed after Nesbit's death, and while rescues take place on the East Face just about every year, none of these accidents resulted in death. Then in August 1988, a two-man climbing expedition from Morrison, Colorado, took a sudden and devastating turn for the worse.

According to a detailed report in the 1989 edition of *Accidents in North American Mountaineering*, Kevin Hardwick, who was 30 years old, and his climbing partner—whose name we never learn—planned to take the route leading to the Notch Couloir. "On the drive in, Kevin had sorted the climbing gear, which included seven ice screws and rock protection, and discussed his selections," the report notes. "At 0540, they reached the Longs Peak trailhead. They did not stop at any of the information boards on the trail, nor did they or had they contacted any other climbers or rangers regarding the climbing conditions on their chosen route."

They stopped on their way to the East Face at 7:15 a.m., watching from Chasm Lake as climbers already on the mountain tackled the Diamond. An hour and a half later, they reached the bottom of Lambs Slide and paused to put on their climbing boots and gear. They were prepared for ice climbing with the gear appropriate to that endeavor, so when they saw that the Notch Couloir was not encased in ice as they had expected, they decided to change their plans and take Kiener's Route. This meant that they would climb Lambs Slide's 40-degree ice slope, cross to Broadway Ledge, and continue up the fourth-class climb to the summit.

Kiener's Route generally poses the least challenge of any route up the East Face, though saying this is much like saying that a fever of 104 degrees makes you slightly less delirious than a fever of 104.1. "Ice conditions on this day posed moderate difficulty," the report notes. The two men went over their climbing strategy and decided to keep to the right side of the route, where they thought their chances of a free fall would be somewhat less than straight up the middle. "With this in mind, they agreed not to rope up and belay their ascent, but rather to keep the rope accessible in case a belay was judged necessary."

Hardwick had chosen a pair of hiking boots for the climb, which were made of stiff leather and half-shanked, a detail the reporter felt was critical. The shank, the area of the mountaineering boot between the insole and outsole, takes the load off the climber's feet and calves, allowing him or her to climb longer without debilitating fatigue. This was usually made of metal in the 1980s, but in Hardwick's boots they were only half the size of the usual shank. Hardwick wore a boot too flexible to support his rigid crampons.

Both climbers strapped on their packs and helmets, and they each carried one ice ax in hand, with a second one in their packs for later use. Another pair of climbers passed them as they booted up for the climb, and they began to work their way up Lambs Slide on the left side, opposite what Hardwick and his partner had decided to do. This second pair determined that a belay was indeed a good idea as they ascended.

Soon Hardwick and his partner began their climb. Almost immediately, however, Hardwick began struggling with one of his crampons, which would not stay tightly strapped to his boot. His partner looked up at him and saw him fighting with the device, and they stopped to talk about ways to keep the crampon in place. His frequent pauses for adjustments allowed the partner to get more than three hundred feet ahead of Hardwick on the route, until he disappeared from Hardwick's field of vision.

Hardwick reached a steeper section of ice and stopped again to tighten the errant crampon, while his partner had worked his way past the ice and around a bulging rock on a direct path to Broadway Ledge. Another pair of climbers—a father and son—were about ninety feet to Hardwick's left, and a moment later, the older of the two heard Hardwick use an unspecified curse word. "30–60 seconds later, he reportedly heard what he thought were rocks sliding above him," the report said.

When he looked to see what had happened, he saw that Hardwick was no longer where he had been standing a moment ago. Instead, he'd slid about seventy-five to ninety feet, and seemed to be turning a cartwheel, "with no ice ax and with one crampon in the air, free of his foot."

Hardwick slid into his partner's view and kept sliding headfirst down the ice on his stomach, his arms out ahead of him in a useless attempt to slow himself down. His partner called out to the other climbers in the area as Hardwick began to tumble, falling close to one thousand feet and hitting several rocky areas on the way down, some of them covered in black ice that only accelerated his fall. His body finally came to rest on the talus slope at the bottom of Lambs Slide.

It was about 9:40 a.m. Hardwick's partner reversed his course and made it to the fallen man's side in a scant twenty-five minutes. He was a trained emergency medical technician, so he performed a first assessment of Hardwick's condition. "He was lying on his back and made movements such as opening his eyes, attempting to sit up, and at one point, lifting his hand to his partner's chest," the report said. "He was unresponsive to verbal commands, his pupils remained unreactive, and it was not possible to detect any pulses."

Another hour passed before the next party reached him, but by this time news of the fall had reached the Longs Peak Ranger Station, and Ranger Linda Stuart set out for the base of Lambs Slide at 11:15 a.m. She paused to interview other climbers along the way about Hardwick's condition, so she could radio for the kind of help that might be required.

At 11:55 a.m., Hardwick's attempts to move ceased, and his partner and others began CPR. A team of rangers finally arrived at about 1:10 p.m., followed closely by a Flight for Life helicopter, but by this time, it had become clear that Hardwick had not survived the fall.

The report's analysis suggests that Hardwick had stopped once again to try to adjust the troublesome crampon, setting down or otherwise displacing his ice ax as he did so. "He may have also tried to move with it loosened and merely dropped the ice ax into the moat," the reporter wrote. "The ice tool was never recovered, but the left crampon was retrieved about 2/3 up the Lambslide [*sic*] slope. The straps were still buckled and doubled back, indicating that he had not actually been tightening them when the fall began."

Hardwick apparently had not locked the straps, which would have kept them from continually loosening during his ascent. "It is also significant that he had worn the rigid crampons with a flexible, half-shanked leather boot," the report continued. "The flex in the boot is not accommodated by the rigid surface of the crampon and can cause the straps to loosen or the crampons to brake [*sic*]."

The Legacy of Cameron Tague

We have seen in this chapter that even the most skilled and experienced climbers can encounter the kinds of conditions that bring a dramatic end to their efforts. No one more typifies this kind of bad luck than Cameron Tague.

Tague discovered the wonders of the Rockies as a student at Colorado University in 1985, where he majored in economics and spent all the time he could learning climbing skills throughout the Front Range. Some say he'd been up Longs Peak as many as forty times, mastering the familiar routes and opening new ones. He stayed in Colorado to complete a master's degree in metallurgy, but he placed climbing above all other priorities, according to friends who told his story in *Accidents in North American Mountaineering* in 2001. "He lived intensely, never wasting a moment of life's precious time," wrote his friend Kent McClannan. "He freed long aid routes everywhere from Mexico to Canada. He opened difficult lines in Patagonia and Peru. He climbed the Diamond about 30 times, sometimes solo, sometimes in winter. He climbed in the Black Canyon of the Gunnison religiously, often linking together two or even three routes in a push. His climbing feats were legendary, and his motivation was unreal." McClannan goes on to offer us this marvelous mental image:

Picture him at the door at 1 a.m. with an extra cup of coffee in hand, smiling and telling you that it is going to be a perfect day for the Diamond. The gear is packed, he has lunch and he is not leaving without you. Or see him pumping up Boulder Canyon at the end of the day on his bike with his panniers full of books and his master's thesis, on his way back from school, which is 50 miles away. Watch him take 30-foot whippers into space off the roof pitch of the Wisdom in Eldorado Canyon, laughing like

a child being pushed by his dad on the park swing. Or visual-
ize the image of him walking toward camp, his face and body
covered in Fisher Towers mud. He is carrying a huge pack full
of ropes, pins, and cams. Mr. Hobbes, Cameron's massive Ches-
apeake Bay retriever, is strutting by his side in the exact same
manner as his master, proudly carrying a duct tape–covered,
two-liter bottle in his mouth. Cameron is exhausted but grin-
ning from ear to ear, and as he moves closer, he lets out a huge
"YEHAAAAA!" that echoes through the desert night.

These images are Cameron. He could never be portrayed by
describing accomplishments or by outlining his life. He is feel-
ings, memories, a type of energy that will always make us smile.

On July 6, 2000, Tague and his girlfriend, Emma Williams—
who had recently moved to the United States from the United
Kingdom to be with him—took on the Yellow Wall Route up the
Diamond. This route, opened by Layton Kor and Charlie Roskosz
in 1962, requires free climbers to move straight up a sheer rock face,
following steep crack systems for fingerholds.

With the confidence of one who has climbed hundreds of routes
all over the world, Tague proceeded unroped on a route ranging in
the Yosemite Decimal System from 5.7 to 5.11. The 5.7 ranking
toward the bottom of the wall would be considered easy for experienced climbers, but as they climbed up the Diamond's face, Tague
and Williams would use all of their expertise to work their way up
a wall of rock that stands fully perpendicular to the ground below.

This would have been all in a day's climb for Tague, had it not
been for an area of rotten rock. In simple terms, this weakened rock
forms when a rock face has been exposed to weather for many mil-
lennia, cracking so that it may break or even crumble under the
weight of a climber's step. Tague, of course, knew the look and

location of this hazardous rock, so he traversed in from the side on Broadway Ledge to look for the strongest point, where he could safely attach his belay rope.

"It would be an easy traverse, and to save time for the difficult climbing higher on the face, he didn't even bother to rope up," wrote veteran climber Jim Collins in an article for *Fast Company*. "Then somehow, he lost his concentration, pulled on a loose piece of stone, and stumbled backward. Tague tried to recapture his balance, his hands grasping and waving about as he skittered toward the edge of the ledge."

In an instant, the loose rock under his feet slid away. He tumbled from the Diamond, past Williams and over the Lower East Face, for eight hundred feet, hitting the ground at Mills Glacier.

The shock of his death rippled through the climbing world. "Tague was an outstanding climber," National Park rangers Jim Detterline and Mark Magnuson wrote in an unusually circumspect entry for the following year's *American Alpine Journal* accident report. "His strategy in climbing unroped was to save time and increase his party's margin of safety later in the day by finishing the route before the afternoon lightning storms would arrive. However, in retrospect, it may have been better to simul-climb with protection placed at intervals. The North Chimney [access route to the Diamond] and Broadway Ledge are notorious for rotten rock, conditions that have claimed other capable climbers in these same areas."

No one doubted that Tague knew where the rotten rock was; losing his footing in that exact spot must have been nothing more than bad luck. Whether simul-climbing—that is, climbing simultaneously while tied to the same rope—would have saved his life or resulted in both climbers falling is a question left unanswered for eternity.

Climber Roger Briggs reflected a year later in the magazine *The Alpinist* about opening another free climb, Bright Star, with Topher Donahue in 2001. "Charlie Fowler had freed the first two pitches in the 1980s, and Donahue and Cameron Tague had freed the third pitch at 5.11+R earlier that summer," he said. "Before they could finish the climb, Tague had died in a fall from Broadway. I was a tragic replacement."

The seven pitches proved to be some of the most difficult of Briggs's climbing career, which had begun in the 1960s. "At the end of the day, I managed them all, and we were standing at the top of a beautiful new free climb, the longest on the Diamond. Donahue congratulated me for one of the best climbing days of my life, but an unmistakable sadness permeated the moment. It should have been Tague's hand he was shaking."

Tague's skill and ability left a permanent legacy for climbers throughout Colorado and as far beyond as Chile, Peru, and British Columbia. In Black Canyon of the Gunnison National Park, he established routes including the eponymous Tague Your Time, a 5.12 route with fifteen pitches and a 1,500-foot elevation change. In 1997, he and climber Eric Greene made the first ascent of the Spicy Red Beans and Rice route up North Howser Tower in British Columbia's Purcell Mountains. With Kent McClannan, he made the first ascent of the sixteen-thousand-foot Mission Control in 1999, on an unnamed peak west of Shaqsha in Peru. In a month-long expedition with Michael Pennings and Scott Lazar in the Chilean Patagonia in 1996, he established Via de la Mammas on Torre Central, Vuelo del Condor on the East Face of Cuerno Este, and Anduril on La Hoja. And when Patience and Topher Donahue opened a new route on South Howser Tower in 2000, another 1,500-foot climb with a difficulty factor of 5.11, they named it Cameron's Pillar, "whose spirit they felt during every perfect jam."

Two Unwitnessed Accidents

No one can say exactly what made Benjamin Russell Hebb, a 26-year-old climber aid-soloing his way up the Dunn-Westbay Route on the Diamond, fall off of the wall at eight a.m. on August 27, 2010.

In solo aiding, the climber fixes the rope to an anchor and connects himself to the other end, using one of many devices available, or his own knots. Hebb was an experienced climber who "could lead 5.12 routes and climb 5.14 rock problems," says his father, Mike Hebb, on the web page he maintains as a tribute to his son.

Two park service climbing rangers had reached the third pitch of the Yellow Wall Route at about eight a.m. when they heard rocks giving way and falling. Seconds later, they saw "several large rocks and a person falling in the vicinity of Broadway Ledge," or in roughly the same area where Cameron Tague had encountered rotten rock a decade earlier. Hebb fell all the way down the North Chimney onto Mills Glacier.

"He had started early that morning and soloed up the North Chimney to the base of the route," the report said. "He likely had just started climbing up the route when he pulled a loose rock off and fell to his death. His rope was still in his pack when he was found." The two rangers descended as quickly as they could, but it was ten a.m. before they reached Hebb's lifeless body. He was pronounced dead at the scene.

Ben had moved to Colorado from his family's home in Strafford, Vermont, when he started college at the University of Colorado at Boulder, but he had already developed his passion for rock climbing as a teenager, working to build muscle in daily visits to the gym to maintain the required strength. While he earned a bachelor's degree in physics and a master's degree in biochemical engineering—which he would have completed in December of that year—he lived in Broomfield and worked at the university's Gill Lab. Even with his many commitments, he still found time to improve his climbing skills on most weekends.

On this August day, Hebb wore a helmet and carried all of the right gear, and like most climbers, he chose to forego the rope as he started out up the comparatively easy terrain at the beginning of the North Chimney. "This is not an uncommon choice on the Diamond, where every second wasted means a much greater chance for being caught in a storm," Rich Browne, emergency services coordinator for Rocky Mountain National Park, wrote in his report for the *American Alpine Journal*. On the other hand, he noted, "Making the choice to forego a partner for the entire climb and a rope for part of it heightens the consequences of a slip or fall. A climber choosing to climb in this fashion must be sure of every move and every hold."

Matt Payne, who maintains the website 100Summits.com, provides his own analysis. "While Benjamin was climbing solo . . . it was most likely not a contributing factor to his death. The section of the route he fell from is often not protected because of the comparatively easy terrain it is on . . . The easier sections of any given route are often free-soloed due to the speed by which a route can be accomplished." He concluded, "This accident merely accentuates the fact that even the best climbers can still fall to their death on easy routes or easier sections of a route (which is probably one of the reasons why people climb to begin with—the rush of climbing is a powerful experience)."

The most recent fatality on Longs Peak's East Face came on October 2, 2015. Rangers received word at 10:30 p.m. Friday night that Spencer Veysey, 26, of Missoula, Montana, had not returned from his planned mountain summit. He had not told his girlfriend, Natalie, which route he had intended to take.

Veysey came to Colorado for the weekend with Natalie to attend a wedding, for which she was in the wedding party. On Friday, while Natalie participated in wedding plans, Veysey decided to climb the highest mountain in Rocky Mountain National Park, at a time of year when its trails become treacherous with rime and black ice.

No search could begin until first light, so when Veysey still had not emerged in the morning, rangers began searching by following the Keyhole Route and the area around Chasm Lake. Early October is already winter on the peak, so they found icy conditions that required special care as they combed the most-traveled routes. Late in the afternoon, one of the teams searching the east side of the mountain discovered a body at the bottom of Lambs Slide. It was indeed Spencer Veysey, who had perished there in a fall. By this time it was too late in the day to begin a recovery operation, so rangers spent the night at Chasm Shelter near the body and moved Veysey's remains out of the park by helicopter on Sunday morning.

Veysey grew up in Ames, Iowa, graduating a year early from Ames High School and spending a year working on a commercial fishing boat in Alaska. He moved to Missoula to pursue a journalism degree at the University of Montana, working at the college newspaper and volunteering at the Montana Innocence Project (MIP), working to find evidence that could free people who had been wrongly convicted of crimes. When he graduated from college, he began working there part time, and three years later he became their lone full-time investigator.

"He was just a great, inquisitive kind of kid. So persistent," said one of his professors, Dennis Swibold, to the *Missoulian*, the local newspaper. "When he was suspicious about something, he wouldn't quit until he nailed it down."

MIP legal director Larry Mansch agreed. "The wealth of knowledge he has and is able to retain . . . it truly is irreplaceable," he told the *Missoulian*. "He can tell you everything about every case." Several cases in progress had moved forward because of evidence Veysey had found that had never been heard in testimony in the original trials.

Mansch said that the organization would call on its network of volunteers, students, and pro bono attorneys to fill the gap left by the loss of their investigator. "As much as we miss him," Mansch said, "the work we do here is good work, and it's still got to go on."

A memorial to Veysey in the *Ames Tribune* listed his passions as "rugby, biking, rafting the beautiful rivers of Montana and, of course, his wonderful Natalie."

He may have been inexperienced at climbing a mountain of the magnitude of Longs Peak, however. He was also unaware of the challenges ahead, which led him to choose a route that was a technical climb, at a time of year when snow and ice would make any climb especially dangerous for a first-time visitor out of his usual element.

CHAPTER 4

Deadly Drop:
Falls from Other Mountains

ROCKY MOUNTAIN NATIONAL PARK'S STAR POWER WITH CLIMB-
ers and hikers emanates most strongly from Longs Peak, but the
park contains many other mountains with compelling trails and
climbing routes. Tens of thousands of visitors attempt to conquer
one or more of these peaks every year, and the vast majority of them
have a terrific outdoor experience—but every so often, someone
does not make it back to the valley alive.

Mountains beyond Longs Peak account for fifty-nine deaths
in the park, beginning with the first recorded fatality on Ypsilon
Mountain, in 1905. Patchy historical records limit my ability to tell
you about all of them, and some of the records only provide enough
information for a couple of paragraphs about the incidents. Those
that are not detailed in this chapter are still listed in the appendix
"List of Deaths in Rocky Mountain National Park" at the end of
this book, however—and if you happen to be a relative or friend
and have additional information about any of these, I'd love to hear
it. You'll find my contact information at the end of the introduc-
tion of this book.

TRAGEDY ON YPSILON

Louis Levings, 21, had a promising future ahead of him. At Armour Institute in Chicago—now the Illinois Institute of Technology—he had completed the first three years of his degree, was a member of Delta Tau Delta fraternity, and played on the football team. His grades were excellent, earning him several scholarships, and he "was a great favorite with the younger set," according to the *Inter Ocean*, one of the Chicago newspapers at the time.

On August 2, 1905, Levings and a friend, George Black, had reached the summit of Ypsilon Mountain in the north-central section of the park. Levings's cousin Dean Babcock had joined them for the first half of the day, during which they had climbed to the top of Mount Fairchild, but Dean had split off and returned to the Levings family home, known as Graystone, instead of continuing up the next mountain.

Ypsilon is part of the ridge known as the Mummy Range, and at 13,514 feet, it stands as one of the most easily recognizable mountains in the park. Two couloirs on either side of its central cirque meet in a formation that appears as a large Y, earning the whole feature the name "Y Couloir." Hikers do not need to climb through this couloir, however, as the mountain features some comparatively easy routes to the top, including the Southwest Ridge route, a crossing of an open tundra.

Whether the two young men chose the easy route or hiked another trail to the top is unknown, but somewhere on the mountain, Levings slipped on a loose rock, slid over a cliff, and fell four hundred feet. "[H]e was struck by projecting rocks several times in the descent, and is supposed to have been dead before he reached the bottom," the *Inter Ocean* reported. He landed in a snow-filled ravine.

Black made his way down the mountain as quickly as he could and ran to the nearest ranch. There he borrowed a horse and rode with all due haste to the Longs Peak Inn for help.

No one who witnessed or heard about the fall doubted that Levings had been killed, so a search party formed to bring the body off the mountain, an effort they expected would take two days. Mountain guides including Enos A. Mills, the man credited with convincing the federal government to set aside this area as a national park, hiked into the Mummy Range and reached the ravine where Levings had died—but not without mishap. "Two of the searching party which went after the body . . . narrowly escaped death," the *Inter Ocean* reported. "There is much ice and snow where the body was buried, and two men slid over a cliff because of treacherous footholds, but escaped with severe bruises." George Black himself accompanied the searchers and nearly became a casualty, falling twenty feet, "and was hurt so badly he [could] scarcely walk."

Worse, the recovery effort failed, and the search party returned to Estes Park on the night of August 5 without the body. It became clear that someone would have to be lowered on ropes into the canyon where Levings lay, so the rest of the party could pull him and Levings's body out together. Babcock and Black organized another effort to attempt this on August 6, but after two more fruitless days, the rescuers made the decision to abandon the endeavor.

"Several of the rescuers have been injured by being dashed against sharp rocks while being lowered to try to reach the body," reports from Estes Park explained. "Dr. James was lowered by a rope, and found that every bone in the body was broken. A man, by pushing himself free from the rocks, can reach the place where the body lies, but rescuers say it is impossible to bring up an inert body."

Instead, they buried the body on-site using rocks and cement, marking the spot with a cairn. "In order to get the cement to the place it was necessary for it to be carried in small packages on the shoulders of men up very steep places," the *Telluride San Miguel Examiner* reported in October 1905. "The tomb is located just below the union of the arms of the Y on the easterly face of the mountain and is 12,000 feet above sea level."

The makeshift burial site remained in the ravine until 1929, when its construction had worn away enough that Babcock decided to return and give his cousin a proper burial. He led a party to the site, bringing a galvanized iron casket with them and making their way down into the ravine to transfer Levings's remains into it. They installed a bronze marker, so the family could visit the site and know exactly where the young man had been laid to rest.

Climbers often eschew the easy routes to a mountaintop, choosing instead to use their technical climbing skills for an entirely different experience of Mount Ypsilon. Tom Cunningham, 23, of Ithaca, New York, and 22-year-old Lawrence Berman of Louisville, Kentucky, obtained a technical climbing permit to scale the Blitzen Ridge on July 21, 1978, a route that MountainProject.com describes as "perhaps the best ridge climb in the Park." While it gets a 5.4 rating, indicating a fairly basic climb, this ridge attracts a great deal of lightning in summer, so it requires a fast ascent to reach the summit and be off of it before the usual afternoon storms.

Cunningham and Berman bivouacked on the route on the night of July 20 and started their ascent early the next morning, rapidly climbing 1,200 vertical feet without being roped. Near the top of Blitzen Ridge, they reached a section of very steep rock, which would require them to rope up before proceeding. The section was only about twenty feet, however, and using rope for such a short distance seemed like more trouble than it was worth. Instead, they decided to climb an adjacent twenty-foot snowbank, and Cunningham led the way, kicking steps into the snow as he went. Berman let

Cunningham get about fifteen feet ahead of him before he started up, using the steps Cunningham had gouged in the snow.

How and why Berman fell remains a mystery, even to the ranger who made the report of this event to the American Alpine Club (AAC). The fact remains that he slipped away from the snowbank and began to fall . . . and kept falling. He dropped a full 1,200 feet to somewhere around the base of the mountain.

Instantly Cunningham reversed his course, working his way to the bottom of the route. Here he began to see Berman's equipment, pieces that had fallen away from him as he plummeted to the ground. He began to search for his partner, but when he could not find him, he climbed a snowfield and gazed out over the mountain's base for any clue that might lead him to his friend. "Searching the bergschrund [the top of a snowfield that melts away from rock faces], he began finding blood spots on the snow and followed them down into a crevasse below the bergschrund," the AAC report said. That's where he found the broken body of Lawrence Berman, who had died in the fall.

Cunningham marked the spot with his equipment and hiked out from Spectacle Lake to the Lawn Lake trailhead, where he reported Berman's death to rangers. They evacuated his body the next day.

BRING EQUIPMENT TO SCALE MCGREGOR

The *Greeley Tribune* provided the scantest of details about the death of Forrest Hein on September 8, 1936, under the appalling headline "Labor Day in Colorado Is Uneventful."

"Forrest Hein, 16-year-old Denver high school youth, was killed in a 200-foot plunge down the rocky face of the McGregor peak in Estes Park Sunday," the article said in the sum total of its coverage, as if sudden death were the most banal of occurrences for a teenager on a holiday weekend.

Let's take this opportunity to set the record a little straighter. Hein and two friends, Norman Lovett, also 16 years old, and 18-year-old Jack Ryan, set out on September 6, 1936, to climb to the top of Mount McGregor (also known as McGregor Peak and McGregor Slab), a mountain with a prominent bald dome that tops out at 10,486 feet. They began by hiking up the mountain's lower slope, but when they reached the sheer exposed rock face above the timberline, Ryan looked up at the nearly vertical wall and decided to take an easier trail, following the curve of the mountain up to its ridgeline. He did his best to convince Hein and Lovett to take the trail with him instead of chancing the climb, but they decided their friend was simply being overcautious. The two younger boys tied the end of a rope around each of their waists and began scaling the steep wall.

Beyond the rope, they lacked any other climbing gear, so the going took time. The two boys made progress, however, clinging to the rock face with their fingertips and toes as they attempted what amounted to their first "free solo." What exactly happened next may never be known; perhaps a loose rock gave way, or one of the boys simply could not hold on any longer. Ryan did not see when they lost contact with the rock wall, but he heard their screams as first one, then the other plunged downward, the rope becoming a liability as the connection yanked the second boy off the mountain and into the air.

Ryan took off down the trail at a run and rushed to a nearby Civilian Conservation Corps camp, where he found people ready to help with a rescue. They grabbed medical supplies and reached the bottom of the mountain quickly, finding the two boys lying not far from one another among the boulders. Lovett had a fractured skull and other injuries, but he had survived the fall. Hein had died on impact.

Another climb without proper gear—this one a descent—ended in death on May 11, 1977, more than forty years after Forrest Hein's fatal fall. Aurora resident Asuncion Navarette, 27, had chosen a particularly difficult way to leave Mount McGregor after reaching its summit, especially because reports indicate that Navarette had only one arm.

He had actually managed to descend three hundred feet on the six-hundred-foot exposed rock face before his grip failed him, dropping the remaining distance to the rocks and foliage below. No one witnessed this accident, so it took a call from family members reporting him missing to trigger a search and potential rescue. Rangers on both foot and horseback and a helicopter combed the mountainside on Thursday, May 12, until three members of a climbing party happened upon Navarette's body at the base of the sheer rock face.

As Navarette had no climbing gear with him, park officials speculated that he might have wandered onto the rock face accidentally after hiking up the mountain on a trail. "Climbing ropes, pitons and other technical climbing gear is necessary to descend the face, they said, and Navarette had no such equipment," the AP said.

Less than a week later, another man—this one with the use of both of his arms—fell off the same mountain. Twenty-year-old Harold E. Holtzendorf, a student at Austin Community College in Texas, plunged from roughly the same area of the rock face. "Holtzendorf and two other campers in the area were hiking in the park when the ACC student decided to try to ascend the slab," the park's information officer, Joyce Bennett, told the *Austin American-Statesman*. "The other two hikers took a safer route, and when they reached their meeting place, Holtzendorf was not there . . . The two other hikers found his body at the base of the slab."

Rangers puzzled briefly over what had made the young man fall, but once again determined that a lack of proper climbing equipment had made the rock face virtually impossible to scale. "He did not apply for a climbing permit, which he should have had, but had been advised of rules and regulations of the park," Bennett told the paper.

Seven years later, yet another young man lost his life attempting to climb McGregor Slab without the necessary gear. David Paul Ormsby, 23, had worked at the National Park Village North store and restaurant in Estes Park every summer since his graduation from high school in Marshalltown, Iowa, in 1979. He attended Aims Community College in Greeley and had been a student at Marshalltown Community College before moving to Colorado.

On July 12, 1984, Ormsby and a friend and coworker, Keith Doroff, decided to attempt to scramble up McGregor Slab without any gear. They had made it three-quarters of the way up by five p.m., when Ormsby apparently lost his footing. News coverage noted that he was not wearing a helmet, but headgear may not have been effective in protecting him from the impact of a five-hundred-foot fall to the slab's rocky base. He died of head injuries.

Doroff did not fall, but he saw where Ormsby landed and worked his way down the rock wall as quickly as he could to reach his friend. By the time he got there, he could see that he could do little but watch and try to help as Ormsby struggled to breathe, and soon stopped breathing altogether. Rangers transported his body to the hospital in Estes Park, where he was pronounced dead on arrival.

The last record of a fall on McGregor Slab happened three years later, and seems eerily similar to the others, providing readers with a valuable lesson about attempting to scale this 45-degree, six-hundred-foot-high monolith of bare rock. David Drea Felts, a 21-year-old army veteran from Texas who was now stationed at Fort Carson, chose August 29, 1987, to attempt to free-climb

Mount McGregor with a friend (whose name does not appear in any of the accounts of this event). Felts had trained at Goodfellow Air Force Base in San Angelo and had considerable strength and solid physical conditioning.

They set up camp not far from the mountain, and then, "without packs or any other gear, they left to ascend McGregor Slab," the American Alpine Club's report tells us.

They reached the top without mishap, with Felts, who was the stronger climber of the two, speeding ahead by as much as three hundred feet. When it came time for the descent, Felts decided that the climb up had been too easy, so he chose to seek a greater challenge and move into tougher terrain than his partner wished to attempt. The friend proceeded down the way he had come up, but Felts ventured into an area rated 5.6 on the Yosemite Decimal System—a route requiring climbing gear in order to complete it safely. Eventually, he was so far afield that his partner lost voice contact with him.

When the partner reached the base of the slab, he did not see Felts anywhere. He looked up to the bare dome and soon realized that he could not see Felts on the rock face, either—which could only mean that he had taken a bad fall and lay somewhere nearby, unconscious or injured. The friend ran for help, bringing back rangers Jane Ruchman and Bundy Philips, who located Felts's body hidden in foliage at the base of the slab.

SOLITUDE ENDS IN A SEARCH
Hoyt White needed a break. A prominent young attorney at 33 years old with a promising career already in progress, he served on many committees in his Yates Center, Kansas, community, and was well into his second and final term as the attorney for Woodson County. In the spring of 1940 he drove to neighboring Iola, Kansas, just about every evening to play tennis on courts there, but as

summer ended, he looked ahead to the change of scenery he had craved on an annual basis for several years.

So it surprised no one when White told his friends and coworkers that he planned to take several weeks' vacation in the Rocky Mountains at the beginning of September, leaving August 31 on a solo road trip to a cabin owned by his aunt, Mrs. Henry A. Helfenbine, in Estes Park. They knew he loved climbing mountains, and that he had experience hiking on his own, so they assumed they'd see him back in a few weeks with many stories to tell.

White chose the Estes Park area not only because of the offer of accommodations, but because he found the physical challenge he craved and the solitude he needed in these mountains. While visiting the park five summers earlier, he had approached a couple whose car sported Kansas license plates, and he introduced himself as a visitor from the same area. "Within less than a minute, he was exclaiming over the thrills of mountain climbing, how many summits he had already scaled and how many more he was ready to tackle," said a report in the *Iola Register*, a Kansas newspaper. "'Boy!' he exulted, 'I sure do get a bang out of climbing over these mountains!' He said then that he soon hoped to scale the 3,000-foot precipice that constitutes the east face of Longs Peak."

Mrs. Helfenbine had word from White early in his trip, letting her know that he had arrived, and saying, "I just wish I could tell you how much I like climbing these mountains." After that, it seemed that White maintained a strange silence as he explored his mountain paradise. By September 15, when at least ten days had gone by without any communication from him at all, his friends contacted Rocky Mountain National Park to see if the park had any record of his whereabouts. One friend remembered that before he left, White had mentioned his desire to climb Twin Sisters, a mountain with a well-established trail leading to its 11,428-foot summit.

Rangers headed out to the Twin Sisters trailhead and made an important discovery: White's car was parked at the trailhead, showing signs that it had been there for some time. They went to Mrs. Helfenbine's cabin to see if he was there and found a journal he had kept daily since the start of his road trip. He had made his last entry on September 5, saying that he intended to climb either Longs Peak or Twin Sisters on September 6.

Now believing that some kind of harm had come to White as much as ten days earlier, the park began to organize a massive search effort. More than 125 members of the Civilian Conservation Corps (CCC) joined 35 rangers and volunteers in searching three sections of the park. Two skilled climbing rangers, Ernest Field and Paul Hauk, "worked over the steep and treacherous East Face of 14,255-foot Longs Peak where searchers theorized White may have fallen into a crevice," the Associated Press reported, noting that snow had fallen on the mountain's summit that very day.

An unnamed editor at the *Iola Register*, White's hometown paper, professed to know the Rocky Mountain Front Range and offered his own theory. "If he did try that feat alone this summer—especially in September when sleet and snow are likely to hit the mountain tops any day—he used less judgment than his friends here give him credit for. That particular climb just isn't made alone." He went on to speculate further: "It is the opinion of those here who know the region that he will probably not be found there but in some other area where perhaps a simple accident made it impossible for him to return to where he might have received help."

The rangers leading the search had come to the same conclusion and organized a team to search the area along nine miles of Highway 7 from Longs Peak to Estes Park. "Chief Ranger J. Barton Herschler ordered the highway search on a theory that White might have been hit and killed by a motorist, and his body concealed in a gully or wood," the AP said. "Herschler said the battery on White's automobile . . . was dead. It is possible, Herschler declared, that White, unable to start his car, started walking back to Estes Park."

No sign of an accident, hit-and-run or otherwise, revealed itself along the highway, however. Kansas colleagues and family members, unable to sit still at home and wait for news any longer, began to arrive in Estes Park to assist in the effort to find White. "Undersheriff C. R. Miller and John F. Timm, clerk of court, arrived from Yates Center yesterday," the newspapers reported. "White's parents, Mr. and Mrs. Sidney White of Kansas City, Kas., and Miss Jessie Cooper of Yates Center, arrived earlier."

The ranks of the CCC deployed all over Twin Sisters, working their way both up and down in an effort to glimpse a scrap of clothing, a canteen, or any other personal item that might signal that White's body lay somewhere on the peak. Major W. Whitaker, a 19-year-old recruit from Guthrie, Oklahoma, canvassed an area about 125 feet from the base of the mountain as carefully as he could. He nudged a log out of his field of vision and spotted something that looked vaguely human. Grabbing the log and pushing it aside, he made the discovery of a lifetime: the battered body of Hoyt White.

"The youth ran a mile and a half down the rough mountainside in 17 minutes to report his discovery to [Herschler]," the AP reported.

Herschler praised Whitaker's careful searching to the media, noting that "searchers passed within 25 feet of the body earlier but that the log [had] concealed it."

The chief ranger's examination of the body led him to determine that White had probably died instantly when he hit the ground. "The attorney's skull was crushed and most of his clothing torn away," he said. He hypothesized that White had made a common mistake on mountains with limited sight lines and rugged terrain:

He probably attempted what he thought was a shortcut either up or down the peak. "The body was about a third of the way down the summit, far from the trail usually used by hikers," he told the AP.

White's parents and friends accompanied his body back to Kansas. He was buried in the family plot at Mount Moriah Cemetery in Kansas City, Jackson County, Missouri.

Two other slip-and-fall accidents have taken place on Twin Sisters, though little information is available about either of them. On August 15, 1974, John Berger, who was 11 years old, fell to his death on the mountain. Six years later, on August 24, 1980, 12-year-old Christina Marie Ulbricht's life ended when she slipped from a rock outcropping on Twin Sisters. This is all we know about either of these deaths, beyond the tragic fact that they were both children.

The Unkindest Shortcut

The squadron of US Air Force students stationed at Lowry Field, near Denver, all presented for inspection in "spic-and-span" condition, a rating of excellence that merited a reward. Boarding buses, all two hundred young soldiers rode to Rocky Mountain National Park on June 16, 1946, for a grand Sunday out, with picnicking, hiking, and other leisure pursuits that were entirely new to many of the recruits.

Private Thomas H. Evans of Akron, Ohio, had never been to the mountains before. After a pleasant day of food and fun, he decided he needed a closer look at the most rugged country he had ever experienced, so he told his fellow privates that he intended to take a short hike. He waved to his friends as he began to follow a trail up Flattop Mountain, a 12,362-foot peak towering over Bear Lake Campground. Chances are that Evans did not intend to attempt a summit, or even to be gone for very long.

Soon the day ended and the squadron got back on their buses and rode to Lowry Field, where they would resume their normal duties and drills Monday morning. Commanding officers called roll and found everyone accounted for . . . except Evans. "Fellow soldiers said he had not returned with the rest of the outfit Sunday night," United Press International (UPI) reported later, a detail the others apparently had not seen as significant until then. "Evans was a tenderfoot, and whether he could forage for himself and find some shelter in the snow-swept Rockies was doubtful." Reports indicated that Evans carried no food or overnight gear—something that hadn't mattered before he decided to wander off into the wilderness.

Initial searches turned up no sign of the man, so three days into the endeavor, a team of twenty-nine GI mountain climbers with full climbing gear—twenty of them from Lowry Field—scaled Flattop Mountain, accompanied by a group of national park rangers. The other nine men came from Camp Carson, near Colorado Springs, and they brought along an army "weasel" snowmobile.

"Mountain experts described Flattop Mountain Trail as one of the most dangerous in the Rockies," UPI said in its coverage. "Snow blanketed the crags Tuesday and Wednesday, and fear for Evans's safety was doubled." It added, "All troops were equipped fully for mountaineering and issued a week's rations."

When these troops found no sign of Evans, more arrived, including alpine teams of the 28th Regimental Combat Group, as well as thirty-four army veterans. Army planes and pilots conducted extensive searches from the air. Three weeks of coverage produced not a single clue, however, and finally, on July 6, authorities from Lowry Field recalled the search parties from Flattop and other trails in the park. The formal search came to an end; perhaps Evans would never be found.

Or perhaps he would.

G. Burton Davy and his wife, both from Boston, Massachusetts, started their day in Rocky Mountain on July 8, 1946, with a plan to climb the south side of Flattop Mountain. As they made their way up the steep trail, they stopped to take a closer look at a strange phenomenon: a miniature waterfall "which seemed to end abruptly," according to the International News Service (INS). To their amazement, they discovered that the obstacle to the water's progress was a body. "The body of Evans was impounding the water," the media said.

Davy and his wife cut their hike short and ran to report their find. J. Barton Herschler, chief ranger, noted that he had personally led a search party along that same stretch of trail, and they had passed within fifty feet of Evans's final position. "He believed that Evans fell from a twelve-foot ledge as he was hurrying down the slope after a solo ascent of the rugged peak," the INS said. A twelve-foot fall might not be fatal in many cases, but Evans had the misfortune to land on his head. Assistant park superintendent George H. Miller also speculated that Evans might have fallen farther, from some height well above his final position, before the last twelve-foot drop from a ledge.

"NOT CONSIDERED DIFFICULT"

Rocky Mountain contains some of the most challenging climbs and hikes in Colorado, but it also offers a number of hikes that don't require special equipment or anything more than appropriate footwear to complete. This does not mean, however, that hikers can blithely skip along these routes without paying careful attention to where they place their hands and feet.

Fifteen-year-old Kathryn Rees discovered this the hard way on July 31, 1953, when she joined eight other women on a hike up

Little Matterhorn to the summit at 11,586 feet, roughly a 2,100-foot elevation gain from the Bear Lake trailhead. The group had nearly reached the top when a rock Kathryn had grabbed for support wiggled under her grasp, startling her into losing her balance. She fell over a ledge, dropped 150 feet, and died on impact with the rocks below.

Gretchen DeGroot and Sandra Miller, two of the older girls who were serving as counselors for the hike, left to start back down the trail to get help for Kathryn—who, to their knowledge, might have still been alive. The accident did not make them more cautious as they descended, however, and soon Gretchen was well out in front of Sandra. She reached Fern Lake Lodge and asked that a telegraph be sent to get help, and then waited for Sandra to arrive.

Time passed, but there was no sign of the other counselor before a search-and-rescue team started up the trail to bring Kathryn down. Before they could reach the girl's body, however, they came upon the equally deceased body of Sandra Miller, where it had landed when she slipped while hurrying down the mountain to get help.

"There is no great exposure on this route up the Little Matterhorn and it is not considered a difficult or hazardous climb," noted the American Alpine Club's accident report. "Carelessness seems to be the main factor in these two fatalities."

The same may be said for the death of Eula Frost, 19, back in the summer of 1917. Frost came to the park with her mother and several friends, and delighted in the option of playing in the snow on an August day. They decided to cross Fall River Canyon at about four p.m. and climb to a snowbank some distance up a mountain, where they engaged in a vigorous snowball fight, followed by a slide down the snowfield to return to the canyon. She and an unnamed young man joined hands and started to slide, but they soon lost control, and Frost dragged the man over the edge of the snowbank and onto the rocky mountainside, where momentum rolled them both for several hundred feet. Their plummeting descent loosened a large boulder in their path, and when Frost finally came to a stop, the boulder rolled over her head and crushed her skull. The young man walked away from the ordeal, but Eula Frost died on the mountainside.

A DAY OFF GONE WRONG

It's not uncommon, sadly, for summer employees at national parks to become emboldened by the magnificent landscapes around them and the feats of skilled climbers and hikers that they have the opportunity to observe. Some of these employees use their days off to try their own luck at reaching summits, crossing expanses of open terrain, and hiking alone in the beckoning wilderness. Most of them are back in time for their next work shift, but some find themselves the victims of their own spirit of adventure.

A climb up Mount Craig went terribly wrong on August 15, 1956, when two summer employees at Grand Lake Lodge decided to summit the 12,007-foot peak on their day off. George Bloom, 21, and John Carpenter, 23, both students at William Jewell College, reached the summit without incident and were on their way down when a thunderstorm blew up, sending pelting rain down the mountainsides and loose shale off of ledges. The two young men found separate spots to take cover until the storm had passed, but after the rain stopped, the mountain became shrouded in fog, and they could not find one another again. Carpenter finally decided to return to the lodge to see if Bloom had taken a different route down and was already safe and sound.

Bloom had not appeared at the lodge, however, so Carpenter notified the park that his friend appeared to be lost. Search teams including "scores of volunteers, 10 forest rangers and a helicopter," according to the AP, scoured the mountainsides until the following afternoon, when they found Bloom's body in a rock pile at the bottom of a two-hundred-foot cliff.

"It was evident that he had died almost instantly from a crushed skull, crushed chest, broken leg, and other injuries," wrote George B. Hartzog, acting superintendent of the park, in his report to the American Alpine Club.

For 21-year-old Patricia Louise Beatty of Greenfield, Ohio, who would be a senior in the College of Education at Miami University that fall, the backcountry in the vicinity of the Continental Divide became too inviting to ignore. She set out alone on August 13, 1962, from Crags Lodge, where she was working for the summer, toward Hallet Peak, a 12,275-foot mountain, and the rugged slopes around it.

No one saw what happened to her, but later that afternoon, Walter Newport and Morris Albertson, who lived in the park over the summer, went hiking with their families and stopped to admire the scenery near Hallet Peak. They looked down into the canyon and were shaken to see what was obviously a young woman who had fallen a great distance. They made their way carefully down into the canyon to try to help her and must have detected a pulse, because they spent the next three hours trying to revive her with mouth-to-mouth resuscitation. Patricia never regained consciousness, so they went to park headquarters and told rangers where she was.

Rangers set out immediately to find the girl and located her quickly, determining in a few minutes that she had died. They could not bring her out of the canyon without assistance, so they returned at three a.m. with a seven-man crew and cable, which allowed them to raise the body out of the canyon. They could then bring her out using a packhorse.

Nineteen-year-old Myron Fritts, a General Motors Scholarship student at the University of Notre Dame and a summer employee of the Colorado Transportation Company in the park, set out alone on the morning of July 14, 1961, to climb Hallet Peak. When he did not come into work the following day, park rangers began a search that soon grew to include many volunteers, including a group of former Dartmouth College students: Will Bassett, Peter Farquhar, and David Laing. These three young men spotted Fritts's body on Sunday, lying at the bottom of a "deep shaft" at the base of the mountain. "Rangers said Fritts apparently fell 200 feet into a chimney rock formation," the *South Bend Tribune* reported. It was not possible to tell if he had reached the summit.

THE PERILS OF TEENAGE BOYS

A Boy Scout troop camping trip usually allows the Scouts to learn camp skills like laying a fire, pitching a tent, and building a lean-to, but a trip out west often includes opportunities to learn rugged trail skills as well. The twenty-three Scouts of Troop 2 from Lincoln, Nebraska, were supervised by four fathers and a professional scoutmaster, Lorenn Wilson, but somehow, on a hike above Mills Lake on June 14, 1966, none of these adults had taken in hand the reportedly headstrong Jay DuPont, 15, and two Scouts who were with him, Scott Fish and Paul Rohrbaugh.

Jay saw a 350-foot-long rock face on the mountainside and thought it would be more fun and easier to slide down this sheer drop instead of walking down the mountain with the rest of the troop. Adults had told him to keep away from this rock face and to stay with the group, but Jay splintered off on his own, while the other two boys took a different route to return to the troop.

No one saw what happened next, but suddenly Jay was gone. Troop leaders began looking for him as soon as they realized he was missing, and they notified the park as well. It didn't take long to discover where he was: His body lay at the bottom of the sheer drop that he had intended to slide down. Whether he actually attempted the slide or just took a misstep while considering it can never be known . . . but the fall from the cliff he had been instructed to avoid did indeed kill him.

A park search-and-rescue crew brought Jay's body out of the park the following day. The trip was cut short for the rest of the Scouts, who returned to Lincoln that afternoon.

"A small amount of good sense would have saved a life," the American Alpine Club report on the incident said. "DuPont was notorious for doing just as he felt and would not take advice from other people. He was raised in Nebraska and knew nothing of the mountains."

Another teen from Nebraska approached a technical climb with a similar sense of daring and the poor judgment of youth. Early on the morning of June 29, 1990, 15-year-old Andrew Tufly and another boy had reached the top of the rocks in an area of the park near Twin Sisters Peak, where students of technical climbing sometimes go to practice their skills. The group, including the two boys and two counselors from a Nebraska church group staying at a private religious retreat, were not using technical climbing equipment.

The boys made it to the top of the rocks, and Tufly decided that he wanted to try a more difficult descent route. The two counselors told him that this was a bad idea, that his skills were not up to the task, and that it was more dangerous than he realized . . . but a 15-year-old boy believes himself to be invincible, so Tufly ignored their advice and started down.

"Tufly lost his footing after grabbing a rock that came loose, and he slid 20 feet and then fell 50 feet off a cliff to his death," said Christy Metz, spokesperson for the park at the time.

The other boy took an easier route down and was not injured. Park rangers, a Flight for Life helicopter, and the Allenspark Fire Department arrived before eight a.m. and retrieved Tufly's body.

Searchers had a good idea where to look for Jay DuPont, and they knew exactly where to find Andrew Tufly, but the disappearance of 12-year-old Robert Baldeshwiler of Lansing, Illinois, became a far more baffling conundrum. Robert and his family began a hike on Flattop Mountain on June 29, 1982, and, seized with a sudden passion for the mountains, he ran ahead of his parents and sister and out of their range of vision. They stopped to rest and waited for him to return, checking with a passing hiker coming down the mountain to see if he had seen the boy. The hiker affirmed that he had and that Robert was still heading up toward the summit.

When the weather began to change and the family decided to turn back, Robert was nowhere to be found. Other hikers coming down said they had not seen him. The parents slowly realized that he had disappeared.

The family notified the park as quickly as they could, watching with trepidation as a storm began to move in over the mountain. Soon rain and hail began to fall and temperatures on Flattop dropped into the 30s. Robert was dressed in jeans, a T-shirt, and sneakers, with a sun visor to shield his eyes, inadequate clothing for the change in weather.

Despite the storm, the search began almost immediately and continued for six days, slowly expanding to cover nearly all of Rocky Mountain National Park. More than eight hundred professionals and volunteers covered the mountain and the surrounding area, walking twenty feet apart so as not to miss a single sign that the boy might have passed that way, or that he might be injured and lying nearby. By the fourth day, with no sign at all of the missing child, the media began adding up the cost of the endeavor to the American taxpayer—$46,593 after four days, plus the value of $56,000 in volunteer hours. Searchers turned up no clues except a single facial tissue that Robert might or might not have discarded.

On July 5, with no new information or finds, the park closed down the search effort. The Baldeshwiler family returned to Illinois with no idea what had happened to their son, but with the crushing certainty that he had died somewhere in the park.

A week later, on July 12, three hikers taking the trail up Flattop Mountain discovered something that had never turned up in the search: a child's sun visor, stained with blood. They brought it to authorities and told them where they'd found it, and two teams of climbers returned to the mountain. Sure enough, they found Robert's body "on a very steep slope of a ravine that had been searched several times before," the AP reported.

"He may have fallen all the way in one swoop, but since the area was searched before, it's possible the body could have tumbled part of the way, then the rest of the way at a later time," said spokesperson Glen Kaye. He added that the climbers said the boy had "a massive skull fracture and contusions and abrasions from head to foot."

The media lost no time in calculating the total price tag for the search: $130,000 in 1982, which calculates to $396,000 in 2020 dollars. "And that doesn't include about $72,000 in time that volunteers contributed," the AP added. Clearly a sea change had taken place in the public's patience with large-scale searches and rescues, as they began to see them as taxpayer burdens as well as humanitarian efforts.

TECHNICAL DIFFICULTIES

As we have seen in the chapters about deaths on Longs Peak, even the most skilled technical climbers can run into trouble in Rocky Mountain. Some even find themselves in the same kinds of predicaments that endanger first-time mountain hikers like young Robert Baldeshwiler.

Four climbers who intended to take on either Chief's Head or McHenry Peak on July 31, 1960, saw the weather change by one p.m., when they arrived at the ridge between the two peaks. Knowing full well that lightning could mean death if they continued, they turned around and began to head back to the trailhead. Just half an hour later, leader Amel Landgraf "heard a large rock start sliding down the slope. It came from a point about 100 feet below him," the American Alpine Club report said. "Les Reeble was in the lead and Landgraf followed the group . . . [Landgraf] stopped to watch for the rock to appear on the snow slope below. Instead he saw Les rolling and sliding out of control down the snow slope, then over the edge of another cliff to a snowfield below."

Landgraf thought quickly, tying the other two climbers together with a rope to keep them from panicking, and the three of them descended to the spot where Reeble had lost his hold. They determined that a rock had fallen from this point, most likely when Reeble put his weight on it as he used it to lower himself down to a ledge. From here, they continued their descent to a point where they could make their way back to Reeble. It took only a moment to determine that he had died in the fall.

Landgraf took full responsibility for the accident in his analysis for the AAC report, noting, "Les Reeble was a man of good judgment. I'm certain he would not have tried anything beyond his capabilities."

The same could be said for Steve Day and his climbing partner, Dave Whiteman, as they took on Pagoda Peak on June 18, 1972. Their careful ascent attempt took them up a particularly difficult route until it became clear that they could not reach the summit the way they had chosen, so they made the decision to descend. As Day began the double-rope rappel he had rigged, checking first to see that the two rope ends were even, he leaned back, lost the ledge, and began to fall. "Whiteman heard him yell and saw him fall backwards and tumble about 80 feet," the AAC report said. "He hit some outsloping ledges at this point and began to roll. He then hit a 3-foot flat ledge very hard, which slowed his fall. He rolled off this ledge and ended up about 200 feet below the rappel point when the rope tangled in some loose boulders on one of the ledges."

Whiteman, who wrote the report in the third-person point of view, knew that Day could not survive such a drop. He made his way down to Day's body and lowered it to a larger ledge, pounding in a piton and anchoring the body there. With pack and ice ax in hand, he took a long look at the scene to determine what had gone wrong. "It was clear that the bong-bong [a large piton] had failed at the beginning of the rappel," he wrote. "The pin was still attached to the rappel rope and was only about six feet from Steve's brake bar."

Whiteman completed his descent, hiked out, and notified authorities. In writing his report to the AAC, he reflected, "I had rappelled on the same piton. I feel that the piton failed because the friction in the double-rope brake system put an upwards pressure on the piton. This caused it to pull out from its position behind the flake at the start of the rappel. Had the pressure on the piton been from below, the piton would have held."

Ropes, pitons, and other climbing equipment are generally considered critically important to climbers, but some prefer the freedom they feel climbing "free solo," going it alone and using nothing but their fingers and toes to keep them on the rock face. Gary Boyer had been free-soloing once or twice a year for about four years when he attempted to do so on Mount Meeker on July 28, 1992. A hiker spotted Boyer nearing the summit ridge around noon that day, "apparently having some difficulty ascending a section of steep rock," and that was the last time Boyer was seen alive.

The next morning, Boyer's wife, Melinda, called the park to report that Gary had not arrived home the night before. It didn't take long to locate his body some four hundred feet up the mountain in technical terrain, "in the gully on the right side of the East Arete," according to Longs Peak supervisory climbing ranger Jim Detterline's AAC report. "Recovery efforts included a technical litter lowering, several hundred feet of scree evacuation, and a 0.25-mile litter carry to a backcountry helispot, where the victim was picked up by helicopter after inclement weather had subsided." Detterline believed that Boyer had slipped on a rock and fallen about one thousand feet—a fall that might have been avoided if Boyer had been roped.

Richard Ladue encountered the same kind of trouble in an unroped solo of a challenging route on Thatchtop Mountain, known as All Mixed Up. The park described it in a news release: "The base of the climb . . . is approximately 1,200 feet above the lake on Thatchtop Mountain, and is in extremely difficult and dangerous terrain. It is steep, with loose talus, ice and unconsolidated snow."

He had climbed this route before, and, at 37 years old, had had considerable climbing experience, but he chose November 15, 1998, for this particular attempt, when ice encased virtually all of the rock, and winter snows and winds made it even more hazardous.

Two other climbers also selected this day to climb, so they became witnesses to the fall that took Ladue's life. They "were unsure if the fall was due to brittle, broke ice or to faulty technique," the AAC report notes. He dropped some one hundred feet, and although he was wearing appropriate head protection, "it is most unfortunate that he was struck below the protection of the helmet," Jim Detterline wrote in his analysis. Ladue suffered a depressed skull fracture on his left temple and died in the litter during his evacuation.

A belay rope nearly saved the life of Jack McConnell, 59, on May 23, 1994, when he and his son, Thomas, 24, climbed the Left Book formation of Lumpy Ridge on the route known as White Whale II. "The Left Book is a large cliff area with a number of similar-looking intermediate-level crack features, which confuse many climbers even when comparing features with a guidebook," Detterline wrote in his report to the AAC. "The McConnells had a guidebook, but left it with their packs at the base of the route. Most modern guidebooks are not pocket-sized to easily transport on the climb."

Jack had been climbing for fifteen years and often led climbs at the 5.6 to 5.7 level of difficulty, but he and Thomas were off-route and didn't know it. They had veered into the Ten Years After Route, a 5.8 to 5.9 difficulty level that exceeded Jack's experience. He still managed to negotiate it, however, and continued upward and out of view of Thomas, who remained below, belaying the rope.

When just twenty feet of belay rope remained, Thomas heard something high above him that sounded like a crash. He looked up and saw with horror that his father was in the air, falling fast toward Thomas and then past him, until the belay rope brought him up short, preventing him from tumbling down the mountainside.

Working quickly, Thomas tied off the belay and down-climbed to reach his father. Jack was in bad shape, struggling to breathe and bleeding from several gashes on his head. With all of the precautions he had taken for a safe climb that day, Jack had neglected to wear a helmet—a piece of equipment that might have reduced the severity of his injuries, or prevented them altogether.

Thomas climbed back up to where he had stood while belaying Jack and lowered his father as far as he could, until he ran out of rope. He then climbed down on his own and rushed to the Twin Owls trailhead to notify authorities and get an emergency medical team on its way to Jack. As luck would have it, rangers were engaged in a search for another visitor in peril that afternoon, so a technical rescue team and a helicopter stood ready in the park and were dispatched immediately. Two climbing-rescue paramedics immobilized Jack and brought him down to the waiting litter at the cliff base, but as they performed the scree evacuation, Jack succumbed to his head injuries. He died before he reached the helicopter.

Three climbers taking on Taylor Glacier had nearly reached the top on October 16, 2010, when one of them, 54-year-old James Charles Patrick of Littleton, Colorado, fell more than one thousand feet. There was no question between the two remaining climbers that he had died in the fall, but even with the shock and grief of that knowledge, they had to deal with an immediate problem for themselves: Patrick had fallen with their rope, so they were stranded on the glacier.

They managed to anchor themselves securely where they were, one hundred feet below the next ledge, and fortunately, there was enough cellular service to call for help. Patrick had fallen at about 11:30 a.m., but rangers were not able to reach the two surviving climbers until 4:15 p.m., so they passed a chilly afternoon in a fairly precarious position on a wall of solid ice. Still, the climbers were in good enough shape to accept a belay from the rangers once they arrived, and they climbed up to the next ledge under their own power, hiking out of the park with the rangers that evening.

As one team helped the climbers to the top of the glacier, another team reached Patrick's body at about 4:45 p.m. "He had fallen into a steep talus area with loose rock, ice and snow," Kaitlyn Bruce of the *Fort Collins Coloradoan* reported. "Two rangers remained in the area overnight until it was safe to recover the body. His body was flown out of the backcountry at 10:30 a.m. Sunday."

Could the climbers in any of these cases have predicted these accidents, and therefore avoided them? Debates on online discussion boards and Facebook pages, analyses in American Alpine Club accident reports, and conversations between climbers suggest that most of these situations could have been prevented, although it may be impossible to predict everything that can go wrong.

Take, for example, a two-man climb of the south face of Petit Grepon on July 2, 1997, led by 34-year-old Todd Marshall. The day had started with an error: Marshall and his partner, Matteo Baceda, took a wrong turn before dawn and found themselves at Spearhead Mountain instead of Petit Grepon, resulting in a seven-mile hike to the correct climb. Once they arrived, they made good time up the 5.8-rated cliffs, occasionally fighting gale-force winds that made them cling to the rock for balance.

When Marshall arrived on a spur ledge just below the summit, about 150 feet ahead of Baceda, he stood fully upright with his arms in the air and yelled, "Hooray!"

In the blink of an eye, a 60-mile-per-hour wind gust knocked Marshall off his perch and tossed him down the mountain.

"Marshall fell 70 feet and struck the rock face, sustaining a massive depressed occipital skull fracture, and instant death," the AAC report said. His body remained lodged some eighty feet above Baceda.

Baceda, meanwhile, was fairly new to climbing and did not know how to climb down on his own. He remained stranded in place on the mountainside throughout a cold night and into the following afternoon, when two other climbers discovered him and performed an on-the-spot rescue. Luckily, areas of exposure on his lips were the only lasting physical effects of the experience.

This sounds like a completely unforeseeable turn of events, but experts disagree.

"At the very least Marshall should have clipped into the belay before standing up on the ledge," Jim Detterline wrote in his analysis. "Marshall was not wearing a helmet; [had he done so], the impact area on the back of his head would have been covered. However, considering the distance fallen and the force produced, it is not clear if he could have survived."

A bad cam device led to the death of Corey Stewart, 22, a student from Newton, New Jersey, studying natural resources at Colorado State University. Stewart fell thirty to fifty feet from Batman Pinnacle on Lumpy Ridge on August 22, 2013, landing on his head in front of several witnesses. Although they attempted to revive him with CPR, he died at the scene.

"It appears an equipment failure contributed to his fatal fall, with a cam that seemed stable failing to hold his weight," Larimer County Coroner's Office investigator Greg Fairman told the *Fort Collins Coloradoan* several weeks later.

By the time a recovery team could get there, thunderstorms had moved in with heavy rain and intense lightning, so they delayed removal of his body until the following day. Rangers remained with his body overnight until the weather had cleared and they could complete the recovery the next morning.

Hiking Alone
George Ogden, a 21-year-old Southern Methodist University student, had just finished a summer course at the University of Colorado in Boulder when he decided to go hiking alone in Rocky Mountain National Park on August 15, 1988. No stranger to the mountains, Ogden was considered "an accomplished mountain climber and outdoorsman," according to an article in his hometown newspaper, the *Duncanville Suburban*.

He "was scoping several hiking trails on which to take friends later in the week," said Ken Pritchett, a family friend who had spent the week with Ogden at a Pritchett family reunion in Estes Park. "He climbed many areas of Colorado, Texas, and Oklahoma . . . He was in an area you didn't need to be in unless you were good, and George was very good."

Even the best hikers and climbers can meet the unexpected in Rocky Mountain National Park, and Ogden certainly did: He fell at least two hundred feet on Spearhead Mountain, and was killed on impact.

"He had a glass eye from having been hit with a BB from a BB gun when he was little," his cousin, Rebecca Winn, told me in an e-mail conversation. Winn is a writer and a fellow Authors Guild member, and offered the information when she saw I was working on this book. "We always wondered if his limited vision might have played a part in the accident."

"George's great loves were his family, friends and God," his mother told the *Suburban*. "He felt closest to the Lord in the majestic beauty of the mountains. He will be remembered by everyone as generous, thoughtful and happy."

"He was much beloved," Winn concurred. "His funeral had so many young friends who spoke really highly of him."

A similar fate came to Kurt Zollers, a 33-year-old researcher with Colorado State University (CSU), while he was on a backcountry patrol surveying bighorn sheep. Zollers served as a field technician for the CSU Fishery and Wildlife Biology Department, and on July 26, 2003, he did not return from a day trip to Baker Mountain. Coworker Brent McClintock called park authorities, and a search for him began that evening. They discovered Zollers's body at the base of a cliff, where he had died of traumatic injuries from a fall.

McClintock called Zollers "a Renaissance man in the full sense of the expression. He was an avid outdoorsman, a poet, a painter; he wrote screenplays and loved music. But he really found his calling when he got into wildlife biology two years ago. I don't think he could have been happier since he started."

When Richard Frisbee, a 66-year-old resident of Fort Collins, fell from a steep snow slope above the western edge of Emerald Lake on June 7, 2008, several witnesses saw the accident happen, called the park on their cell phones, and rushed to his aid. By the time they reached him fifteen minutes after his fall, however, he had no pulse and had clearly suffered massive trauma. He had fallen more than five hundred feet.

Frisbee was no stranger to the mountains and maintained an excellent physical condition, participating in "dozens of triathlons, bike races and marathons, where he ran a 2:38 time in the Boston Marathon," his lengthy obituary tells us. "He recently enjoyed a wonderful climb with his son, in Rocky Mountain National Park, sharing his love of the outdoors." Park records note that he was wearing crampons and a helmet, knowing that June conditions in the park would require protection against icy trails and snow-covered slopes. Unfortunately, these precautions could not save him from so dramatic a drop.

For Ken Teselle, a 73-year-old volunteer in Rocky Mountain, an off-duty summit of Mount Lady Washington on August 23, 2017, should have been just another walk in the park. This was the day that Teselle took a "tumbling fall" while coming down the mountain, according to the park's news release. Many people saw him fall and came to his assistance, performing CPR and calling the park for a rescue. "Rangers were nearby in the Chasm Shelter area and reached the man in 15 minutes," the release continued. The rangers took over CPR, but they could not revive Teselle. Weather conditions did not allow them to bring the man out of the park immediately, so rangers stayed with the dedicated volunteer's body overnight and completed the recovery in the morning.

Several weeks later, bystanders witnessed another solo climber's fall, and once again, they hurried to his side to help. Henry L. Gholz, a 65-year-old ecosystem scientist from Fort Collins, had recently retired from the National Science Foundation. He had gone to the park to indulge in his passion for climbing, choosing the Batman and Robin Route on Lumpy Ridge on September 30, 2017. He began a technical climb, reaching Batman Pinnacle before he fell from the spire to the rocks below.

The fifty-foot fall happened in front of a number of park visitors, and they reached him in minutes, beginning CPR and continuing until rangers arrived. The rangers employed Advanced Life Support, but Gholz soon died of his injuries, and his body was recovered by long-line helicopter in the morning.

DEATH OF A RANGER

For rangers who patrol the Rocky Mountain backcountry, hiking alone may be a requirement of the job, as it was in 2006, when ranger Jeff Christensen departed on his patrol of the Mummy Range on July 29. A 31-year-old veteran ski patroller in his fourth season as a park ranger, he was scheduled for a solo backcountry patrol beginning at eight a.m., when he arrived at the ranger operations center to complete paperwork and prepare for his day on the trail. Rules at the time did not require him to file a written plan with his route and expected schedule.

At eleven a.m., a coworker drove him to the Chapin Pass trailhead, and they discussed his intended patrol route—a 22-mile hike to Lost Lake. Later, Christensen decided that this route was too long, as he was only scheduled to be on patrol until four p.m., so he set off with a shorter plan.

The ranger spoke with a trail crew foreman at the Chapin Pass trailhead at about 11:05 a.m., and then headed down the trail toward Mount Chiquita. Here he stopped to speak with a couple from Oklahoma City at 12:30 p.m., and mentioned that he intended to hike to the mountain's summit and then go on to Ypsilon Mountain. "The couple also thought Christensen might have mentioned something about Lawn Lake," the *Fort Collins Coloradoan* noted in their review of the investigation report published by the National Park Service several months later.

More hikers chatted with Christensen as he approached the Chiquita summit, and another one remembered seeing the ranger at the saddle between Mount Chiquita and Mount Chapin. Later, photos recovered from Christensen's camera in August revealed that he had taken a route from Chiquita to Ypsilon . . . and here is where the trail ended for the backcountry ranger.

He had told the ranger who dropped him off at the trailhead that he would call for a ride back, but the lack of a call from him went unnoticed until eleven p.m., when two fellow rangers saw that Christensen's car was still in the parking lot at the ranger operations center. They called Dispatch and his home to see where he was, and drove over to the Lawn Lake trailhead to see if he had made it there. When the rangers found no sign of their coworker, they notified their supervisors.

Dispatch tried to call the missing ranger over all channels but received no response, so search-and-rescue operations began at sunrise the next day. They followed the route Christensen had described to the ranger who drove him to the Mummy Range the previous day, checking drainages between Old Fall River Road and the Lawn

Lake Trail, from Fairchild Mountain to the Lawn Lake trailhead. When this route provided no clues, they put out a bulletin asking anyone in the park who had seen Christensen on July 29 to call with information, and they received the tips that helped them put together a timeline of the ranger's whereabouts. Searches of these areas over the next eight days produced no additional clues, leaving the park with few options for continuing the effort to find their colleague.

On August 6, the eighth day since Christensen's disappearance, three hikers in the Mummy Range found the ranger's body. "Investigators weren't able to determine where Christensen fell or whether he might have been hit by falling rocks and tumbled down the mountainside," the *Coloradoan* noted when he was found.

In retrospect, the park determined that he fell somewhere below Chiquita's eastern summit between four and eight p.m., hitting his head and fracturing his skull. The injury triggered the formation of a blood clot on his brain, which the Larimer County coroner later determined had been the cause of death.

The fall didn't knock him out, however. Christensen performed basic first aid on himself, taking a T-shirt from his backpack and tying it around his head to stanch the bleeding. He put on his rain jacket and started walking until, presumably, he could go no farther.

Why didn't he call for help? His radio was damaged, the report said, but it still worked, so he could have sent and received calls and notified the park that he needed assistance. The radio coverage in that area was "excellent," according to the park, so a distress call should have been possible.

"One theory is that he didn't know how badly he was injured," the *Coloradoan* said. "Another is that he was unable to talk after the fall." There's a third possibility as well: Park Dispatch received a series of clicks at about four p.m., just when the coroner estimated that the ranger had fallen. He might have attempted to call for help, but anything from a low battery to difficulty speaking could have prevented him from completing the call.

This much is known for certain: Sometime between six p.m. and midnight, after a period of several hours of unconsciousness, Jeff Christensen passed away alone in the shadow of Mount Chiquita.

The accident triggered an investigation by the National Park Service to determine what policy and procedural changes needed to take place to help prevent such a tragedy from happening again.

"Only 10 other rangers have died on backcountry duty in the 89-year history of the National Park Service . . . and two of them suffered heart attacks," wrote Kim Nguyen of the Associated Press. "Rangers go through extensive training and refresher courses in emergency response, search and rescue, and other fields, but most visitors are far less prepared."

National Park Service spokesperson Al Nash added, "We don't know what the public brings as far as knowledge and experience. The public is an unknown quantity for us. But our personnel are a known quantity to us."

Solo patrols continue to be a standard practice in the national parks, especially with the availability of cellular phones, satellite phones, stronger radios, and personal GPS beacons. The dwindling number of rangers in modern times also means that rangers often must patrol the backcountry alone, as the National Park Service budget becomes more and more strained. Some forms of patrol, including climbing patrols on Longs Peak and other challenging mountains, do require rangers to work in pairs for their own safety and to cover ground more quickly.

ALONE AND OUT OF SIGHT

Hiking alone certainly does not guarantee an automatic death sentence, but if a hiker or climber does meet an unfortunate end on a solo expedition, it may become very, very difficult to locate the lost person's body. This can create a miserable situation for parents, family members, friends, and the dozens or even hundreds of searchers who may be called to duty to find it.

On the morning of Saturday, June 30, 2018, Brian Perri, 38, told his friends in Fort Collins that he planned to hike Mount Meeker on his own and would be back by evening. Later that day, he texted a photo of himself at the summit of the 13,911-foot peak to a friend in the eastern United States. It looked like he was having a great day and that he'd be home as scheduled.

Friends tried to get in touch with him the following day, and the day after that. When they had had no response from him for five days, one of his friends called the Fort Collins police and asked them to do a welfare check at Perri's home. Perhaps he'd fallen in the shower, or maybe he'd gone out of town unexpectedly. No contact from him definitely was a sign that something was up.

Police went to his house and found signs that he had not been there for several days. They listed him as missing and sent out a Be On the Look Out, or BOLO, to law enforcement agencies across Colorado, including the National Park Service at Rocky Mountain.

"Later that day, Rocky Mountain National Park crews located Perri's car in the parking lot of Sandbeach Lake trailhead, and the search for him began that evening," Sady Swanson of the *Windsor Beacon* reported. "The only clue search crews had to go off of was the photo of Perri at the summit of Mount Meeker [that Perri had] sent to a friend on the East Coast."

The first helicopter pass took place that afternoon, with a Flight for Life ambulance scanning the mountainside. At dawn the Rocky Mountain National Park Search and Rescue Team deployed on the ground, focusing on the mountain's summit and ridges above the tree line. Soon Northern Colorado Interagency Helitack arrived to assist from the air, and on Sunday, Larimer County Search and Rescue and Rocky Mountain Rescue out of Boulder County joined the effort, bringing the total number of searchers up to sixty-four people. They expanded the search area to include the Loft Route via Keplinger's Couloir, the Dragon's Egg Couloir and Meeker Ridge, and lower sections of the mountain as well.

On Monday, July 8, helicopters left the area to assist with wildland fires in other parts of the state, but a dog team from Larimer County's search organization arrived to attempt to track Perri by scent. By Monday, the park had added an unmanned aircraft system (UAS)—a drone—to help them view terrain that human searchers could not reach. The drone had the ability to get closer to areas than a helicopter could, increasing the possibility of finding clues that helicopter crews might have missed.

Five days into the search, however, not a single clue had come to light. "Since Thursday, the search area has encompassed significant sections of 22.5 square miles," the park's news release said on July 10. "The area has been searched by helicopters, ground searchers, dog teams, and UAS reconnaissance, providing a great deal of coverage. Today, search managers are analyzing the UAS reconnaissance footage and information from the previous days' search efforts, and [are] continuing to adjust search tactics accordingly."

The area where Perri might have fallen, been injured, or become lost stretched for considerable distance over varied terrain, the park explained. "Perri's destination was believed to be the summit of Mount Meeker," a news release on July 15 said, updating the media on progress. "This would be approximately 14 miles round trip from the Sandbeach Lake trailhead. His exact route was unknown. Most of the route is beyond trail access, which would necessitate bushwhacking, mountaineering and route finding through thick forests and the ability to travel in rugged remote terrain with loose rock, steep ridges and exposed cliffs."

Another two weeks passed with no sign of Perri coming to light, and the park quietly stopped providing daily updates to the media. Searchers and volunteers continued to go out from the Sandbeach Lake trailhead daily, however, including Perri's best friend, JC Fischer.

"Fischer said he isn't an experienced hiker like 38-year-old Perri—he had never actually climbed a mountain in Colorado before this—and the more than 200 miles he hiked over the past month took a toll on his body," the *Beacon* reported. Still, despite significant foot and leg injuries, he had a powerful motivation: He told reporter Swanson, "I didn't want that mountain to be my best friend's grave, and I was going to hike until my body broke or until he was found. And it just so happened that both of those happened on the same day."

That day was Saturday, July 28, when climbing rangers received word of a GPS tracking signal device set off by a hiker somewhere on Mount Meeker, indicating that he or she might be injured and in need of assistance. The rangers set off to follow the beacon to the proper coordinates. They did eventually find and assist the visitor, but they also came across something they did not expect: the remains of a hiker's body.

More rangers arrived and stayed in the area with the body until it could be removed from the mountain on Tuesday. They conducted an investigation and gathered what clues they could about what had happened to the man whose body they believed to be Brian Perri.

"He was found downhill and southwest . . . of the photo he had texted a friend at the summit of the mountain June 30," Swanson reported in the *Beacon*. "He was above tree line at the base of a steep, nearly vertical drop-off with large boulders and loose rocks."

The park added, "Unfortunately, the steep terrain, angle, sheer size of the rocks and boulders, as well as the coloring of his tan and green clothing made it extremely difficult to see him."

The Boulder County Coroner's Office confirmed the identification on August 6. "Perri took an approximate 25- to 40-foot tumbling fall and appears to have died instantly," the park confirmed.

CHAPTER 5

Falling Snow and Rock:
Avalanches and Rockslides

GIVEN THE HEIGHT OF THE MOUNTAINS, THE VOLUMINOUS AMOUNTS of snow every winter, and the length of the snow season in Rocky Mountain National Park, you might expect that avalanches would cause many climber fatalities throughout the coldest months. Remarkably, this is not the case: Only six deaths in the park can be attributed directly to massive snowslides that tore climbers away from their gear. Three of these deaths came in two incidents in the early 1990s, while the last one took place in 2013—and this one involved two of the most experienced climbers in the Estes Park area. Even those with consummate skill and knowledge can find themselves in a situation they did not expect, and while survival skills can help a climber survive, they can't save everyone.

Long before dawn on Saturday, March 16, 2013, David Laurienti, who was 43, and 45-year-old Lisa Foster set out from the Lawn Lakes trailhead to climb Ypsilon Mountain. They carried all the necessary gear to climb the Blitzen Ridge route, a Class 5 technical mountaineering route. Normally rated 5.4 to 5.7, this type of trail requires that climbers be roped and use protection hardware—a fairly easy climb for well-seasoned mountaineers. Laurienti and Foster expected to complete their ascent in about half a day and descend on Donner Ridge on the south side of the mountain. If all went well, they would be back by dark, or shortly thereafter.

Foster had hiked virtually every trail and climbed every accessible mountain in the park, and she had the credits to prove it: She authored *Rocky Mountain National Park: The Complete Hiking Guide*, a book released in 2005 with a second edition in 2013, and was widely considered the ultimate reference to the park's many trails, as well as a wealth of off-trail options. She also held a unique record: She was the only woman to have climbed Longs Peak in every month of the year, a feat she completed in 2012.

Laurienti had earned a bachelor's degree in outdoor recreation from the University of Northern Colorado, beginning his career as an outdoor educator for Kent Mountain Adventure Center of Estes Park. He maintained his passion for the mountains even as he became the owner of custom home-building and construction companies in the area. "Whether on a rock-climbing route, a fishing trip, mountaineering, mountain biking, or simply enjoying the sunset around a campfire, he was at home in the backcountry," an article in the *Estes Park Trail-Gazette* said about him later in 2013. He also passed on his love of the outdoors to his children, Emma and Marlon, and shared it with his wife, Liesl.

Laurienti and Foster arrived at the mountain and began their ascent, reaching the most technical section of Blitzen Ridge at about 9:45 a.m. Here they began to work their way around and past the Four Aces, a series of four sharply pointed, jagged peaks that stand between the climber and Ypsilon's summit. Whether the general winter conditions, blowing snow, or rising winds hampered their progress, the result was not what they expected. The two climbers finished the fourth Ace at about seven p.m., reaching this point in darkness. They had two choices here: They could relinquish their summit plans and head down a couloir toward home, or they could continue to the summit and take a less-technical route down. Either option required them to spend at least part of the night on the mountain—and despite all of their experience, they had not brought bivouac gear, extra food, or a stove, all of which would have allowed them to pass the night on the mountain in relative safety and continue their ascent or descent in daylight.

They quickly ruled out a descent through the Northeast Couloir, seeing precarious overhanging snow that could break free in an avalanche if they attempted to climb down that way. The wind had picked up as well, creating dangerous climbing conditions that appeared too risky, especially in darkness. Instead, they decided to continue to the summit and descend on a less technical route, an option that not only seemed more prudent, but would most likely get them home that night. By 7:30 p.m., they were on their way to the summit.

Climbing in the dark, they lost track of the correct route, an error that slowed their progress to a literal crawl as they found themselves north of Blitzen Ridge, where the terrain becomes even more technical. Dawn saw them still climbing, and as the day wore on, they crossed the Northeast Couloir below ledges weighted with snowdrifts—exactly the conditions they had wanted to avoid. "Wind erodes snow from the windward (upwind) side of obstacles, such as a ridge, and deposits the same snow on the leeward (downwind) terrain," the Avalanche.org website tells us, a partnership between the American Avalanche Association and the US Forest Service National Avalanche Center. "Wind-loading is a common denominator in most avalanche accidents. And no wonder, because wind can deposit snow 10 times more rapidly than snow falling from the sky. Moreover, wind-drifted snow is ground up by bouncing along the snow surface, and when it comes to a rest, it is often much denser than non-wind-loaded snow."

Late in the day on Sunday, March 17, they reached a notch roughly 200 feet below the summit, at 13,300 feet in elevation. Foster could see that Laurienti had begun to show signs of hypothermia. They had been out in frigid March temperatures and working at the limits of their endurance for more than thirty-six hours, and they still had a long way to go. The summit was now out of the question; they needed to descend as quickly and efficiently as they could, before one or both of them succumbed to the cold.

The way home down the Northeast Couloir, however, remained as hazardous as they had judged it the night before. The two climbers used all of their rope—nearly two hundred feet of it—and began to simul-climb their way down the massive crevasse, assisting one another, with Foster in the lead.

Halfway down a narrow section of the couloir, a wind slab suddenly broke free just above Laurienti. One of the two pieces of climbing equipment, a nut, pulled out of the rock wall and fell down the couloir. The other, a camming unit that expands in a crack in a rock face, held firm.

Laurienti and Foster fell about one hundred feet, banging into jutting rocks and hard-frozen ice on the way down. The avalanche debris missed them for the most part, but it buried their rope, essentially ending their expectation of a reasonably safe descent down the rock face. Laurienti believed that he had not been injured in the fall, but Foster could not make the same claim. Later reports indicated that she had multiple broken bones and damaged soft tissue, including broken ribs, a torn MCL (medial collateral ligament), a broken coccyx, and injured wrist ligaments.

"It is unclear whether he triggered the slide from below or if it released naturally from wind-loading," American Alpine Club reporter Joe Forrester wrote about the incident, "but given the start zone and the position of the climbers at the time of the avalanche, wind-loading was suspected."

Somehow, despite searing pain, exhaustion, and their already depleted condition, they both got on their feet and made their way to the bottom of the couloir, one step and one handhold at a time. Once they reached the base, Foster removed her crampons and replaced them with snowshoes and they set out across the snow-whitened trail in the dark, limping from multiple injuries and moving slowly against the stiffness of their joints and numbed hands and feet.

Barely a quarter mile down the mountain slope, Laurienti reached the limit of his endurance and collapsed into the snow, his consciousness and coherence ebbing away rapidly. Foster had no choice but to stay with him and attempt to keep him alive. Perhaps help would come their way soon, now that they were a full day past the expected return time they had recorded when they registered their climb with the park rangers. Foster did what she could to make Laurienti comfortable, but around 8:30 p.m. he became completely unresponsive. She had to face the fact that her friend was dying.

At first light, with her ribs and other injuries aching and cold penetrating every inch of her body, and with Laurienti never regaining consciousness, Foster set out for the trailhead, making slow progress across the difficult terrain in the Upper Fay Lakes drainage area. She had walked just two painful miles and had begun to consider the consequences of spending another night in the bitter cold and wind when, at about 2:45 p.m., she spotted the first human beings she had seen since she and Laurienti had started their climb: a team of National Park Service rangers and members of Larimer County Search and Rescue (SAR), on their way to look for her.

Grateful to turn over her own care to the rangers at last, she told them where they would find Laurienti, and then she accepted emergency medical care and assistance in returning to the Lawn Lakes trailhead. The team of thirty-two rescuers from the park staff and six from Larimer County SAR evacuated her using a toboggan, finally reaching the trailhead around one a.m., where EMTs transferred her to a waiting ambulance and brought her to Estes Park Medical Center.

"Lisa's survival is impressive and improbable given the length of time exposed to brutal weather conditions and the extent of her injuries," noted the American Alpine Club's accident report. Then, giving with one hand and taking with the other, it continued: "It seems that the biggest contributor to this fatality was not the avalanche per se, but the climbers' inability to traverse the technical portions of the ridge quickly enough. Blitzen Ridge is long even in ideal summer conditions, and in winter conditions it can be very committing. It would have been more prudent to descend, given the length of time it took the climbers to pass the Four Aces."

The process of recovering Laurienti's body began on Tuesday, the day after Foster's rescue, with a six-person search team heading out from the trailhead early in the morning. They found him at about two p.m. exactly where Foster had described, but subzero cold, blowing and drifting snow, and high winds with gusts exceeding 60 miles per hour made an immediate evacuation impossible. The team moved his body to a safe location to await a day with less volatile weather conditions and hiked out of the backcountry with plans to return when the weather improved.

On Wednesday, March 21, a team of park rangers and two members of Rocky Mountain Rescue left the Lawn Lakes trailhead at dawn to return to the place where Laurienti's body awaited recovery. When it became clear that gusting winds would prevent the use of a helicopter, a second team, including park rangers and members of Larimer County SAR, followed them at eight a.m. "The safety of the teams has been the top priority of today's efforts," a park news release about the operation made clear. Even with this caveat, the two teams brought the body to the trailhead by four p.m. that day, a notably brisk and efficient recovery in difficult terrain and continued brutal weather. An autopsy revealed that the final cause of Laurienti's death was hypothermia, although despite his initial protestations, the coroner discovered that he had also sustained some injuries in the avalanche.

It wasn't long before Foster recovered from her injuries and returned to her passion for climbing mountains in the park. On August 16, 2015, she broke the world record for female ascents of Longs Peak held by Ruth Ewald Gray, completing her 73rd ascent of the 14,259-foot mountain. "I have climbed the peak 73 times, by 17 different routes," she reported on the Longs Peak Summit Club's Facebook page. "I have climbed it 46 times in summer, 8 times in calendar winter, 12 times in calendar spring, and 7 times in calendar autumn."

NOTHING CAN PREPARE YOU

David Emerick, who was 24, and his friend Robert Hritz, 19, both from Boulder, appeared to be fully prepared to take on an autumn climb somewhere above Taylor Glacier in the park's southeastern region. They wore crampons and carried ice axes, and they were roped together—all signs that they had some inkling about ice climbing in the Front Range. The fact remains, however, that little can prepare even the most experienced climbers for a wall of seemingly stable snow to dissolve above them, breaking into a storm of snow masses, ice chunks, and gravel cascading down on climbers in one gargantuan dump. Not only can such a phenomenon cause extensive injuries, but it can also bury the climbers in its path, cutting off their air supply and causing a terrifying death by asphyxiation.

No one can say exactly what happened to these two young men, but when two other climbers from Boulder came upon them on October 13, 1973, at the base of Powell Peak, it appeared that they had "been caught in a snow avalanche which swept them down a steep snow shoot," an unidentified park spokesperson told the Associated Press. They remained connected by their rope, and while this did not save their lives, it did aid in locating them both in the heap of tumbled ice and snow.

When Joe Massari, a highly skilled and experienced climber, set out in the volatile conditions of early spring to attempt Kiener's Route on Longs Peak, he had the requisite experience and all of the equipment he needed to climb this particularly difficult route to the summit. Massari, who was 45, had never succeeded in a winter climb up Kiener's, so he had a certain zeal to reach the top that may have overridden his otherwise excellent judgment. For reasons of his own, he chose to climb unroped.

"Joe Massari had a long history of solo climbs and was very familiar with Longs Peak," noted Rocky Mountain supervisory climbing ranger Jim Detterline in his report to the American Alpine Club. "However, he had never succeeded on Kiener's Route, and had been avalanched from it twice before."

Massari filled out a backcountry permit from the self-service registration box at the Longs Peak ranger station before beginning his climb, but he didn't include his planned route on the form, and he didn't share the information with anyone else before starting up the mountain on April 20, 1991. He'd chosen a particularly difficult day, with heavy snowfall and intermittent whiteout conditions, as well as arctic cold and "extreme avalanche danger."

As he made his way upward, he encountered a local guide with experience in climbing Mount Everest in Nepal. This guide had several climbers with him, but he had turned his party around when he realized that conditions were too treacherous to risk the summit. He urged Massari to turn back as well, but the solo climber decided to ignore the guide's advice. Instead, he "continued up Lambs Slide, across Broadway, and onto upper Kiener's Route," Detterline's narrative said.

What exactly happened next can never be known for certain. Experts believe that Massari triggered a mammoth avalanche, one that knocked him off the mountain and into clear air for at least part of the 1,500-foot drop to Mills Glacier, probably tumbling him like wet clothing in a dryer down the lower slopes of the peak. "He died of massive injuries," the report tells us, sparing us the details. The avalanche's momentum continued to drop deep snow on top of Massari, burying him entirely.

The following day, a Longs Peak ranger noted that Massari's car remained in the parking lot, despite his notation on his permit that he had expected to return the previous night. He notified authorities, who began a lengthy and detailed operation involving forty ground searchers, two teams of dogs trained in searching avalanches, several technical climbing teams, and two helicopters.

"Detterline said he and his partner set off several avalanches Wednesday as they climbed to the summit," noted the Associated Press. Park spokesperson Jim Mack put a number on it: Searchers had triggered nine avalanches in one day. As hopes diminished that Massari might be found alive, park officials began to consider that conditions on the mountain might be much too hazardous to conduct a thorough search, as it put too many people at risk.

"We haven't much evidence," Mack continued. "We know he did not reach the summit . . . he did not log in at the summit." He might have made it to a higher elevation, however, so helicopters brought some searchers to areas close to the top to see if they could find clues there. "Searchers spent Tuesday night in shelters near the summit, flashing light signals periodically through the night and listening for any cries for help," the AP said. "They were to repeat the all-night vigil Wednesday night."

Four days of this intensive searching revealed not the slightest clue, though the searchers triggered six more avalanches. As weather continued to hamper progress and it became clear that Massari would not be found alive, the park finally decided to end the formal SAR operation, at least until the snow began to melt and more clues—scraps of clothing, climbing equipment, or the missing climber's body—might be revealed.

On June 18, two months after the formal search had ended, a team of five backcountry rangers and Williams Sarmiento, a visiting rescuer from Venezuela, set out on a routine climb of the East Face of Longs Peak. They had hardly begun their climb when at 7:15 a.m., they saw what looked like a body amid the melting snow on Mills Glacier. They went closer and determined that they had indeed found a missing climber, along with two cameras he had been carrying. They began a body recovery operation immediately and radioed for a helicopter to complete the mission.

Detterline's report minced no words in defining the responsibility for this death. "If Massari had used a rope during his solo efforts and had left a properly detailed plan with someone, it is possible this this tragedy could have been prevented," he said. "Given the adverse conditions that he started his climb with, it would have been better mountain sense to turn around and reschedule the climb. One should consider the possibility of adverse consequences to others before setting out on solo climbs in desperate conditions. The search efforts were quite hazardous considering the weather, avalanche conditions, and flying conditions. Fortunately, no rescuers were injured. The accident cost nearly $35,000," or the equivalent of nearly $66,000 today.

In the case of two climbers swept away by an avalanche on November 1, 1992, all evidence suggests that they never had an inkling they were in imminent danger.

Todd Martin, 24, and Brad Farnan, 30, chose the Central Couloir on the northwest face of Flattop Mountain as an appropriate place to practice snow- and ice-climbing techniques. Martin, a native of Ohio, had taken up mountaineering five years earlier as part of his recovery during a drug treatment program. Climbing became his passion—so much so that he moved to Denver and planned a career as a mountain guide, while climbing mountains in twenty-eight states as well as Canada and Mexico. Farnan, a guide with the Colorado Mountain School (CMS), brought Martin and two female climbers (whose names never appeared in the press) to the mountain for some challenging ice climbing.

"Farnan was an experienced and respected mountain guide," the AAC report said. "This was a trip among friends, and not a CMS class. He had been climbing and guiding in these gullies of Flattop all during the autumn season without incident . . . Conditions in the gully were stable [with] excellent climbing. He had also been there the day before."

As they made their way up the couloir, snow began to fall and the wind started picking up. They reached the junction with the West Couloir, but seeing the route ahead and watching the change in weather rolling in, the two women decided that they were not prepared for these conditions. They turned back, leaving Martin and Farnan to continue up the mountain on their own.

During their descent, something happened that made the women pause. They were sheltered by what the AAC report refers to as a "rock island," a spot where they managed to avoid the worst of the wind and snow, when they felt an atypical gust of wind come down the couloir, followed by a swirling cloud of snow. At the end of the gust, they spotted one of Todd Martin's gloves.

This alarmed the women, so they yelled up to Martin and Farnan to make sure they were all right. No one answered their cries, and blowing snow blocked their view of the couloir above them. The women headed down the mountain as quickly as they dared and notified the first ranger they found.

Search-and-rescue personnel knew that what the women described was an avalanche, and that if there was any chance of finding the climbers alive, they would have to act quickly. The ensuing search effort began in the midst of what became a miserable storm, "with some rescuers in snow up to their shoulders despite snowshoes," the AAC report said. Knowing where the two climbers had last been seen aided in focusing the search effort, but with heavy snowfall and single-digit temperatures, SAR activity proceeded with extreme caution.

Two days passed before the first and only clue revealed itself: two backpacks, each with an ice ax placed on top of it, sitting together on a wide ledge at about twelve thousand feet. The two female climbers confirmed that the packs belonged to Martin and Farnan. Both sides of the ledge were covered in avalanche debris. Park spokesperson James Mack speculated to the Associated Press that the men may have been just a few feet away when an avalanche rushed down the mountainside and swept them off the ledge. If they were buried by an avalanche, he said, the bodies might be hidden under snow and ice until the summer thaw.

The first winter storm passed, but more snow and wind followed closely on its heels. Sub-district ranger Kurt Oliver told the *Dayton Daily News* in Martin's hometown in Ohio that winds had allowed a helicopter to make only a few passes over the search area, with the rest of the search taking place on the ground. The helicopter crew had not seen any sign of the missing men. Search operations chief Drew Davis of Larimer County Search and Rescue told the *Colorado Springs Gazette Telegraph* that heavy snows and high winds had made some parts of the search area inaccessible, with more than two feet of snow falling since the men had disappeared.

"Rangers have remained at the climbers' base camp around the clock with lights and strobes in case they return," the *Gazette Telegraph* reported. "But as the weather worsened and time passed, hopes of finding the two men alive faded."

Finally, after ten days, it became clear that the climbers could not have survived in the cold this long, and that bodies buried in several feet of snow and avalanche debris would not come to light over the winter. The searchers left the mountain with the intention of returning once the weather had warmed the following summer, with the hope of bringing closure to Martin and Farnan's families then.

Nearly two years passed, however, with no sign of the missing men. Not until August 10, 1994, did the body of Todd Martin come to the surface, discovered by a climber who spotted a hand sticking up out of a pile of snow. Martin's ice-encased remains were recovered and returned to his parents for burial in Ohio after an autopsy. With the best information they had to date on where Brad Farnan's body might be, the search resumed and finally had success, with the discovery of the climbing guide's remains on August 25, 1994.

Experts believe that while the two men took a break and sat on a ledge, the overhanging snow cornice just above them gave way. "It was unusual for the cornice to have persisted this late in the season," the AAC report said. "On this mountain face, the cornices generally form at the beginning of winter, and drop off in late spring to early summer. Although Farnan correctly judged conditions on the route itself, there was no way of knowing that the cornice had been sufficiently weakened to unload."

DANGER FROM FALLING ROCKS

A climb up Notchtop Mountain's Spiral Route in winter comes with its own set of challenges, though experienced climbers consider this a good technical route for people who want a first sample of climbing in Rocky Mountain National Park. Mark Frevert, 28, of Niwot, Colorado, chose this route to introduce 19-year-old Colorado State University student Samuel Mitchell to the pleasures of climbing in the park. Mitchell hailed from Lafayette, Louisiana, where he lived at sea level, but the lure of the high country had taken hold, and he was eager to explore the mountain. Frevert had been climbing since he was a teenager and was considered a skilled climber, certainly capable of guiding and instructing Mitchell and helping him stay safe.

The fact that they chose this route for a February climb in 1983 did not have a significant impact on their plans. The Spiral Route usually remained covered in snow throughout the year, with 60- to 70-degree inclines that could be filled with soft snow in summer or hard, crusty ice suitable for steps in winter. Their chosen day, February 6, dawned cold with wind gusts, but this was a fairly typical winter day in Colorado, with no major snows predicted.

They set out early Saturday with the expectation that they would be back by nightfall, so when they didn't return that night, Frevert's wife called the park first thing Sunday morning. Park searchers moved out onto the mountain immediately and asked for helicopter assistance, but wind chills between 30 and 50 degrees below zero made the use of aerial reconnaissance impossible. The search effort expanded on the ground despite the cold, however, with participants from SAR teams in Boulder and Larimer counties, Colorado

Mountain School, park staff, and personnel from sporting goods stores in the area.

At 10:30 a.m., searchers found Frevert's body at the base of a steep slope, at about 10,800 feet. Glen Kaye, spokesperson for the park, told the Associated Press that Frevert had probably died instantly, and that searchers assumed he had fallen. They soon discovered a trail of footprints in the snow speckled with drops of blood, and began to follow them. The footprints continued for more than a mile and led directly to Mitchell's last resting place, at the end of a zigzagging route that eventually brought him to within 100 yards of Lake Helene and the route back to the trailhead. He had "suffered a severe injury to the right side of his head, and in his effort to find help had discarded most of his climbing gear," the AP reported. "His path appeared 'aimless,' according to Kaye." In speaking with United Press International, Kaye added: "We don't really know where he was headed. He was sort of floundering."

The park worked to reconstruct the accident to understand what had gone wrong. Three weeks after the incident, Kaye announced that the climbers had already climbed Notchtop Mountain and begun their descent. They had nearly reached the base of the mountain when something happened that they could not have predicted or prevented: They were caught in a rockslide.

"Their deaths were not due to human error," said Kaye. He explained that the rockfall hit both climbers' heads, killing Frevert within minutes, and Mitchell, an hour later, from blood loss and shock, as well as hypothermia. Through no fault of his own, the younger man's first climb turned out to be his last.

Falling rock can be a legitimate danger in the park, but only one other rockslide has resulted in death. On June 25, 1999, Reverend Charlie Harrison, the 47-year-old pastor of Aldersgate United Methodist Church in Wichita, Kansas, took his son Chris, newly graduated from college, hiking in the park. They chose a moderately difficult trail in the Windy Gulch Cascades, one they normally could have handled without mishap. On this day, however, rock came loose above their heads and came rolling down the side of the mountain. Chris managed to catch himself and regain his balance without falling, but the rocks swept the pastor off the trail and down into a ravine. He died in the fall.

"Harrison was known as an innovative pastor whose blessing of the animals and Western-themed worship services attracted attention in the church's northwest Wichita neighborhood," the Associated Press reported. In addition to his son, he was survived by his wife and daughter.

CHAPTER 6

Tallest Object:
Lightning Strikes

It may seem like a wonderful way to spend a summer afternoon: hiking to the open, bald top of a mountain in Rocky Mountain National Park and standing at the summit to admire the spectacular view. On summer afternoons in the park, however, rainstorms with lightning can form rapidly and arrive with little warning. Watching a storm roll in can be an unforgettable experience, but doing so from the top of a mountain can literally kill you.

Why is this the case? The ground's positively charged electrons attract lightning's negatively charged ones, so the ground becomes a strong conductor of electricity in the air. Tall objects offer lightning the literal path of least resistance, making a steeple, a tower, a mountaintop, or the person standing on top of the mountain the fastest route to the ground. A lightning bolt delivers 100 million to 1 billion volts of electricity to whatever it hits, according to the National Severe Storms Laboratory (NSSL), a department of the National Oceanic and Atmospheric Administration (NOAA). That's why most people die instantly when hit by lightning, making it particularly remarkable when someone survives.

Of course, the vast majority of lightning strikes reach the ground without coming in contact with a human being. The NSSL tells us that lightning strikes the ground about 25 million times annually in the United States, and in any given year, the odds of a person being struck by one of these bolts is 1 in 1.2 million. If you have a knack for computing probability and statistics, you may have the ability to determine the exact odds of being struck over a person's eighty-year lifetime, but the NSSL has done that work as well: The odds drop to 1 in 15,300, a much more frightening figure.

Now, consider the possibility of standing at a mountain summit in Rocky Mountain National Park in late afternoon on a July day, just as the near-daily thunderstorm crackles over your head. The park tells us that eleven people in the state of Colorado die from lightning strikes every year on average. "Most of these victims were in places where lightning is common: on mountain tops, under a lone tree, in flat wide open areas, and on bodies of water," the park's website notes. "Lightning strikes occur most often after [12:00] noon, but can happen anytime."

There's no doubt that pioneer Alexander MacGregor would have benefited from the knowledge that he stood directly in harm's way on June 17, 1896, when he and his son George performed an assessment on a mining claim "on a spur of the Continental Divide at the headwaters of the Big Thompson and Grand River," as the *Denver Republican* reported a week later. A rancher who also served as justice of the peace for Estes Park's twentieth precinct, MacGregor and his wife, Clara, had begun construction on a home larger than the one they had built when they arrived in the area.

Sadly, MacGregor, who was 50 years old, did not live to move into that new house. He and George "were prostrated by a flash from a sudden electrical storm," the newspaper tells us. "When the son recovered consciousness, his father was dead. Finding he could do nothing for his father in his lame and dazed condition, he crawled to his pony and went for assistance." Six friends of the family formed a recovery team and went back to the mountain summit, carrying down Alexander about twelve hours later.

We don't know exactly where Dr. William Edward Dillingham and his 7-year-old son encountered lightning on August 20, 1914, while exploring in the mountains "about 20 miles from Estes Park," according to the *Boston Globe*. Dr. Dillingham, who was originally from New Bedford, Massachusetts, had moved to Colorado fifteen years earlier, "on account of his health," and four years later had met and married Marion Emery, who hailed from the same area back east.

On this bright Colorado day, he led a packhorse with his son astride it as he, his wife, and two or three neighbors followed a trail somewhere in the park. "Dr. Dillingham and his boy were some distance ahead of the party . . . when a thunderstorm broke," the *Globe* said. "A lightning bolt struck Dr. Dillingham and the horse, killing both. The boy was stunned but not seriously hurt."

You can imagine the horror Marion Dillingham and her friends felt when they came up the trail and discovered her husband, the horse, and her son lying in the dust. All we know of her life after her husband's death, however, is that she remained in Colorado to settle his affairs and then most likely headed back to the Boston area and her family there.

Lightning on Longs Peak

Bolts from the blue find their way to Longs Peak, the highest point in the park, on a regular basis throughout the midsummer, late summer, and fall months, but just three of these strikes have turned deadly.

Jesse Kitts, a 37-year-old real estate dealer from Greeley, reached the mountain's summit on August 1, 1922, just in time to encounter an approaching electrical storm. He and his climbing partner, J. E. Bullas of Topeka, Kansas, both served as the tallest objects in the area as they stood on the mountain's flat summit, but they seemed to have no awareness of the danger in which they had placed themselves. Lightning struck them both, killing Kitts and leaving Bullas with some burns on his head, the bolt's impact blowing Bullas's shoes right off his feet. Other hikers attempted to help him, but he eventually regained consciousness on his own and actually started picking his way down the mountain without shoes. By this time, however, hikers had gotten word down to rescue personnel that Bullas was injured but alive. Rangers and a doctor met him partway down the mountain, treated his injuries, and helped him descend safely. The following day, a rescue party climbed Longs Peak to bring Kitts down the mountain, completing their dismal mission early the following morning, before that day's thunderstorm brought more lightning to the peak.

Attaining the summit is not a prerequisite for death by lightning strike, as Rena Hoffman discovered on August 15, 1956. She and three climbing companions, one of whom was her husband, had reached the area just east of Chasm Lake by 2:30 p.m.—an elevation of about 11,500 feet—when lightning found its way to them in a split second. All four hikers felt the effects of the blast, but Rena died instantly and her husband lost consciousness, while the two other hikers sustained only minor injuries.

Decades passed before another hiker lost his life to lightning on Longs Peak, and even attempts to recover his body became treacherous amid continued electrical storms. Andy Haberkorn, 28, and his climbing partner, Stanley Smigel, were working their way up the Casual Route on the Diamond on July 12, 2000, at about 3:00 p.m. Haberkorn was about forty feet above the Yellow Wall bivouac ledge when Smigel saw a blinding flash right where his partner stood. Lightning had struck Haberkorn square in the chest, penetrating to the ground beyond him. Smigel moved quickly to reach Haberkorn, but the injured climber died of internal injuries in minutes.

"Haberkorn's fatal strike occurred about 15:00 [3:00 p.m.], a most dangerous time of day to be high on the face in midsummer," said Jim Detterline in his report to the American Alpine Club. "There is a past history of a climber struck by lightning at this same spot. Usually lightning strikes the summit and outstanding points on ridges. Also lightning usually strikes the leader or higher individual."

He added, "Mr. Smigel must be commended for his efforts in tending to his partner, and in getting down the Diamond under the most difficult conditions."

"Both climbers were well-equipped and probably very experienced," Dick Putney, a spokesperson for the park, told the *Denver Post*. No amount of climbing knowledge can protect a mountaineer from a bolt of electricity descending from the sky, however, even if he or she knows not to be the tallest object in a storm-prone area. This particular spot some distance from the summit would not necessarily trigger a cautionary response, even for the most skilled climbers.

Continued storm warnings hampered the body recovery effort over the next two days, as a helicopter and fourteen climbers worked for twelve hours to bring Haberkorn's remains off the mountain. Lightning strikes and so much activity on the mountain created an increased danger of falling rock, so the park closed much of the mountain to hikers and climbers until they could complete the recovery operation.

THE HIGHEST NATIONAL PARK ROAD

When a road rises to the kinds of heights that Trail Ridge Road reaches in Rocky Mountain National Park, those who use it can expect to encounter some issues that they won't face on any other road in the national park system. Trail Ridge Road tops out at 12,183 feet, crowned by the Alpine Visitor Center and magnificent views of the Colorado Front Range in every direction. Such a road makes visitors want to leave their vehicles and experience the open vastness on their own, standing well above the timberline and losing the protection of tall trees as they gaze out over the expansive Rockies. Nearly everyone who enjoys this experience returns home alive. Every once in a while, though, someone does not—and some of these unfortunate souls die of a lightning strike.

The first person to lose her life in this fashion, 46-year-old Leola H. Swain of Archie, Missouri, stood "near a stone retaining wall at Medicine Bow Curve," about twenty-five miles west of Estes Park on August 6, 1964. She, her husband, and two friends in the car all got out at the pull-off to gasp with admiration at the gorgeous view. Seconds later, Leola Swain lay dead on the pavement, while her husband and friends, standing a good one hundred feet or more away from her, received no injury at all.

Ten years later, on July 1, 1974, 17-year-old Barbara Gully of Farmington Hills, Michigan, and her parents left their vehicle in a parking area along Trail Ridge Road at about one p.m. and walked out toward Iceberg Lake. As they returned to the parking area, Barbara climbed up on top of the rock wall barrier—the one placed there for the public's safety. While she was surrounded by mountain peaks, she managed to be one of the tallest things in the area. The shaft of lightning found its target, and barely a heartbeat later, Barbara crumpled to the ground.

The girl's father began mouth-to-mouth resuscitation as he and his wife moved her into their car and drove to the Alpine Visitor Center for help. Here they found a medical student and a nurse who were visiting the park; they came forward instantly to offer first aid, and the medical student managed to restore Barbara's heartbeat, giving the family hope as she was rushed to the hospital. That evening, UPI reported that she was in "very poor" condition. She died of her injuries at 5:45 a.m. the next day.

"Officials [have] warned park visitors that severe storms move in quickly, exposing visitors to the dangers of low temperatures, rain, snow, sleet and lightning," the Associated Press took the opportunity to reiterate. "Visitors should stay away from open and elevated places during lightning storms, they said."

Park superintendent Roger Condor added that Barbara "may not have read the National Park Service pamphlet which included warnings on the dangers of lightning storms," UPI noted on July 4. "A person above timberline as Miss Gully was is likely to be the highest object in the area and attract lightning," he said.

Twenty-five years passed before lightning killed another visitor along Trail Ridge Road. On July 21, 1999, 35-year-old John Retting of Brooklyn, New York, put his 2-year-old daughter Katherine in a child carrier on his back, and he and his wife Carol set out from the Alpine Visitor Center across open tundra to enjoy the flowers blooming there. Well above the timberline, at 11,700 feet, this expansive area provides no cover in the event of a storm.

They were about half a mile from the visitor center at 12:37 p.m. when gathering clouds generated a lightning strike. John took the brunt of it, but Katherine and Carol both received burns as well. Park personnel saw the flash and ran out to the Rettings to help, immediately beginning CPR on John and first aid for the others, but John had died on the spot. He was pronounced dead at the Estes Park Medical Center at 1:10 p.m.

Emergency medical technicians rushed Carol and Katherine to separate hospitals in Denver. "Mrs. Retting was burned over 5 percent of her body and Katherine had second-degree burns on her left thigh and abdomen," the *New York Post* reported. Both of them survived.

Two other lightning strikes in the Trail Ridge Road area led to fatalities. What makes these particularly unusual, however, is that they occurred just a day apart.

On July 11, 2014, Rebecca and Justin Teilhet of Yellow Springs, Ohio, and six other hikers left Trail Ridge Road to hike the Ute Crossing Trail, a fairly easy hike that loops across the open tundra and back to the road some distance down from the original trailhead. "A storm blew in, and it came very fast," Justin said to the Associated Press a few days later. "It started raining a little bit. We were hearing claps of thunder everywhere, but there wasn't any lightning."

He had seen one of the signs posted about lightning danger in the park, he noted, but it didn't make the group want to change their plans. "When you see a sign warning you about lightning, you just sort of file it away with the things you already know are dangerous," he said. "This is a huge, beautiful, dangerous, amazing place, and they've done a lot to make it accessible to the public."

One moment the group was walking down the trail and enjoying their surroundings, and the next, Justin found himself regaining consciousness, flat on the ground, with his friend Nick Tertel of Fort Collins giving CPR to his wife. "It was a lightning bolt, he learned later," the AP reported, "and it killed his wife and left him with a burn on his shoulder and scrapes on his face when he was knocked unconscious."

Despite the storm, an air ambulance managed to land close by to take Rebecca to a hospital. The effort could not help her, however, as her restarted heartbeat could not sustain itself, and she died on the scene.

Justin remembered lying in an ambulance and seeing two emergency responders come into the vehicle and take his hand. They were there to tell him Rebecca had died, he said. "They were both next to tears."

Tragedy would come to Trail Ridge Road again the very next day, July 12, 2014, at about 3:50 p.m., this time in the Rainbow Curve pull-off area at 10,829 feet in elevation. Fifty-two-year-old Gregory Cardwell of Scottsbluff, Nebraska, took the brunt of a strike that affected four people.

"We didn't see the bolt. It was just a white flash," said Mary Ivarson, who was nearby when Cardwell was hit. "It just felt like something hit you on the back of the head and just kind of jolted [you] forward."

She and others tried to revive Cardwell with CPR until rangers and medical personnel arrived. "His T-shirt and stuff was burned from the lightning, but we were just trying to help him," she said.

Cardwell never regained consciousness. Three other people who were injured by the lightning strike left the park in ambulances, while several others drove themselves to Estes Park Medical Center for medical attention.

Of the remaining three deaths in the park from lightning strikes, we have few details. Fifteen-year-old Andrew Paton of Madison, Wisconsin, perished on Twin Sisters Mountain when lightning found him on August 24, 1979. Glenn McDonald, 31, climbed a ridge near Hallet Peak on June 28, 1992, and became a target for lightning there, while his climbing partner, Wayne Smart, escaped unharmed. And Michael Hines, who was 23, led a church group on the Bridal Veil Falls Trail, becoming a conduit for lightning on August 7, 1999. No one else in his party received serious injuries.

CHAPTER 7

Swift Current:
Death by Drowning

LONG BEFORE THE SELFIE AND DIGITAL PHOTOGRAPHY CAME INTO vogue, sightseers with cameras and film spent a great deal of time finding the perfect shots in national parks. The slogan "Take only pictures, leave only footprints," cautioned visitors to leave the parks as they found them so that others could enjoy them in their pristine splendor. As each click of the shutter represented an expense in film and processing, amateur and professional photographers selected their shots with great care, whether the resulting photo would go into a scrapbook of memories or on the cover of *National Geographic*.

This made setting up a shot a bit of an obsession, even for families collecting vacation snaps. Members of today's millennial generation were not the first to risk their lives to get a photo of themselves having the time of their lives; this bewildering behavior started long ago, probably with the first tourist to bring a Kodak Brownie camera into the wilderness in 1900. In Rocky Mountain National Park, the first death-by-snapshot incident took place in 1947, on the banks of North St. Vrain Creek.

We call this waterway a "creek" today, but in the park's early days, it was known as a river—one trickling between snowdrifts in winter and swollen with snowmelt in summer. So much water ran into the

North St. Vrain in late spring and summer that its current increased its pace, forming Class IV and V rapids that still delight whitewater kayakers today. Too narrow for rafting, the creek may look relatively harmless to visitors, but its power has taken the lives of six people in the park—five of whom were under the age of eighteen.

Six-year-old Robert Earl Briggs stood patiently on rocks along the riverbed on July 7, 1947, while his father, Albert Briggs, fussed over the perfect pose for a photo. He and his wife had brought Robert with them from Wichita, Kansas, for a special vacation in the American West, and they chose a hike in the Wild Basin area. The roiling river carried meltwater down from the surrounding mountains, increasing its usual activity and repeatedly splashing the rocks along its banks, including the one on which Albert perched Robert.

Albert stepped up on the same rock, and in an instant, father and son slipped on the wet surface and fell into the river. Instinctively Albert reached out for his son, but the boy was gone in seconds, swept downstream on the current and calling out for his father as he disappeared into the foaming rapids.

Albert, gasping and coughing as he fought to keep his head above water, managed to scramble back up onto the bank. He ran along the river, but he could not see his son in the churning whitewater.

Later in the afternoon, Ranger Carol Gilbert recovered Robert's body, which had been carried some distance downstream. Coroner George Howe confirmed that the boy had drowned, and blamed the speed and force of the current for the father's inability to save him.

Just two months later, on September 14, 1947, 30-year-old William S. Holley fell into the North St. Vrain and drowned. As no one saw this happen, we have no further information about the incident, and more than twenty years passed before the river—by then known as a creek—claimed another life.

This time, no one saw 12-year-old Danny Saucier of Boulder fall into the water at the junction of Cony and North St. Vrain creeks during a fishing trip, but his father, Donald, realized Danny was missing at about 3:45 p.m. on Sunday, July 30, 1972. When he couldn't find the boy, he rushed to the Wild Basin ranger station a mile and a half away and appealed for help, and a search began in and around both creeks. No clues emerged on land, so search teams focused their efforts on the waterways.

Sunday and Monday passed with no success. On Tuesday, as two park rangers donned scuba gear and worked with the Rocky Mountain Rescue Group to probe into the creek's deep pools, they finally found Danny's body, lodged about twenty feet deep.

The following year, on July 6, Mr. and Mrs. Bernard Primosch of Wichita Falls, Texas, brought their 5-year-old son, Kurtland Brandon Primosch, on a vacation to the park. As they enjoyed a break in a picnic area on North St. Vrain Creek at about four p.m., Kurt wandered off on his own. Moments later his parents began looking for him, and rapidly realized he was truly missing. Rangers started a search and discovered his body at about seven p.m. Kurt had most likely slipped and fallen into the creek, and was overpowered by the flowing water.

When Ellen Marx fell into the creek on July 13, 1986, her 18-year-old brother and two girlfriends saw her slip over a six-foot waterfall before she disappeared entirely. The Marx family had come to the park on vacation from Minneapolis, to which they had recently moved from Kansas City, Missouri. Ellen, who was 13, remained pinned underwater for fifty minutes before rangers spotted her about half a mile from where she had fallen, and to their amazement, they discovered that she still had a pulse; the frigid water had helped to keep her alive even though she had been deprived of oxygen. They began resuscitation immediately and kept it going until EMTs arrived with a medical helicopter.

She arrived at St. Luke's Hospital in Denver at about 8:15 p.m., and went into the intensive care unit in critical condition. Here she remained for two days, but Ellen never regained consciousness, and she passed away quietly on the afternoon of Tuesday, July 15.

Remarkably, only one more death in the park took place in the North St. Vrain Creek. Seventeen-year-old Glenn Hays, an honors student from Loveland, made a valiant attempt to jump across the creek at the top of Ouzel Falls on July 3, 1993. Visiting the park with a group of twenty-four high school students who were part of a four-week science-studies program for gifted students, he applied his skills as an Eagle Scout and cleared the creek, landing on slippery rocks on the opposite bank. He couldn't regain his balance quickly enough, however, and he slid off the rocks, into the water, and over the falls.

Hays dropped fifty feet into the pounding water and the plunge pool below. Rangers brought in dive teams from Estes Park and Boulder County and rescue teams from around the area, and they recovered his body before the day ended.

THE BIG THOMPSON

Lois Lee Matthews and Sheryl Hargis, both 19, had saved their pennies for eight months for the cross-country road trip of their dreams, camping in national parks and exploring the American West. Living in Orlando, Florida, they both worked at Walt Disney World, and Matthews was a freshman at Florida Technological University. As soon as the school year ended in May 1973 and before the long summer at Disney began—where the management did not permit its employees to take vacations during the busy summer season—the two girls set off in their 1971 automobile packed with a tent, sleeping bags, and their backpacks. They drove through the Southwest and into California, where they stopped to compare the original Disneyland Main Street with the one they knew so well in Florida.

With the theme park stop behind them, they continued through Hollywood to San Francisco, and then began exploring some of the nation's most stunningly beautiful places, including a stop at Rocky Mountain National Park on May 27.

"We knew what they were doing practically every night of their trip," Lois's mother, Mrs. Joseph Matthews, told a reporter with the *Orlando Sentinel*. "They would call us frequently and we would tape the conversation."

In the park, the girls stopped for photos of themselves by the swiftly flowing Big Thompson River, an impressive sight in May, when spring snowmelt swelled it and drove its churning current even more powerfully than usual. Lois stood on a wet boulder as Sheryl set up the shot—and Lois suddenly lost her balance. She slid off the rock and into the river, and vanished from the surface.

The details of the attempt to rescue Lois were not reported in the press, but we can guess the story: Rangers, knowing that the chances of finding her alive were almost nil, worked to locate her anyway, and eventually discovered her body. The dream trip had ended in tragedy.

"They were having an absolutely beautiful time," Mrs. Matthews told the *Sentinel*. "[Lois] told us Saturday when we talked with her [that] she loved it in Colorado."

Barely a month later, another young woman lost her life on the Big Thompson River, also by slipping off of rocks. On June 27, 1973, Sherran Joy Haley of Canyon, Texas, and her husband, Dennis, who was 25, attempted to cross the rushing river together near its bridge in Moraine Park, by hopping from one rock to the next. A particularly heavy late-spring snowfall that year had resulted in higher-than-usual water levels and currents that would thrill a whitewater enthusiast, swirling over the rocks and making them particularly slippery. Sherran fell, pulling Dennis in with her, and the water's force pulled them down the river, slamming them against other rocks as they went.

Dennis's brother Arthur, standing safely on the bank, saw them fall into the water and ran to help, and several other bystanders came to his aid. Dennis managed to grab hold of a rock and keep his head above water until these helpful visitors pulled him out, and while he sustained some bad bruises, he was otherwise unhurt. Sherran, however, had disappeared entirely. By this time a search-and-rescue team arrived, and searchers continued to look for her until dark, beginning again at daybreak. They finally located her body about three hundred yards downstream from where she and Dennis had fallen in.

Tragedy returned to the Big Thompson on May 14, 1978, when 6-year-old Christopher Ermijo, visiting the park with his family, drowned in the river west of the bridge at Bear Lake Road. Not until 2001 did another child become the river's victim, however. This time, 9-year-old Scott Johnson of California drowned on May 12, at a time when melting snow swelled the river as it did every spring.

FALLING WATER

Only one death in the park has taken place at Chasm Falls, where visitors who take Fall River Road through a remote part of the park often stop to view the spectacular cascade on ledges well above the water. On June 19, 1964, 43-year-old James Keller, an estimate assigner with Southwestern Bell Telephone Company in Corpus Christi, Texas, brought his wife, three children, and a nephew to the park for a family vacation. Keller served in the US Marine Corps in World War II and was decorated for heroism during the invasion of Guam, according to the *Corpus Christi Caller-Times*.

As they stood on a ledge seventy-five feet above the falls in the Fall River gorge, Keller simply slipped and fell, tumbling down the side of the gorge and hitting jagged rocks before landing in the water and washing away over the falls. His body was recovered late that night, and the coroner suggested that Keller may have died from injuries suffered in the fall, even before he reached the river.

When 7-year-old Rey Alexander Dermody visited the park with his parents, Marco and Phoung Dermody of Baton Rouge, Louisiana, the family made a stop at the Roaring River to admire Horseshoe Falls. They chose to walk in an area "marked with red and white warning signs because of unstable banks, slick rocks and falling debris next to the river," park spokesperson Glen Kaye told the media.

At about two p.m., Rey slipped into the river before his parents' eyes. A park search-and-rescue team found the unconscious boy in the river some forty-five minutes later and began efforts to revive him while waiting for a helicopter to arrive. He was airlifted to St. Anthony Hospital in Denver, where he died early Saturday morning.

Signs, guardrails, fences, stone walls, and other warnings and barriers in national parks are meant to keep visitors safe, not to limit our view (although this is sometimes necessary) or restrict our experience. Park officials know where the hazards are that can lead to serious accidents or deaths, and they do their best to keep us from doing the foolish things that can turn a great vacation into an unspeakable tragedy. People who heed these warnings tend to go home in one piece, even if they do choose to take calculated risks in other parts of the parks. If a sign suggests that entering an area, leaving a boardwalk, or stepping over a railing could be dangerous, it most likely is. Ignoring these warnings may kill you; following directions may save your life.

CHAPTER 8

Airborne Accidents: Plane Crashes

First Lieutenant Cranston Harvey Dodd, 23, had served for eleven months in the Pacific Theater of World War II, where he logged more than four hundred hours of flight time in an FG-1D Corsair, one of the war's premier fighting planes. After the war he became a Denver resident instead of returning to his native Dallas, Texas, attending the college of business administration at the University of Denver and serving as a Marine Corps reservist. He continued to fly FG-1Ds, however, maintaining his skills as a fighter pilot while planning for his future outside of the military.

Originally designed by Chance M. Vought of Vought Aircraft and subcontracted to other manufacturers to speed production, the FG-1D was built by Goodyear and rose to prominence as the fighter of choice for more than fifty US Navy and Marine Corps squadrons, both on land and on aircraft carriers. The sturdy bomber earned the respect of enemy pilots as it racked up an eleven-to-one kill ratio during the war, and it continued to provide service and maintain solid results in Korea in the early 1950s. By the late 1940s, however, some of the Corsairs had been reassigned to reserve bases throughout the United States, while others made their way to air shows and museums.

Lieutenant Dodd knew the power, service record, and maneuverability of this aircraft well; in fact, in the several weeks before August 27, 1948, he had logged 31.9 hours in the air in this and other FG-1Ds. He frequented the Marine Corps' Buckley Field in Denver and took a Corsair out regularly, cruising the skies over northeastern Colorado on military business.

What exactly happened on this clear day in late August has been reconstructed from bits and pieces, assembled by experts who examined the remains of FG-1D Corsair #92255.

Dodd took off from Buckley Field and headed northwest to Estes Park, where residents and visitors to Rocky Mountain National Park could see his plane make "several low passes thereabouts & to N & W of that area," an unidentified examiner noted on the Marine Corps' Aircraft Accident Card. "He was noted to make pass up Fall River Canyon, around Sundance Mt., down Forrest Canyon, then back up Fall River Canyon toward Trail Ridge."

This placed a number of particularly tall mountains in his path, but on a day recorded as having unlimited visibility at the stroke of noon, the high peaks should have been obvious to the young pilot. While Dodd's specific purpose in this area cannot be known some seventy-plus years later, his intention seems clear: He was there for fun, flying low and performing some steep turns and banks as he zigzagged through the mountains at a dangerously low altitude.

"He was believed to be in climbing attitude at 140 [knots]," the one-page report continues. "Pilot apparently realized he could not gain altitude in time to clear approaching ridge."

How had he not anticipated the twelve-thousand-foot peak that rose abruptly in front of him, much closer than he had expected or intended? Dodd executed a sharp left, climbing as fast as he could as he tried to avoid the towering mountain and head for Fall River

Canyon. Before he could complete the move, however, a downdraft from Trail Ridge interfered with his climb, pulling the craft into the face of solid rock. The FG-1D Corsair struck it head-on, 400 feet below the top of the ridge, at roughly 11,600 feet in elevation. The International News Service described the location as near Trail Ridge Road and Iceberg Lake.

"[Aircraft] completely demolished as result of crash & following fire," the terse report continues.

Dodd had survived dogfights with Japanese fighters just a few years earlier, but he did not survive this impact.

The inspectors who analyzed the crash cut Dodd no slack at all in their estimation of the cause of the accident. "Opinion of [board] that pilot in unauthorized area at time of crash, that he was conducting unauthorized low flying in mountainous terrain & that he failed to observe ordinary precautions for flying in mountainous terrain."

This could be construed as carelessness, but the report went on to imply intent: Dodd "hit [the] ridge while flat-hatting in canyon." *Flat-hatting*, a well-known term among fighter pilots, refers to any style of flying a plane that disregards basic safety in favor of thrill-seeking or showmanship. In other words, the pilot was showing off.

Chances are that this was not the first time Dodd sought some fun in the air, but this time he began his flat-hatting maneuvers at insufficient altitude to pull them off safely.

The report concluded by recommending that "single plane flights be restricted to local area," and "that pilots be cautioned against low flying in mountainous terrain." Apparently Dodd's compatriots in the Marine Corps Reserves heeded this advice, for Dodd remains the only pilot from Buckley Field to lose his life in a plane crash in Rocky Mountain National Park.

GONE FISHING

April in the Rocky Mountains may be a little early for a fishing trip, with the probability of lingering spring storms ready to hamper the fun of the rugged wilderness. For pilot Jack D. Henander and five friends, all from Louisville, Colorado, the threat of early April snow should have made them reconsider their plans to head home after spending several days along the rivers of Wyoming.

Henander, who was 28 years old, piloted a single-engine Piper PA-32 private aircraft, and he had already logged a total of nine hundred hours at the helm, earning an instrument rating—meaning that he could fly in weather that occluded his vision in the air, using the plane's instrument readings to guide him. He was employed by Kensair Corp at the Jefferson County Airport, and this fishing trip would mark the last one of his life as a single man: He was engaged to marry Linda Condy of Longmont on Sunday, April 16, 1967, just a week after his scheduled return.

As he and his friends arrived at the airport on April 9 to begin their trip home from Wyoming, Henander received an in-person briefing from airport staff about the weather along their route, a forecast the ensuing report by the National Transportation Safety Board (NTSB) noted was "substantially correct."

The forecast called for obscured visibility as the plane crossed through Colorado, particularly in the Rocky Mountain National Park wilderness area. Airport personnel at their departure in Rock Springs, Wyoming, warned Henander about the potential for blowing snow, icy conditions, and zero visibility as he reached the Colorado mountains. Nonetheless, Henander filed a VFR flight plan—that is, he intended to use visual cues instead of his instruments to guide the plane through the inclement weather and high mountains.

The men in the party included Dow Chemical employee William P. "Dixie" Elrod, who was 55; municipal utility employee Charles DeNovelis, who was 54; 27-year-old Jack De Giacomo, who worked with Elrod at Dow; Charles Grosso, who was 35 and owned the Primrose Bar in Louisville; and Albert Romano, a 49-year-old construction worker. They climbed into the plane and made ready for what they expected to be a fairly rocky trip, based on the weather reports, but one that would bring them across the mountains and to the Jefferson County Airport in Broomfield, Colorado, by 4:30 p.m., well in time for supper.

Shortly after takeoff, Henander radioed from his position over Laramie, Wyoming, that everything was going fine. As they crossed over the national park, however, the promised weather changes began to blow up around them. Wind whistled past the little plane. Visibility dropped to zero as snow fell and formed an impenetrable wall, making it impossible to see in front of them. Soon they were shrouded in thick snow clouds as the ceiling lowered to zero. The forecast they had been given did indeed turn out to be "substantially correct," as the NTSB report would later confirm. They had flown right into the weather they had been told to expect.

Henander had the ability and the rating to switch from visual flight to instruments, but for reasons that will never be explained, he did not do so. This turned out to be his undoing. As ice encased the plane's wings and the extra weight dragged them toward the ground, he had no way to see what might be ahead of him. The plane reached Signal Mountain—at 11,262 feet, not the highest mountain in the park, but a formidable edifice with which to collide—and Comanche Peak, significantly higher, at 12,702 feet. Whether it collided head-on with one of these mountains or had a more controlled descent, the little Piper PA-32 dropped out of the sky in the vicinity of these two landmarks.

The mountainside tore the wings from the plane. The force of the forward thrust buried the fuselage under at least six feet of snow, wedging it into a narrow canyon.

De Giacomo and Grosso realized in short order that neither of them had been seriously hurt. Albert Romano was not so lucky; significant pain in his back told him that he was injured, but somehow his condition did not appear to be fatal. The three of them turned to Henander, Elrod, and DeNovellis and found them to be unconscious. Efforts to revive them failed, and after an hour of attempting to restore a pulse or breathing, the three survivors had to accept the fact that their friends had perished in the accident.

Now they faced a major dilemma: whether to stay put and wait to be found, or to find their way out of the Colorado backcountry in the midst of a violent snowstorm. Logically, they knew that someone would start looking for them when their plane did not arrive on time, but finding a downed small plane in the mountains, especially one shredded by impact and mostly buried in deep snow, could be a losing proposition in the best of weather. Staying put seemed like a bad option, especially since two of them had only minor injuries, and the third was determined to do what was necessary to survive despite his physical discomfort. On Monday morning, when the weather had let up enough to allow them to see where they were going, they set out in what they hoped would be a direction toward civilization. Despite the pain, Romano had enough range of motion to make it out of the plane when his two companions determined he needed to do so.

Sure enough, when the plane did not reach the Denver airport on time on the evening of April 9, 1967, officials began to organize a search. Hampered by weather, the Civil Air Patrol had to wait until Monday, April 10, to send a total of twenty-four planes into the air while twelve ground units deployed across the mountainous terrain.

As the search progressed, however, weather and other issues began to rack up additional casualties. First a search plane piloted by Dennis Harmon, deputy sheriff of Boulder County, clashed with a ridge and made an emergency landing, managing to avoid injury of himself and his two spotters, Sil Jones and Jack Varra. The men were "shaken but not hurt," the Grand Junction *Daily Sentinel* reported.

Hours later, search pilot Billy Mitchell of Golden, Colorado, crashed in Poudre Canyon, delivering a severe concussion to Mitchell and facial cuts to one of his spotters, Gordon Gibson of Lafayette, Colorado. The second spotter, Dave Ferguson of Louisville, escaped injury and walked out of the canyon to seek assistance for Mitchell and Gibson. He reached the search command without further mishap, and they sent a helicopter piloted by Ken Hoffman of Boulder to retrieve the injured men.

Monday stretched into Tuesday, and Tuesday into Wednesday, and still the searchers had not found the plane. Finally, a plane containing antelope counters from the Colorado Game, Fish and Parks Department saw a wisp of smoke rising from a campfire early Wednesday afternoon. Pilot Wayne Russell descended carefully to investigate and spotted the three plane-crash survivors waving frantically at him. Remarkably, his plane had a public address system, so he determined that these were the crash survivors and they needed assistance. He maintained position and radioed for helicopters, and soon Grosso, De Giacomo, and Romano were airlifted out of the wilderness one by one and transported to the nearby Lazy D Ranch. From here, another helicopter took them to the hospital in Fort Collins.

With no map and no clear idea of where they might be, they had wandered in the mountainous terrain for three days, sustaining significant sunburn under the bright, high-altitude Colorado sky. Thanks to their rugged fishermen's clothing and outdoorsman skills, they had avoided hypothermia, but trudging through deep snow had taken its toll on all of them.

"As far as we could tell, the other three are dead," Grosso told the rescuers. "We checked for pulse and heart."

De Giacomo and Grosso received treatment for their injuries, which were comparatively minor considering the ordeal they had experienced, and were released the same day. X-rays of Romano's back revealed broken bones, however, along with a minor skull fracture, so he remained in the hospital for treatment. "In spite of his injuries, Romano wandered about the national park for three days with the other two survivors," the *Daily Sentinel* noted, perhaps making him the most stoic of the men involved in the crash.

Descriptions from the rescued men helped the search commanders determine the most likely area where Henander's plane went down. Sheriff Ray Scheerer told the media he believed that the plane had crashed into the side of Comanche Peak on the park's northern boundary, some twenty-five airline miles west of the route Henander had filed in his flight plan before the plane left Rock Springs. From here, the survivors had walked five miles through deep snow, making their way fairly steadily to a lower altitude.

On Thursday, another winter storm came through and dropped visibility down to two hundred feet. The Larimer County sheriff called off the search and recovery of the three remaining bodies and closed the section of the park believed to be the crash site, declaring it a disaster area.

Nearly another week passed before searchers could reach the accident site on April 18, the Tuesday after the three survivors had been found. It took two more days to remove the bodies of Henander, Elrod, and DeNovellis, two of them on Wednesday by helicopter, the third, stymied by bad weather, eventually transported out by mountaineers hiking through snow as they carried the body to waiting snow vehicles.

Investigators determined that Henander had continued to fly using visual cues instead of his instruments, resulting in a "controlled" collision with the side of a mountain as visibility dropped to zero. Miles from his intended route, he may never have known that he had strayed across the northern boundary of Rocky Mountain National Park until he collided with one of the highest peaks in the region.

INTO SOLID ROCK

It's hard to say exactly what caused the crash of N4132C, a single-engine Maule Bee Dee M-4 personal aircraft owned by Martin Ryan, on August 16, 1977.

What we do know is fairly gruesome: A small group of eye-witnesses saw the plane approach the east wall of Fall River Pass at about 6:30 p.m., attempt to climb over it, lose speed, and smash directly into the granite wall, 10,300 feet above sea level. The plane burst into flames, killing the two people inside.

"Skies were overcast and scattered showers were reported in the vicinity at the time of the crash," the *Colorado Springs Gazette Telegraph* reported the following day, but two investigators from the National Transportation Safety Board were not so generous. They noted that the pilot had received an accurate forecast by phone from the flight service personnel before taking off from the airport in Broomfield, Colorado, and that visibility remained clear and unlimited as the plane crossed the park.

Examination of the crash site and the plane's remains revealed that the pilot had "failed to follow approved procedures [and] directives," and that he had "misjudged distance, speed, and altitude as he approached the canyon wall." Once he realized that he had put himself and his passenger in a dangerous situation, he "failed to obtain/maintain flying speed."

The NTSB struggled to identify the plane itself as well as the travelers inside. The fire had burned so hot that it destroyed the numbers on the hull, making an immediate identification impossible. The Federal Aviation Administration finally located the plane's flight plan the following day, discovering that the two travelers were pilot Ryan, who was 23, and 19-year-old Janet Bonneville, both from Vancouver, Washington. Ryan had logged 195 hours in the pilot's seat—enough to recognize the gravity of his situation and determine a way out. In this instance, however, quick thinking seemed to elude him as the canyon loomed large in his sight. His attempt to execute a steep climb resulted in a stalled engine, eliminating any option that might have saved his and his passenger's lives.

A CHRISTMAS MIRACLE

Barry L. Krieger knew his way around a twin-engine plane, logging more than 6,200 hours in the air as a licensed noncommercial pilot and countless additional hours in his several years as a federal air traffic controller in Longmont, Colorado. On December 23, 1979, he loaded his Piper Apache PA-23 with gifts and food for a Christmas visit to Fullerton, California, and took off from Longmont with his 62-year-old mother, Virginia Krieger, and his three daughters: Kathy, who was 17; 15-year-old Connie; and 10-year-old Clare.

Not long after takeoff, the plane entered the airspace above Rocky Mountain National Park. Here clouds gathered for a sky the NTSB calls "broken"—heavy cloud cover with breaks between layers or clusters, obstructing some of the pilot's view. Visibility, however, remained "unlimited" in the reviewing team's estimation. No storm gathered as the plane crossed above the Never Summer Mountains, and no snow or icy precipitation fell or gathered on the wings.

As Krieger guided the plane over the mountains, the wind began to gust with ferocious strength. Clouds closed above and below him, and he began to circle, looking for a break that would allow him to rise above the turbulent air. The heater inside the plane shut down altogether, and the girls gathered together for warmth, with Clare sitting on Kathy's lap.

That's when the wind grabbed the little plane with all of the power of nature and pulled it down toward the mountains below. Updrafts and downdrafts buffeted the craft as Krieger struggled and failed to regain control. "Clare was on my lap, and I knew we were going down," Kathy Krieger told media sometime later. "I just closed my eyes and held tight to my baby sister."

The Piper Apache belly-flopped on the side of Chippler Mountain at about twelve thousand feet. Mercifully, the impact drove its nose into a snowfield that cushioned their landing, keeping the plane from shattering into bits when it hit the mountainside. Krieger and his daughters found themselves largely unhurt, but Virginia sat unconscious in her seat. Luggage piled behind the plane's seats had sailed through the air and rattled around the inside of the plane, and one heavy suitcase had struck Virginia in the back of the head.

The worst appeared to be over, but the Kriegers quickly understood that they had another ordeal ahead of them. They had no way to know how long it would take for rescuers to begin looking for them. Krieger had not filed a flight plan, so it could be some time before anyone realized that they had not arrived in California as scheduled. They had not prepared for the possibility of days and nights at high altitude in the dead of winter, so frostbite and hypothermia loomed on the near horizon. A quick assessment of their food situation revealed some oranges and a pecan pie, but little else. Krieger also knew that the continued high winds would hamper any aerial search effort. The plane had an emergency locator beacon, however, so he activated this, giving himself and the children hope for eventual discovery.

They huddled together inside the plane, and Krieger had the girls unwrap their Christmas presents: Bibles, which seemed especially appropriate in this life-and-death situation. They kept themselves occupied by reading aloud from the Bibles, singing Christmas carols, and sharing what food they had. Sunday stretched into Monday, and Monday gave way to Tuesday—Christmas Day, with food running low and no sound in the mountain wilderness.

Then, on Tuesday afternoon, a distant whirring broke the silence. It took only a moment for the girls and their father to realize that they could hear helicopter rotors.

Kathy, Connie, and Clare sprang into action, grabbing loose clothing, leaping out of the plane, and standing on its wing to wave frantically at the helicopter. "It came back again," said Kathy. "The most glorious sound I've ever heard was the first helicopter to spot the wreckage."

Soon a Colorado Civil Air Patrol plane appeared, piloted by Major Harvey Siegal of Littleton. Siegal had been tracking the emergency beacon, which searchers had detected for the first time on Monday, and he breathed a sigh of relief when he spotted Clare standing on the downed Piper's wing, waving at him.

"It was quite a Christmas present for us," he told the Associated Press. "It's a beautiful sight when you see a [crashed] plane with someone waving from it."

Siegal summoned more helicopters, and St. Anthony Hospital, Fort Carson Army Base, and KBTV all sent aircraft to transport the survivors and their grandmother's body out of the mountains. The girls and Barry landed at Longmont United Hospital, where they were treated for exposure, and Barry received additional treatment for potentially frostbitten legs and feet. The girls were released later that day and stayed with friends in Niwot until their father recovered.

Kathy told reporters that "every day for the rest of her life, she is going to think about how wonderful it is to be alive after surviving the plane crash."

A Mountain out of Nowhere

On April 5, 1989, at about 12:30 p.m., pilot Terry Bentley, operator of the Bob Adams Memorial STOLport ten miles north of Steamboat Springs, Colorado, left the STOLport in a Cessna 182P Skylane, a single-engine four-seater, bound for Fort Collins. Bentley was scheduled to take a "check ride" with the Federal Aviation Administration later that day to assure his competency and proficiency, as required by Title 14, Section 135 of the Code of Federal Regulations for pilots with certain authorizations.

Most pilots would consider the flight from Steamboat to Fort Collins to be a short hop, but it crosses some of the national park's most mountainous terrain, with mountains as tall as 13,500 feet. Chances are Bentley knew this area well, however, as he had logged more than 9,000 hours as a pilot—including more than 2,100 hours in this make and model airplane—and probably took this route on a regular basis.

On this day, Bentley decided to fly using VFR, but as he entered the park, he encountered heavy cloud cover and mountaintops obscured beneath low clouds, and tailwinds as strong as 100 miles per hour. No one can say exactly what happened next, or why Bentley made the decision to continue to fly through instrument meteorological conditions (IMC) using VFR, but suddenly his plane was no longer in the sky. The last anyone saw of it, the plane had flown low over Cameron Pass.

Bentley had not filed a flight plan, but the FAA representative he was supposed to meet at Fort Collins airport knew immediately that the Cessna was overdue. A search began quickly as seven aircraft and a Denver news helicopter took off from the search base in Kremmling to look for the cream-colored Cessna among the snow-covered mountains.

Late Friday morning, however, the wind picked up again. "The wind is really making it difficult for us to search," Civil Air Patrol (CAP) mission headquarters representative Steve Budd-Jack told the Associated Press. He told the reporter that the search aircraft were turning back early on the second and third days of the search because of winds gusting up to 100 miles per hour. Ground searchers continued to cover the area along Bentley's assumed route, led by the Routt County Sheriff's Department.

At its peak, the search involved twelve aircraft and as many as thirty people, with hopes that Bentley had enough survival gear with him to sustain himself in the high-altitude wilderness for days, or even weeks.

Days passed with no sign of the missing plane or its pilot. Eight days into the search, a pilot and observer made an emergency landing in their Cessna T-41 when they lost an engine, putting it down in three feet of snow about fifteen miles north of Kremmling. Fortunately, pilot Dana Ramsey of Aurora and observer Scott Mathena of Castle Rock were not hurt, and rescuers soon reached them and transported them to the search base at Kremmling. The plane "was not seriously damaged," according to CAP spokesman Dieter Hantschel.

Searchers continued to canvass the area for another ten days, but on April 24, the CAP called an end to the operation when the last of the leads to the plane's possible crash site finally ran out. Hope remained that with the summer thaw, the plane's location might finally be revealed by visitors or by increased flightseeing traffic.

As it happened, a park researcher exploring Rowe Glacier stumbled upon the plane. He found debris from the crash scattered on the glacier on Thursday, June 29, and reported it to rangers, who flew in to investigate. They found Terry Bentley's body still in the plane, where he probably died on impact.

With the crashed plane in hand, the NTSB had the opportunity to determine a probable cause for the accident. Their report states that the pilot's "failure to discontinue the VFR flight when he encountered IMC; and the [pilot's] failure to maintain adequate altitude to clear the mountainous terrain" caused the in-flight collision with the terrain. The report notes that the lowest cloud ceiling was at about ten thousand feet, while the plane crashed at roughly thirteen thousand feet. Why Bentley did not switch to instruments in such conditions remains a permanent mystery.

WEATHER OR NOT

Peter Smith, a 46-year-old Littleton resident, was no ordinary pilot. His nearly seven thousand hours in the air spanned roles as a flight instructor, a military pilot, and a helicopter pilot, with considerable experience flying single-engine and multi-engine aircraft. Before he took off from Erie, Colorado, north of Denver, on the evening of January 31, 1996, he filed an instrument flight plan and headed northwest toward Rock Springs, Wyoming, on his way to Boise, Idaho, flying a Piper PA-34-220T Seneca with no passengers.

The night was overcast but bright, according to the report compiled by the NTSB, with ten-mile visibility and calm winds. Smith received his IFR clearance in flight and then requested a visual rating once he had climbed above the cloud cover. He then requested a vector heading for Rock Springs, "just to verify . . . a radar vector heading just to check that . . . ," the recording of the conversation with air traffic control said. "I'm having a little heading problem here, but switching to compass nav, but we're VFR on top. In fact, it's pretty much VFR below us now." After that, Smith continued on his way to Rock Springs, as he would on any other flight.

Nine minutes later, his plane disappeared from air traffic control radar.

"Radar data indicated the airplane descended from an encoded altitude of 15,100 feet to 13,900 feet in 1 minute, 31 seconds, or about 800 feet per minute," the report says. "No distress call was received. Wreckage examination failed to explain why the airplane descended or anything causal to accident."

To make matters worse, it took searchers a month to find the aircraft, lodged in the side of Ypsilon Mountain. Weather events and forest fires kept crews from removing the plane from the mountain until late July, six months after it crashed, but careful examination of the plane did not provide clues to an event that forced it out of the sky. "Descent into mountainous terrain for reasons undetermined," the report concluded, drawing no clear inference from its disastrous end.

In contrast, the most recent fatal crash in Rocky Mountain National Park—now more than twenty years ago, in April 2000—turned out to be fairly easy to analyze. Pilot Robert Donoho, who was 52, and his 47-year-old wife, Terri, were flying from Page, Arizona, to their home in Fort Collins in a two-engine Smith Aerostar 601 when they encountered stormy weather above the park. Robert had more than four thousand hours of flight experience, but he was not instrument-rated, so he maintained visual flight in a snowstorm that required instruments to navigate.

Ahead of the Donohos' plane stood Comanche Peak, a rugged, 12,176-foot mountain, and the last peak they needed to pass before they cleared the Rockies and headed for home over flatter terrain. Clouds obstructed the pilot's view, however, and his altitude dropped to about one hundred feet below the top of the peak. He ran smack into the side of the mountain. Robert and Terri were killed instantly.

It took four days for the Colorado Civil Air Patrol, Larimer County Search and Rescue, the Colorado National Guard, and park employees to locate the downed plane and determine that there were no survivors of the crash. In addition to the high, mountainous terrain and clouds, the NTSB report lists all of the errors that led to the Donohos' deaths: inaccurate weather evaluation on the pilot's part; VFR flight in IMC conditions; and inadequate clearance.

But the more important message here is not about a single pilot's error. The high peaks region of Rocky Mountain National Park generates some of the most volatile weather in the country, with gusting winds and rapid changes from clear skies to heavy precipitation. Pilots who intend to take in the spectacular scenery below must pay heed to weather forecasts and take the warnings of potential changes very seriously. Some find themselves virtually sucked out of the air by high winds, driven to low, unsafe altitudes by ice and snow, and shrouded by heavy clouds at the very moment when visibility is most required. This is not an area for flat-hatting, or for taking previous knowledge of the terrain for granted. If weather threatens, small-plane pilots should consider a less dangerous route.

CHAPTER 9

Rising Waters:
The Lawn Lake Flood

On the cloudless, sunny morning of July 15, 1982, campers began to rise from slumber in Aspenglen Campground, ready to enjoy a quiet breakfast and spend the day exploring the park. Some planned to pack up and head into Estes Park, where they could purchase food and supplies, or return to the luxuries of vacationland civilization. Others were just beginning a long weekend of hiking, campfires, and family time in what promised to be a beautiful few days of sunshine and clear air.

In town, business owners swept the sidewalks in front of their establishments, set out sidewalk signs to lure customers in, brewed coffee, fired up grills, and readied themselves for a busy day of commerce at the height of the tourist season. With thousands of visitors filling hotel rooms and campgrounds throughout the area, this promised to be a solidly prosperous day for restaurateurs and owners of bars, gift shops, and other businesses that graced Elkhorn Avenue and other thoroughfares.

This, however, would be no ordinary day.

Eleven miles from Estes Park stood the Lawn Lake Dam, built in 1903 and operated by the Farmers Irrigating Ditch and Reservoir Company in Loveland. The aging dam had recently received a rating as a "moderate hazard dam" from the Colorado State Engineer's Office, allowing its management to inspect the earthen structure once every two years. In the thirty-one years before this warm July day, however, it had been inspected just four times, and issues had been found each time, including a leak discovered in 1977. An inspector in 1978 recommended that "subsequent inspections be made when the lake was full or near full, so the dam could be checked for seepage," the Associated Press reported in 1982. This more thorough inspection was planned for sometime in 1982, but it had not taken place by July 15.

Exactly when the twenty-four-foot-high dam began to crack remains difficult to say. Sometime around 6:00 a.m., however, one man realized something was amiss: Stephen Gillette, a driver for A-1 Trash Service, making a pickup at the Long Lake trailhead, heard a sound he'd never heard up there before. He called park rangers at 6:26 a.m. and reported dirt and debris floating in the air and a roaring sound he could not identify. "It was like a jet had crashed into the mountain," he said during a 1982 interview. (Gillette, whose quick realization that something bad was happening on the mountain probably saved hundreds of lives that day, eventually became an Estes Park town trustee.)

Alert personnel at Estes Park's only radio station, KSIR, heard their police scanner crackle to life as Gillette contacted the rangers. Listening to the details of the call, they determined that a potential public safety crisis might be in progress, so they confirmed the report with the rangers and took to the airwaves. They monitored the rangers' radio channel throughout the early morning and broadcast updated reports to the six thousand residents of Estes Park—and to as many as forty thousand tourists who crowded the town in mid-July, the height of the vacation season.

The Lawn Lake Dam split open moments after dawn. From its elevated position at roughly 10,987 feet, its weakened walls washed away in seconds, releasing millions of gallons of water into the Roaring River. The lake's contents—219,724,000 gallons of water—emptied rapidly and rushed downward, gaining speed and energy as it descended nearly 2,500 feet in minutes. Hydrologists from the US Geological Survey's water resources division estimated that between 2 and 4 million gallons of water a minute pounded down the watercourse and into the Fall River—a massive change from the river's normal flow of 9,600 gallons per minute.

Stephen Cashman had risen early in the backcountry campsite he shared with his friend, 21-year-old Stephen See, with whom he had driven to Rocky Mountain from Hilbert, Wisconsin, in a 1968 Mercury Cougar. Cashman went about the simple tasks of making coffee in the peaceful park. Suddenly a loud crash made him look up from his camp stove.

"All he said was that there was one hell of a racket, and then all of the sudden there were boulders and trees," said Sylvester See, Stephen See's father, to *Daily Sentinel* staff writer Steve McMillan on the day his son disappeared. "That was the last Stephen saw of any camping equipment, the tent, and my son, who was in the tent."

Cashman reacted quickly and managed to get out of the way, but See, still asleep in his sleeping bag, had no opportunity to escape. In seconds he was gone, submerged and swept away by a wall of dam debris, trees, and rocks powered by the force of the flood.

By the time it reached the Horseshoe Park area, the giant mass of debris had taken on a life of its own. It towered twenty to thirty feet high, darkened by dirt and mud and propelled forward by its long downhill slide, and headed straight for Aspenglen Campground.

At this hour, between 7:00 and 7:30 a.m., some of the campers had already awakened and had begun to prepare for that day's exploration of the park. One by one, campers began to realize that the sound of the merrily burbling river had become much louder.

"It sounded like distant thunder," said one of eight campers from Chicago to the media later that day, "but then a wall of water filled with huge boulders and trees came roaring down the river, accompanied by a thick mist." They bolted for higher ground, as did a dozen or more other campers, while others awoke to discover that water was streaming through their tents.

"You didn't really have time to get scared," Kacie Cavanaugh told reporter Steve Krizman of the *Daily Sentinel*. Cavanaugh had camped at Aspenglen with her husband and two-year-old son. "But you just had the idea that you didn't know if you were all of a sudden going to be under 10 feet of water. But as it turned out, we had room to maneuver."

Those on the campground's higher ground found themselves dry but surrounded by water on all sides, cut off from their cars by deep, fast-moving water. Tony and Peggy Donovan and their two young daughters waded across water up to their knees, escaping to higher ground before they were completely trapped. Comfortably above water level, they watched as the water propelled boulders the size of cars in its path, broke off tall trees, and destroyed the paved road that could have led them out of the park. When the waters finally subsided, they explored the damage in its wake, carefully negotiating around standing rubble and huge holes in the road, and watching National Park Service personnel attempt to create some kind of passage to allow the campers to return to civilization.

One topic quickly became unmentionable among the stranded campers: the people who could not move quickly enough to escape the hastening flood. Three campers had made it out of the water's path, then paused momentarily and turned back to attempt to gather their personal belongings. They remained in the flood's path for an instant too long. The sheer force of the flood dragged them under, treating them like so much more debris in its wake. The three campers vanished from the view of the others who had managed to reach unaffected land.

"They were trying to get out of the water that was rising around their tent, and they haven't been seen since," said Glen Kaye, park spokesperson, to the *Denver Post* the day after the flood. "But nobody actually saw them washed away."

Bridget Doris of Arlington, Texas, usually went camping with her husband, Rod, and her parents, Ingrid and Don Thomas. This time, however, Bridget and Ingrid had decided to make it a girls' weekend, arriving Wednesday night and choosing Aspenglen and its stunning views of the Rocky Mountains.

"Bridget came here because she loved it," Rod Doris told reporter Steve McMillan the day after the flood. "She loved it here, and she loved camping."

When the floodwaters hit, Ingrid Thomas managed to run away from the water's path. Bridget hesitated, and attempted to retrieve her tent and belongings before her campsite was completely inundated. Terry William Coates, a 36-year-old vice principal of an elementary school in Peoria, Illinois, saw Bridget struggling with her tent and stopped to help her. His wife, Rosemary, and their two children ran for higher ground.

An instant later, churning floodwaters covered the campsite. Bridget and Terry vanished from view.

Campers also told authorities about an unidentified white man in his mid-30s, camping alone, who also disappeared when the floodwaters hit.

When the rushing water reached Horseshoe Park and Aspenglen, it washed away the campground's access road before the flood's momentum ceased briefly as a small dam on Cascade Lake contained it. Here the marshy ground provided room for the waters to expand and their force to dissipate, with the area's numerous beaver dams providing short-lived obstacles to the flood's progress. Still six miles outside of Estes Park, the Cascade Lake dam provided the respite people in town needed to get out of the way of the potential deluge. Townspeople rapped on one another's doors to be sure everyone had heard about the emergency and that they were taking precautions to protect their lives and property. Authorities warned motel owners just before 7:30 a.m. and instructed them to alert their guests to the approaching crisis. At 8:00 a.m., according to county employee Jim Crowe, the streets of Estes Park remained dry, and people began to hope that the flood had come to a standstill in Horseshoe Park.

Indeed, for precious minutes, the dam in the park held back the water. It had not been built for this kind of pressure, however, and within an hour it collapsed, and a fresh deluge began. Water flowed from Horseshoe Park into Fall River, where it quickly crested the river's banks. Dyed dark brown by mud, it coursed down the normally clear river and onto US 34, the main road through the eastern part of the park, where the combined force of floodwaters and river turned the road into a soggy thoroughfare several feet deep.

Seeing the potential route the flood might take as it rushed toward Lake Estes on the east end of town, the Larimer County Sheriff's Office dispatched officers to close US 34 through the western end of Big Thompson Canyon. In 1976, a flood along the Big Thompson River had killed 139 people, so the sheriff's office lost no time in taking this precaution. Closer to town, they also closed US 34 and 36 and State Route 7, allowing no one to enter Estes Park until they could be sure the floodwaters had been contained.

Then, said gift-shop owner Forest Johnson to the *Denver Post*, "We looked up the highway and the first thing we saw was a string of trailer houses coming down the highway, but there weren't any cars pulling the trailers." The flood virtually cleaned out Fall River Trailer

Court, washing away nearly every home there. "There was a four-or five-foot wall of water; whole trailers were floating out of those mobile home parks. Then the trailers would hit things and clobber them. There were automobiles, tractors and everything under the sun, floating down the road." He added, "It screwed things up real good."

At 8:12 a.m., the column of water reached the west end of Estes Park. Mobile homes bowled over by the speeding waters drifted for a block or more, and then smashed against permanent buildings and shattered into pieces. One observer reported pieces of log cabins and other sections of a motel carried off, tangled in twisted metal and unidentifiable building parts. Later it became clear that the properties that had taken this extensive damage were Nicky's Resort and the Ponderosa Lodge.

The flash flood not only swept away mobile homes and automobiles; it had also scooped up boulders and silt on its way down the Rushing River and through Horseshoe Park. Now it sent a moving wall of debris straight through town, collecting more and more items as it rocketed past buildings and businesses on US 34, and veered right onto Estes Park's Elkhorn Avenue to follow Fall River. The four- to seven-foot-high column of water tossed cars and trailers into shop fronts, smashing plate-glass windows, yanking street signs out of their foundations, mangling door frames, and knocking down support structures. Deep floodwaters poured into stores and restaurants. Cars parked on the street lifted off the pavement and drifted—some of them turned upside-down—until the river gave them up some distance down the road.

When dentist Bill Pike heard the warning of the approaching flood, he closed his office and drove to his home on Fall River. "My wife and I looked out the window and we heard the roar coming," he told the AP. Normally about twenty feet wide, the river was "suddenly 200 feet wide . . . It must have been a 10-foot wall of water. Pine trees were falling down like matchsticks, a small bridge floated by, followed by lots of camping gear—thermoses, blankets, fishing tackle boxes, nylon jackets . . . we had a front-row seat, but it was terrible to watch."

The moving wall of debris raced along the river from one intersection to the next, destroying a total of eighteen bridges as it passed. Floodwaters collided with a total of 108 homes, causing extensive damage, but the worst of the impact took place in town, where 177 businesses—75 percent of Estes Park's entire business community—took on as much as three to four feet of water, which left behind two-foot-deep mud.

By nine a.m., even before the flooding had come to a standstill, some opportunists began looting the compromised stores. They battled the waters still flowing down Elkhorn Avenue and gathered whatever appeared to still have value after a thorough soaking in muddy water, followed by a coating of settling silt. This nefarious effort did not last long, however; local police moved quickly to seal off the affected areas of town and post guards to prevent further destructive action.

Finally, the floodwaters reached the western end of Lake Estes and dumped tens of thousands of gallons of water and tons of debris into the lake. Officials and residents began to worry that the lake might overflow its own shores, but the lake remained firm, turning dark with added soils and solids, but supplying a final resting place for the roiling flood. The dam at the lake's eastern end held up against the massive pressure, keeping the waters from cascading down into the canyon beyond.

The Lawn Lake Flood was contained.

Word of the disaster reached the Colorado governor's office by late morning. Governor Dick Lamm was attending a Democratic Party meeting in Washington, DC, but Lieutenant Governor

Nancy Dick toured the Estes Park and Rocky Mountain National Park area by helicopter with the first aerial survey to assess the damages. She moved quickly to sign a state disaster area proclamation that afternoon when she returned to her office. This allowed emergency services to begin, including the deployment of fifty-five military police officers from the Colorado Army National Guard, who arrived to safeguard homes and businesses and prevent looters from causing even more destruction.

With the floodwaters finally contained, both town and park had monumental challenges ahead: determining how many people had perished in the flood, how extensively the park and town had been damaged, and what kind of effort and resources it would take to recover. Search parties sprang into action as soon as the water's force subsided and its levels began to drop, signaling that the abnormally high flow down the Roaring River had finally emptied Lawn Lake. They moved up along the Roaring River to find the twenty-five people with overnight camping permits along the flood's route. "We've already found out that there were at least four illegal campers in that area," said Glen Kaye to the AP, increasing the number of people search parties would need to locate. By this time news of camper Steven See's capture by the flood had reached the park's offices, but searchers fully expected to discover that more people had vanished in the wake of the floodwaters.

By day's end, most of the campers had been found alive, but as many as six still had not been located. The search halted for the night as dusk settled over the park, where water three feet deep still covered the Horseshoe Park area.

The search continued for the missing campers on Friday morning, July 16. Stephen See's body came to light first, "pinned among debris where the Roaring River empties into the Fall River," according to the *Daily Sentinel*.

Rod Doris and his father-in-law, Don Thomas, came to Estes Park from Texas to conduct their own search for Bridget Doris. They took a flight from Dallas to Denver on July 15, landed at about 11:00 p.m., rented a car, and arrived in Estes Park at about 1:30 a.m. on Friday, the morning after the flood. They found the town barricaded by National Guard soldiers, but they finally found their way to the municipal building and met a park ranger there, who brought them up the road into the park and as close to Aspenglen Campground as they could reach by vehicle. From here, Rod and Don put on hiking boots and backpacks, loaded up with search-and-rescue equipment, and hiked in another mile to the soggy campground.

Here they left their packs, grabbed flashlights, and waded into the still-swollen river to begin their search. After two hours, it became clear that Bridget was not to be found there. Hope left them that she might not have drifted down the river with the flood and debris, or that she might be injured and stranded fairly close to her campsite.

"If she was alive, she would have turned up somewhere Thursday—maybe hurt," Rod Doris told the reporter. "I expected to find her that way when I got here. But I had no illusions that she would be found alive today [Friday]. If her body doesn't turn up by tomorrow, we may never find that either."

On Saturday, a cadre of six searchers focused their efforts on an area downstream from Aspenglen. By this time, park staff had come to the conclusion that the four missing people were almost certainly dead, so "there isn't the urgency we had before," park spokesperson Mary Karraker told the media. The searchers concentrated on a number of piles of uprooted trees, boulders, and mud that had come to rest between Aspenglen and Estes Park, as these seemed to be the most likely places to find a body hidden from view or even buried among the debris.

It took three more days for Terry Coates's body to come to light, discovered by construction workers clearing the debris from the Fall River channel a mile below Aspenglen Campground. Coates's wallet remained in his pocket, making the identification certain.

A month passed before Rod Doris's dire prediction could be proven wrong. On August 14, state highway construction workers clearing debris from a fish hatchery bridge south of Fall River Road discovered the body of Bridget Doris, buried in mud and gravel at the base of the bridge.

No fourth body was ever located, and the identity of the missing camper in his mid-30s—if he existed at all—remains a mystery.

Meanwhile, Estes Park neighbors broke out their snowplows and bulldozers to begin clearing the deep mud, silt, branches, roots, and other debris from the streets, filling dump trucks with the stuff to be hauled off. Workmen clad in fishing waders and hip boots caught and secured damaged power lines, examined broken gas mains, contained gas leaks, and provided boards and tools to help business owners close up their establishments, making it more difficult to loot them.

Business owners, finally allowed to reenter the town on the evening of the flood, got their first looks at the massive damage done to their stores, gift shops, and restaurants, and began to understand the effort it would take to repair the damage to the structures and recover from the loss of so much inventory. "We've got at least $100,000 in damage," said June Bartlett, who owned one of the town's largest gift shops with her husband, Norb. She waved a hand to encourage an Associated Press reporter to take a good look inside her destroyed store, where jewelry, crystal, and china lay splintered and crushed amid three-foot-deep gravel and silt on the floor. Tree branches stuck out at angles, and a pair of someone's shoes sat atop the heap. "Look—just look at this," she said.

She was far from alone. Every store along Elkhorn Avenue had suffered similar damage. "There's never been anything like this to hit the town since I've been here, and I arrived in 1945," Herzog's Gift Corral owner Charlie Herzog told the AP.

Dwayne and Carol Herman, who owned the Village Goldsmith shop, had managed to use what few moments they had before the flood to move much of their merchandise up to the store's second floor. Dwayne caulked around the windows and doors as well, an effort that did not keep all of the mud and water out of the store, but significantly reduced the damage. With these tasks completed, Dwayne and Carol climbed up to the roof of the Village Goldsmith and waited out the flood, watching as the high water and its heavy cargo sluiced through their town.

"It was scary, friend," Dwayne told reporter Steve McMillan. "It's one of those things you will remember for a long time."

These precautions kept the Hermans from losing most of their inventory, but many other stores were not so fortunate. Tom Morrow, owner of jewelry store Peacock Limited, saw the majority of his expensive merchandise wash out of display cases and down the road in the floodwaters, most likely coming to rest at the bottom of Lake Estes.

Despite the sudden destruction and the overwhelming level of cleanup and repair ahead of them, however, many of the merchants and restaurateurs reopened their businesses in just a few days, serving the customers who remained in town as best they could with the supplies and wares they had available. A number of tourists pitched in to help clear water and mud from shops, deepening the proprietors' commitment to restoring normalcy and reopening as quickly as possible. They saw themselves as having only two alternatives: declare a total loss, as many did, or make the most of the area's short tourist season and bring in whatever money they could to aid in their own reconstruction.

State funds became available, but "those who stayed faced a long, harrowing, and expensive cleanup process," noted John Cordsen of the *Loveland Reporter-Herald* in the paper's coverage of the flood's thirtieth anniversary. "They had to rebuild during the busy summer season in Estes Park."

Facts also came to light about the rarity of inspections of Lawn Lake Dam, and the distinct possibility that other dams around the state might also be in danger of collapse. The state had just seven dam safety inspectors for 2,249 dams across the state—not nearly enough to make certain that dams were inspected in a timely manner, which for most meant annually.

"[This] understaffing has left the residents of Estes Park steaming about government negligence, because the Lawn Lake Dam had been inspected just four times in 31 years, most recently in 1978," an editorial in the *Daily Sentinel* noted on July 19, 1982, four days after the flood. "The cost of hiring more inspectors probably doesn't seem that high to the resort community of Estes Park, which sustained approximately $75 million damage . . . The people of Estes Park aren't labeling the disaster an 'act of God.' They're calling it an 'act of government.' Or, more precisely, lack of government."

Inspections after the dam break revealed that "water had been seeping through the earthen dam for some time and . . . peat moss and tree roots were found in the earthwork," the Associated Press reported on July 18.

On Thursday, July 22, President Ronald Reagan approved federal disaster relief for Estes Park, making funds available for individuals and agencies to repair and rebuild their homes and businesses, as well as roads and other structures damaged by the flood. This was good news for the town, especially because Colorado governor Richard Lamm announced that the state could not legally reimburse private property owners for their losses, though it would assist with rebuilding bridges and roads.

That weekend, the annual Estes Park Rooftop Rodeo went on as scheduled, beginning with a parade through the center of town led by men in muddy clothes, carrying a banner that read, "The Gutsiest Little Town in CO." The *Estes Park Trail-Gazette* echoed this sentiment, declaring:

Estes Park WILL be back, stronger, tighter, and better than ever, even though we may not reach full blossom for some weeks or months to come.

If money is what it takes, we'll find it.
If a miracle is what it takes, we'll pray for it.
If cooperation is what it takes, we'll work for it.
If guts is what it takes, we've got 'em.

It will surprise no one that a flood of lawsuits followed the news of limited state aid, most of them directed at the Loveland irrigation company that owned the Lawn Lake Dam. In this generally dry area, most of the residents and businesses did not have flood insurance. "A spokesman for the National Flood Insurance Program said he had only 38 flood insurance policies on file from Estes Park," the Grand Junction *Daily Sentinel* reported. "More than 100 businesses and homes were flooded."

In the end, 62 percent of these business owners either lost their businesses or gave up and moved away, leaving many empty storefronts on the town's main strip. Nonetheless, Estes Park rallied; the remaining businesses were repaired, homes rebuilt, lawsuits settled, and the town recovered from the single worst disaster in its history. The fact that so few lives were lost is a testament to the quick reactions of a handful of individuals who recognized danger, took quick action, and got the word out to townspeople and campers in time to keep people safe.

CHAPTER 10

Off a Cliff:
Homicides

BAD BLOOD CAN MAKE AN OTHERWISE CIVIL DISPUTE GO HORRIBLY wrong, especially in a place where people habitually take the law into their own hands. In northern Colorado in the 1920s, statehood required this largely unsettled frontier to practice law enforcement like everywhere else in the United States—but this was the American West, and remnants of the lawless 1800s still lingered among some segments of society, especially in remote areas like the Rocky Mountains. Some still settled a dispute with a lynching instead of a lawsuit, thinking they could somehow escape prosecution for what was inarguably a capital crime. Remarkably, just one of these cases took place within the boundaries of Rocky Mountain National Park, on a hot July day in 1926.

Born in Colorado, Fred N. Selak grew up in Georgetown, where gold mining became familiar to him. He later went into the mercantile business and owned a store in Grand Lake, where a 1911 advertisement tells us he dealt in "general merchandise, ranch produce, real estate, loans, saddle horses and teams for rent."

When the federal government drew the park's boundary, Fred Selak's land ended up just inside of it. This had no real effect on his property or ownership, as the government permitted anyone who owned land within the park to remain on it for the rest of their lives, with the option to sell it to the National Park Service at any time. So Selak, who was 61 years old (newspapers reported his age as 75, but his tombstone says he was born in 1865), had the final say about anything that might go on within his acreage, a fact that irked a father and son, Alonzo and Arthur Osborne, and their employee, 21-year-old Ray Noakes.

The Osbornes and Noakes wanted to cross this land regularly, but Selak had erected a fence that forced them to go around his property. They visited him and demanded access, but the reclusive Selak wanted none of this, and told them so in no uncertain terms—a choice that earned him a severe thrashing from the three men. Selak knew his rights, so he filed charges against the men and prosecuted his case in court. The Osbornes and Noakes were found guilty and forced to pay a fine of $16—not a large sum even in 1926, but enough to make them even angrier at the obstinate landowner.

In small communities, people talk. In Grand Lake, just a few miles from Selak's property, neighbors speculated about Selak— whom they called "The Hermit of Grand Lake"—and how much money he must keep in his cabin. As anyone who has ever heard a rumor knows, facts inflate as gossip travels, so much so that people began to tell tales about Selak's great fortune of as much as $500,000 stored somewhere in his home. They came upon their facts honestly, relatively speaking: Selak was said to boast of his wealth and sometimes show it off. "Selak became a legendary Midas, and now the gossips declare that at least $60,000 in currency and gold lies buried near his cabin," a news story suggested. "Relatives of the . . . man claim to have found a large sum deposited in a Denver bank in Selak's name, but the queer habits of the aged hermit lead his neighbors to the suspicion that most of his wealth is hidden."

Selak's hired man had told Grand Lake townspeople a whopper of a story: "I cleaned up around the place once and found an old baking powder can. When Selak heard I had unearthed it, he frantically searched till he found it, and when he opened it, there was $5,000 in gold." In another tale, Selak asked a visiting Easterner for advice on investments. The banker asked, "How much do you want to invest—a thousand dollars?" Selak was said to have laughed. "I have $60,000 buried at my ranch right now," he told him. No one ever forgot hearing that from the lips of the wealthy man.

The men who had beaten Selak listened to these rumors and took them to heart, deciding that the potential rewards of a robbery could be great enough to warrant the satisfaction of killing the man in cold blood. They hatched a plot and waited for an opportune time to carry it out.

Still fuming about the original dispute, Arthur Osborne and Ray Noakes paid Selak a visit on July 21, 1926. Osborne and Selak quarreled again, and suddenly Osborne pulled out a gun and threatened Selak, demanding that the old man give him his money. Selak pleaded for his life, but Noakes grabbed a halter rope they found in his cabin and looped a noose around Selak's neck. They dragged him out of his cabin and into a canyon on the property, where they chose a tree, tossed the end of the rope over a branch, and strung up the elderly man, hanging him until he strangled to death.

When they ransacked his cabin and ripped up the floor, however, they came up with little besides disappointment: a paltry $75, plus some old coins they did not recognize as worth anything beyond their face value, and some clothing that they took as well. The two men came away dissatisfied with the entire affair, although they had finally gained the right-of-way they had wanted, in order to trespass on Selak's property—now a small comfort compared with the expected fortune they had not acquired.

When Selak had not been seen for several days, some of his neighbors went to his cabin on July 25 to see if he was ill. Instead, they found Selak's belongings tossed and the room torn apart, and no sign of the elderly man. They alerted law enforcement immediately, fearing that something dreadful must have happened to Selak, and police and ranger Fred McLaren, who lived nearby, began a thorough investigation, even bringing in experts from other towns to examine the crime scene and determine who might have been inside. No clues came to light right away, and heavy rains for several days hampered efforts to search the countryside for Selak's body, making the case even more baffling. Soon Selak's nephew, S. R. Oliver of Denver, offered a $2,000 reward for any information leading to Selak, dead or alive.

Newspapers continued to carry stories about the great fortune that must have been stolen from under the floorboards. One referred to the missing man as a "money lender," and repeated the rumor that he had an aversion to banks and kept his money hidden in his cabin.

A few days later, Arthur Osborne and Ray Noakes went into Grand Lake and did some business with local stores. In one shop, they paid for their purchases with the old coins they had stolen from Selak. The proprietor recognized the antiques and knew that Selak was a collector, so he called the police, essentially sealing their case against the men they had suspected were the culprits all along.

On August 12, officers picked up Osborne and Noakes, as well as Osborne's father Alonzo, and two other men, Barney McCoy and Gerald Reese, and brought them in for questioning. McCoy and Reese, who had nothing to do with Selak's death, were subsequently released.

With the arrests came another development: the appointment of an administrator for Selak's estate. Newspapers reported that the estate might be worth between $65,000 and $200,000—not the rumored half million, but a princely amount that the killers would have loved to have found in his home.

Faced with a roomful of police and detectives, Noakes confessed quickly, both to the robbery and to participating in Selak's murder. He told the police officers where to find the body, still hanging from the tree where he and Osborne had left it three weeks earlier. Officers went to Selak's property with Noakes and a dog trained in locating bodies, searching "across trackless mountains, which for weeks have defied every effort of posses," the Associated Press waxed dramatically, and finally found the man's hanged remains in a canyon on his own property.

The two killers spent the rest of their short lives in prison, with their conviction recorded on March 7, 1927, and their execution a year later, on March 30. They had appealed the death sentence, but the State Supreme Court determined that it was indeed justified for their merciless act of murder.

"The murder of Fred Selak, 'the hermit of Grand County,' is one of the most gruesome and diabolical crimes in the history of Colorado," an impassioned editor of the Grand Junction *Daily Sentinel* declared the day after the details of the crime came out. "Surely there should be no delay on the part of the law in dealing with the two confessed murderers, and, if ever a crime justified the administering of capital punishment, then this particularly brutal murder affords that justification."

The method of capital punishment was hanging, an irony not lost on the press. "It was believed that Colorado's mechanical gallows, by which the doomed man hangs himself, was used," the United Press reported. "When the noose is placed around his neck and he steps on a trap, water is released from a keg. As the last drop falls out, a weight jerks the doomed man upward, breaking his neck."

This should be the end of the story, but there's one more thing. Selak's neighbors, still convinced that gold and cash must have been buried somewhere on his property, returned to his land in the spring of 1927 to search for it. If anyone found anything, they didn't tell the media. So as far as anyone knows, no evidence of the rumored wealth came to light. Today this land remains part of the national park, where digging is not permitted, even if you could be sure you were looking in the right place.

THE SECRET INSURANCE POLICY

Celebrating a wedding anniversary with a hike in Rocky Mountain National Park may sound like heaven for people who are passionate about the outdoors, but Toni Henthorn, a 50-year-old Denver ophthalmologist, did not belong in this category. She probably would not have chosen to take such a hike, as the terrain her 56-year-old husband Harold chose involved scrambling and high cliffs, at a time of year when trails could be made hazardous by snow and ice.

Nonetheless, the couple from Highlands Ranch, Colorado, set out on September 29, 2012, on a trail along the north side of Deer Mountain. As they made their way up the trail, they stopped on a ledge to take a photo of the spectacular view of colorful fall foliage and white-capped mountains. Suddenly, while Harold glanced away to read a text from their daughter's babysitter, Toni teetered, lost her footing, and fell headfirst over the edge, dropping 130 feet to the jagged boulders below.

Harold climbed down the cliff face as rapidly and carefully as he could, reaching Toni and moving her gently to a flatter spot where he could assess her injuries and try to resuscitate her. Later he told police that he had administered CPR, but his efforts could not save her. Forty-five minutes into his attempt to save her life, he called 911 from his cell phone. It was too late for Toni; she died at the bottom of the cliff.

At least, that's how Harold told it.

Rangers saw Toni Henthorn's death as a tragic accident, but all deaths in the park require investigation, so they began to assemble the facts. It didn't take long before things about this case began to look irregular.

First, Toni wore her wedding ring when she fell, but the high-value diamond in the setting was gone. "Ranger Paul Larson said he could not find the diamond in the craggy, secluded area where authorities found the body," the Associated Press reported. The gem was sizable—Harold readily told investigators that it was worth more than $30,000, adding that "the missing stone did not matter at all at this point." The missing diamond raised eyebrows among investigators, however, because Toni's hand did not take the brunt of the fall, and in fact showed little damage at all.

Harold knew the trail well, it turned out, as he had recently hiked it nine times before bringing his wife there. Detectives later considered this as evidence that Harold had researched trails in order to find a cliff that would provide a particularly deadly fall. "It didn't make sense that she would have gone willingly to such dangerous terrain," coroner James Wilkerson said later.

As with most deaths in the park, the coroner performed a thorough autopsy and determined that Toni died of "serious brain and chest injuries and severe blood loss," according to the AP, but despite what Henthorn had told dispatchers, Wilkerson found no evidence that Harold had performed CPR on his wife. "I couldn't determine whether it was an accident or whether, with some of the unusual or suspicious circumstances, it was a homicide," he said later in court.

Then, Harold's phone records didn't add up. His claim that he had a text from the babysitter and called 911 forty-five minutes later turned out to be false. Worse, he had a park trail map with him that included an X drawn at the exact point where Toni had fallen.

The investigation revealed two other pieces of information that pointed in one direction. First, Harold's first wife, Sandra Lynn Henthorn, had also died in a tragic accident twenty years earlier. She and Harold were changing a tire on their car when the auto slipped off the jack, crushing Sandra beneath the car's bulk. Coincidentally or not, this accident also took place shortly after Harold and Sandra's twelfth anniversary, and Harold collected a sizable life insurance payout. No one had investigated Sandra's death at the time, but as details of Toni's death began to contradict Harold's story, police reopened the earlier case.

Second—and this will surprise no one—Harold had taken out life insurance policies on Toni without her or their family's knowledge, listing Harold as the sole beneficiary. The payout would be a staggering $4.7 million.

After two years of collecting evidence, the Henthorn case resulted in Harold's arrest on November 6, 2014, for "willfully, deliberately, maliciously, and with premeditation and malice aforethought" committing first-degree murder. If convicted, he faced life in prison and a $250,000 fine.

Defense attorney Craig I. Truman called Toni's death a "tragic accident" in his opening statement, and addressed the question of Sandra Lynn's death as well. "The government thinks lightning never strikes twice," he said to the jury. "Wait until you see the evidence."

Truman described Harold's quick reaction to the fall in detail, finishing with, "As he tried to help her, he saw her life slipping away. He loved her very much." He told the jury that any inconsistencies in Harold's story at the accident scene were the result of hysteria from watching his wife die in his arms.

Assistant US Attorney Suneeta Hazra disagreed in her opening statement. "These deaths were not accidents," she said to the jury. She revealed that Toni's fall was not the first "accident" to befall her with Harold as the only witness. In 2011, while doing some construction work on their cabin in the mountains, a twenty-foot beam had dropped from the frame and struck her on the head, fracturing a vertebra. Harold's nine trips to the park before his day out with Toni provided strong evidence of intent, the prosecutor said. Harold sought the "perfect place to murder someone," where no one would see it happen and there was no chance of Toni surviving the fall.

The evidence convinced the federal jury, so on September 21, 2015, after ten hours of deliberation, they convicted Harold Henthorn of murdering his second wife. Applause erupted in the courtroom after the jury's dismissal, and one juror went so far as to hug Toni's mother, Yvonne Bertolet, as she left the courtroom.

The conviction came with a mandatory life sentence. "We are overjoyed with the verdict and relieved this won't happen to any other lady," said Barry Bertolet, Toni's brother, to Sadie Gurman of the Associated Press. "We don't have to worry anymore."

Rangers working with local law enforcement and the FBI played a vital role in the investigation, said chief ranger Mark Magnuson to Erin Udell of the *Fort Collins Coloradoan*. "When a violent crime such as this occurs in a national park, one of our nation's most treasured places, we work hard to ensure that those responsible are held accountable."

Many national parks have a homicide like this one in their history—one spouse pushing the other off a cliff and attempting to make it seem like an accident, thinking that they will collect a big reward when they cash in on the life insurance. The fact is that park rangers and investigators at insurance companies recognize these crimes for what they are, based on the collective knowledge gained from investigating many fraud attempts. This particularly insidious get-rich-quick scheme comes with consequences too severe to risk.

CHAPTER 11

Lost Forever: Missing Persons

On a sunny morning in August 1933, Joe Halpern, a 22-year-old employee of Yerkes Observatory in Green Bay, Wisconsin, and his friend Sam Garrick (or J. H. Garrich, in media reports) set out to hike to the top of Flattop Mountain. Halpern drove his Ford sedan to the Bear Lake trailhead and parked it there, and the two young men carried army knapsacks filled with sandwiches and fruit to the mountain's summit at 12,362 feet.

They had been on a road trip with Halpern's parents, Fanny and Solomon, crossing South Dakota and exploring many places before arriving at Rocky Mountain National Park for some rugged hiking. Once Joe and Sam arrived at the top of Flattop, Joe urged Sam to keep going, encouraging a traverse to the top of nearby Taylor Peak, at 13,153 feet, a route that would take them over Hallet Peak and Otis Peak before reaching Taylor. Sam said no, he'd had enough hiking at altitude and was ready to return to their campsite, so they agreed to meet back at Bear Lake trailhead at a specific time. Sam saw Joe go off up the trail to Taylor at about 2:30 p.m. and started to descend Flattop on his own, without a clue that he would never see his friend again.

Sam arrived back at the trailhead at about 6:30 p.m. Three hours passed as he waited at the car, and as darkness fell in the park, he realized that Joe had to be in some serious trouble. Sam notified the park's rangers, triggering a search that began at 10:00 p.m. as rangers with floodlights ventured up the trail to Taylor. They found no sign of Halpern that night, so at daybreak the search expanded, and over the next several days it expanded further, involving more than one hundred searchers who braved snowstorms and overnight drops in temperatures as they covered the mountain peaks.

Rocky Mountain's assistant superintendent John Preston led much of the effort, which involved members of the Civilian Conservation Corps (CCC) and many other volunteers. With no clues coming to light after four days of constant searching, he told the Associated Press that "he feared Halpern had perished." The young man had worn only a light shirt and pants and heavy boots when he'd headed toward Taylor Peak—not enough to keep him alive night after night in near-freezing cold. That being said, he underscored that the search would continue. As if to emphasize this, search officials put out a call to the Denver police department the following day to request bloodhounds and their handlers, but Denver did not have a canine force, so the police there referred the park to Colorado Springs.

As the search ended its fifth day, the *Green Bay Press-Gazette* sounded the first alarm that something fishy might be going on. "No Joseph Halpern is listed in Green Bay directories as far back as 1927, nor can anyone be found who knows of him," an unnamed reporter wrote.

His parents certainly knew him, however, and they had waited in Estes Park throughout the search for any evidence that their son might still be alive. At the end of the day on August 21, the park terminated its search, leaving the Halperns with no choice but to let go of the hope that he might yet emerge from the wilderness. They left Colorado and headed for their home in Chicago. Sam Garrick wrote to his brother Isador, Joe Halpern's best friend, and broke the news to him: "Joe Halpern disappeared in the mountains last Tuesday and nothing has been heard of him since . . . The last couple of days have been miserable out here with a deadly gloom prevailing. Mrs. Halpern cries all night long."

Park superintendent Edmund Rogers guessed that as darkness fell on Taylor Peak and its adjacent glacier on August 15, Joe Halpern had become lost and confused, and had fallen into a crevasse somewhere in the area. If this was the case, his body might never come to light.

This summation, of course, could not keep wild theories from simmering into a full rolling boil. Over the next several years, members of the Halpern family, their acquaintances, and a host of strangers began to entertain ideas that they felt might lead to Joe Halpern's "true" whereabouts, all based on the theory that he had used this solo hiking outing as his chance to escape a life in which he had felt trapped. These concepts came to the public consciousness again just recently in a feature story by Erin Udell in the *Windsor Beacon* in August 2018, in which the writer interviewed Joe's cousin, Roland Halpern, who continues to search for answers.

Roland told Udell that Joe's parents became convinced that Joe had ditched his life in academia to become some kind of transient, or even a sailor.

Then, in 1934, an acquaintance visited the couple and spotted a picture of Joe. Not knowing who he was, or what had happened to him, the acquaintance claimed that he saw Joe in the winter of 1933, begging for a meal outside of a Phoenix restaurant.

The Halperns sent Joe's picture to the restaurant owner, who gave it to the Phoenix police. The police then showed it to boys in a local transient camp who said, yes, Joe had been there months earlier under a different name.

The Halperns began to hope beyond hope once again, speculating that Joe may have taken a fall on the mountain and hit his head, giving him amnesia that made him wander out of the park and onto the streets. Or perhaps he had planned all of this, stealing away to a new life under an assumed name. More "clues" added fuel to this fire: A friend wrote to the FBI claiming that Joe now called himself Louis Hollenbuck and worked for the Lewis Brothers Circus. Another suggested that Joe had joined the CCC and was in a camp in Alliance, Nebraska, hale and healthy and doing physical labor.

The question remains, however: Would this 22-year-old man who still vacationed with his parents change his life so secretly and dramatically that he caused them tremendous pain and grief? Would he simply run off and join the circus or the CCC without ever contacting them again, and let them think that he had died alone on a mountain?

Roland Halpern told Udell that while he attempted to find credence in these and other theories, he didn't buy any of them. "My own feeling is that he never left the park," he said. "He was probably going to run down Tyndall Glacier and beat Sam back to the trailhead as a joke . . . and somewhere along the way, he got sucked down into the glacier or one of the cliffs."

If this is the case, and Joe met his end in a crack in a glacier, he may yet be found after all these decades. Climate change has increased the pace of glacial melt in the Rocky Mountains and elsewhere; as the glacier melts, it may reveal just what happened to Joe Halpern.

A FOUR-YEAR-OLD DISAPPEARS

On a jolly Independence Day weekend in 1938, Mr. and Mrs. William H. Beilhartz of Denver rented a cabin in Rocky Mountain National Park near the Roaring Fork River and brought their ten children, including their four-and-a-half-year-old son, Alfred, to the park. Early on their first morning in the park—Sunday, July 3— Mrs. Beilhartz spotted a blister on the bottom of Alfred's foot. She bandaged it carefully with gauze and adhesive and slipped a pair of new canvas shoes on the little boy's feet. By eight a.m., the family was outside and enjoying their first full day in the park.

Moments later, the pleasure of the great outdoors shattered for the Beilhartz family. Alfred had disappeared.

It took only a few minutes before the parents notified rangers that their son could not be found. They feared that the boy might have fallen into the river, as he had gone with his father to the river to wash that morning and might not have understood the danger of playing in the river alone.

When the first day of searching yielded only a child's leather shoe—not a canvas one, like the ones Alfred had put on minutes before he vanished—the search expanded significantly, with more than two hundred CCC workers, park rangers, and sheriff's deputies covering the ground around the campground and well beyond. Bloodhounds arrived from the Colorado State Penitentiary on the morning of July 5, picking up the scent at the last place where Alfred had been seen and following it along the edge of the river for a mile and a half to the junction of the Ypsilon Peak and Lawn Lake trails. Forest ranger Burt Fraser, limping from leg injuries he had suffered the day before when he fell down an embankment during the search, brought the dogs back to the beginning to see if they diverted from their course, but each time, the bloodhounds came to the same point on the banks of the river and stopped. The message was clear: Alfred must have fallen into the Roaring River.

Search supervisors devised a labor-intensive but surefire way to find the boy's body in the river: They would build a temporary makeshift dam and divert the river's waters from the campground to its junction with Fall River. This would reveal the river bottom, where the body should come to light fairly quickly.

The CCC men set to work building the dam out of sandbags, rocks, and logs, but when the water no longer flowed through the riverbed, they found only rocks, vegetation, and sand. They poked through the remaining pools of water with pikes and grappling hooks and crawled through mud and sand on all fours to move boulders and peer around them, to be sure the body had not lodged beneath the surface. "Weary mountain men who pushed forward Wednesday in the 80-hour search thru the timbered fastness of the Fall River country, eight miles above Estes Park, and along the boulder-studded bed of the Roaring River, diverted from its channel by a dam of bags, rocks and logs, failed to find a trace of Alfred Beilhartz," the Associated Press reported. "With each passing hour the mystery of what happened to the blond child becomes more baffling."

Some still clung to the idea that the boy had drowned, perhaps sweeping farther down this tributary and into the larger Fall River—though a wire net installed by the Public Service Company of Colorado would have caught the boy's body, even if he had done the impossible and somehow managed to pass five beaver dams between the campground and the net. To be sure that one of these dams had not snagged the body, they dynamited them, but this activity proved fruitless as well. Others thought he might have fallen prey to a black bear. "But clinging to an almost forlorn hope were his grief-stricken parents, who still insisted that the child had become lost in the heavy timber and was probably alive."

As a crew removed the temporary dam and restored the river's flow, the rest of the searchers began to comb through the surrounding forest even more carefully than they had before. "Every inch of the high country now will be covered," the *Greeley Daily Tribune* promised on July 7. "Already the workers have gone over an area ten miles square."

On July 8, park officials heard from William J. Eels, a radio appliance company employee from Denver, who described a child he had seen by himself on the slopes of Mount Chapin. "He and his wife saw a child on the mountain early last Sunday afternoon," the Associated Press reported. "Eels said he and his wife had walked far up the Old Fall River Road until they became tired. He said they stopped to rest, and then looking far up the mountainside, saw a boy sitting on a rock. When the couple climbed to the point near the rock, Eels said the child had disappeared. He expressed belief no child could have reached the spot without assistance."

By this time, the Beilhartz parents had come to the inevitable conclusion that their son had been kidnapped. Park superintendent David H. Canfield expressed reticence to accept that theory, however. "He considered the kidnap theory was born largely of their hope the child was still alive," the AP said.

Canfield did send fresh search parties of newly arrived CCC enrollees up the slope of Mount Chapin into the region known as Devil's Nest, even though "park officials were convinced it would be utterly impossible for him to have climbed alone to the high mountain spot where it was believed he might have been sighted," the AP reported. "Equipped with blankets and provided with lunches, these new searching parties, each carrying a portable radio set, were under orders to push on into the mountains until they had exhausted every hope of picking up a trail which might lead to the boy or his body." Eels himself returned to the point where he believed he had seen the boy, accompanied by US commissioner Wayne Hackett, chief park ranger J. Barton Herschler, and assistant park superintendent Don S. McLaughlin.

While the Devil's Nest search yielded no new information and no sign of Alfred, another discovery lent credence to the concept that the boy might have been taken out of the campground by an adult. Searchers discovered a discarded gauze bandage about a mile from the last place Alfred had been seen. The child's parents took this as conclusive proof that Alfred had not fallen into the river, declaring that Alfred disliked bandages and always tore them off. (This being decades before the use of DNA evidence to determine if the bandage was indeed from Alfred's foot, the Beilhartzes surmised this solely by instinct, and faith.)

The following day, a report came in from Mrs. C. A. Linch of Big Spring, Nebraska, that she had seen a man walking along a highway in her state with a blond five-year-old boy who she believed looked like Alfred. Colorado authorities asked Nebraska officers to investigate, but the child was not Alfred.

On the night of July 12, when three hundred CCC searchers had not produced any sign of the child, Superintendent Canfield called an end to the search. He assigned selected CCC enrollees to watch the Fall and Roaring Rivers in case Alfred's body came to the surface, and he announced that the Public Service Company of Colorado intended to drain the Cascade Dam on the Fall River to see if Alfred's body might be in the pool beneath it. The formal search activity, however, was over. The Beilhartzes returned home to grieve for their son, although they had not given up hope that he was still alive and might one day return to them.

Then, on Sunday evening, November 27, a man in a messenger's cap and overalls knocked on the Beilhartzes' door in Denver. The man handed Beilhartz an envelope and walked away. When Beilhartz opened it, he cried out, "What is this?"

The *Greeley Tribune* summed up the contents of the note:

We have gone out west. We are now out of money. Your boy has not taken to us. We will return him to you if you will secure $500 in old $1, $5, and $10 bills and place them in a kettle at the corner of East Thirty-Second Avenue and Syracuse Street.

Beilhartz and his son Matthew ran from the house to try to stop the man, but they could not find him. They came back and read the rest of the note with the family gathered around their father. It said that if he followed the instructions, Alfred would be returned twenty-four hours later.

At first the family decided they would handle this privately and not inform the police. By morning, however, they realized that this might be some kind of extortion scheme, so they got in touch with authorities and made a realistic plan.

"Monday night six carloads of officers, including the crack detectives of the police department, went to the scene," the *Tribune* reported. "It is wide open country around the Beilhartz home, located near the municipal airport. Barricades of police cars were set up to block all roads leading out of the district. Detectives and patrolmen hid among the hillocks and lay in wait."

Sure enough, a car drove up and stopped at the intersection the note had specified. Beilhartz placed a kettle at the corner. It had no money in it; instead, he had written a note: "If you will give me any proof that you have my boy, I will pay the money."

Police watched and waited as a man pushed a dog out of the car in front of him, then got out himself. They could see a woman in the car as well. They waited silently until Beilhartz, hiding with one of the officers, could stand it no longer and yelled, "Stop!"

The man shoved the dog back into the car, climbed in himself and closed the door, and sped off. He could not go far, however, as police barricades stood in his path. The police took the man, woman, and dog in for questioning but soon let them go when it became clear they were just a couple out walking their dog.

The police turned the case over to the FBI for further investigation. "We do not believe Alfred is alive," said acting captain of detectives O. A. Carter to the *Tribune.* "We believe this whole thing is a cruel hoax. Naturally, Beilhartz and his wife have clung to the hope that Alfred is still alive. They would be most willing to pay if they could get their boy back. The father told us he would mortgage his home, do anything to get the money. This, we believe, is just a vicious thing without a single bit of truth behind the statement that the boy is alive."

He added, "Every resource of this department will be put forward to find the writer of the note."

In the end, the extortionists were never found, though it became clear to the Beilhartzes that the note had not come from a legitimate source who intended to return their son. A year after Alfred's disappearance, as the United Press news service checked in with the family, Beilhartz remained firm in his conviction that his son was alive. "I know he didn't fall in the river," he said. "I'm confident he is in some distant city today. We have his toys just as he left them. Someday we will find him—somewhere."

Alfred Beilhartz has never been found. If alive, he would be in his eighties today.

An Aggie Outing

When students from the hiking club at Colorado Agriculture and Mining (A&M) College boarded a bus for an all-day outing in

Rocky Mountain on Sunday, October 9, 1949, they numbered forty in all. They broke into smaller groups to head out from Grand Lake to hike to Bear Lake, a rugged, eighteen-mile hike over the Continental Divide.

Two sophomores, Bruce W. Gerling, from Phoenix, Arizona, and David O. Devitt of Arvada, Colorado, joined nine club members for the challenging hike. This was their first hike with the club, and they hoped that when they finished it successfully, they would be pledged to the club and become permanent members.

As the eleven hikers approached a shelter on Flattop Mountain, a high point on the trail at 12,300 feet, Bruce and David decided that they had gone far enough. They stopped at the shelter for a rest and told the others that they would catch up with them.

As we have seen throughout this book, October hiking in Rocky Mountain can be unpredictable, and this day was no exception. The nine remaining hikers soon found themselves in the midst of a snowstorm, covering the trail and clouding visibility. They continued to the end of the trail, however, and felt particularly grateful to see the bus waiting for them there. The students clambered onto the bus and out of the wind and weather, and the driver returned them to campus on schedule.

Not until Monday morning did the hikers realize that Bruce and David had not been on the bus the night before.

The hikers believed at first that the missing boys must have turned back to Grand Lake. They reasoned that Bruce and David had been wearing plenty of warm clothing and carried packs with food and supplies, so they had probably holed up somewhere overnight and expected to reconnect with transportation to campus that day. Perhaps this was all some kind of prank by the two sophomores as payback for not noticing that they were not on the bus when it drove away. Whatever their hopeful suppositions, however, the club members did not notify authorities about their missing friends until late in the day on Monday. By then the trails and roads in the Flattop Mountain section of the park had become impassable because of heavy snow and whiteout conditions.

When Tuesday brought fresh snow and more driving winds, park employees braved the blizzard and set up a search headquarters at Bear Lake, sending two search parties up the trail to look for the missing students. Searchers set up a portable transmitter and gave walkie-talkies to the leaders of each party, with plans to help guide them to specific places on the mountain, but an incoming snowstorm soon cut off the transmitter and prevented contact with the searchers. No trace of the boys came to light on the first day. "Some searchers have expressed fear that Devitt and Gerling fell into Tyndall Glacier from the steep slopes of Flattop," the United Press reported on October 12.

A fall into a glacial crevasse can kill a hiker in the space of just a few hours. Wedged between walls of ice with no climbing gear to free oneself, a hiker may be unhurt by the fall but still be in grave danger. Body temperature begins to drop slowly, then faster as the hiker succumbs to the enveloping cold. Even if he calls for help at first, the trapped hiker loses the ability to speak or move, and eventually perishes from hypothermia.

After two days with no sign of the boys' whereabouts, the park called in trained mountaineers from Camp Carson, the US Army training center in Colorado Springs, to expand the search area and refresh the teams on the mountain. The army responded with a contingent from the 14th Regimental Combat Team (RCT). "Rocky Mountain National Park officials held little hope the pair would be found alive after three nights of subzero weather and howling winds which froze [the] hands and feet of searchers," the Associated Press reported.

The enemies of the search, park officials knew, were the four- and five-foot-high snowdrifts that piled up all over the mountain, filling in crevices and obscuring any sign of where the boys might have gone. "We're just groping," chief ranger Barton Herschler told the Associated Press. "We've been all over the trails twice from end to end. We've gone over every conceivable path they might have taken . . . If anyone fell in any of those places, we wouldn't know it."

Nonetheless, the search continued as Bruce's father, W. J. Gerling, arrived from Phoenix, and David's parents, Mr. and Mrs. Oliver Devitt, waited at Bear Lake for any word about their son. Gerling told reporters at the Denver airport that he was disappointed the search had not begun sooner, responding to the news that leaders of the club had not reported the boys missing until late in the day on Monday. Thursday became the first day that searchers did not have to battle snow and wind just to stay on mountain trails; Herschler told the media that while they had done an "excellent job" of canvassing the mountain and surrounding area, searchers found nothing that would point them to the boys' whereabouts.

By the weekend, as many as 150 people had joined the effort, but the deep snow and continued lack of clues persisted on Saturday and Sunday. Chief ranger Herschler held a meeting late in the day on Sunday, October 16, and announced that he saw no choice but to call off the search on Monday, October 17, with the assumption that the boys had not survived and that their bodies could not be found until the snow melted the following summer. Devitt's and Gerling's parents attended the meeting, as did Lieutenant E. C. Gulczynski, commander of the Camp Carson search team, and J. C. Clevenger, dean of students at Colorado A&M.

A further search "would not be worthwhile," Clevenger said to the media after the meeting. "Hope of finding the two students alive is no longer held." Even so, members of the Aggie Hiking Club vowed to continue hunting for the two boys.

Bruce's father managed to accept the chief ranger's decision. He himself had climbed to the crest of Tyndall Glacier and seen the precipitous drop that may have been the boys' last scenic view, ending in jagged, icy terrain below. "If the boys were down there, there's no hope they will be found until next spring, if they are ever found," he said to the *Miami Silver Belt* in his hometown in Arizona.

To this day, no sign of Bruce Gerling or David Devitt has ever come to light. Whether they lost the trail in a snowstorm and fell into a crevice in the rock, vanished into a crack in Tyndall Glacier, or dropped to the bottom of a canyon, their remains are hidden somewhere in the wilderness. If snowmelt has ever revealed their final resting place, no one has stood in the right place at the right moment to find them.

THE LONE SKIER

What makes a person decide to ski into the winter wilderness alone? It seems like a rookie mistake, the sort of adventure a young skier on his or her first overnight trip might find daring and exciting. This was not the case with 27-year-old Rudi Moder, however, an "experienced winter mountaineer," according to the American Alpine Club's accident report, "with two years' experience in the German Army Mountain Corps and two Himalayan expeditions, very fit, and a strong ski mountaineer."

Originally from Augsburg, West Germany, Moder skied into the Zimmerman Lake area with friends on February 13, 1983, with the intention of setting up a base camp at Ditch Camp 3 deep in the park and making day trips from there. At about nine a.m., he left his friends and skied toward Thunder Pass, disappearing into the snow-whitened landscape.

Moder expected to return after spending two or three nights in the backcountry, but six days after he had departed, he still had not come home. On February 19, Moder's roommate Hans Moosmueller called the Larimer County Sheriff's Office and reported Moder missing. By the next morning, search teams had moved into the field and begun a systematic overview of the route he had told friends he would take. They hit their first major clue right away: an untouched food cache Moder had placed at the mouth of Box Canyon, giving them hope that they would locate him nearby. The fact that he had not returned to the cache, however, reduced their hopes of finding him alive.

The following day, the searchers discovered a snow cave just fifty feet from the food cache. Heavy snow had fallen two nights before, so only a small hole gave away the cave's location, indicating that Moder had not been in it recently. His sleeping bag, backpack, and cooking gear remained inside the cave, so if he had run into trouble somewhere in the area, he didn't have the benefit of warmth the bag and stove might have provided.

Sixteen ground searchers and two helicopters investigated Box Canyon but discovered nothing there. He had to be somewhere in the vast expanse of the surrounding Never Summer Mountains— an area so large that his whereabouts might never be known.

"We don't know how much food he had with him," spokesman Glen Kaye told the Associated Press. "We found nothing [Wednesday] to lead us to believe he is alive if he is in the area." Moder's skis, poles, and day pack never turned up either, suggesting that he still had all of these things with him.

A set of ski tracks leading up to a mountain summit and back down gave search teams hope—until they discovered evidence of a fresh avalanche in the area. Their probe of this debris for articles of clothing and Moder's body produced no sign of the man, even with additional assistance from a dog trained to find bodies in an avalanche.

Indeed, after four days of intensive searching, involving sixty-five people and four helicopters, no new evidence of Rudi Moder or his death ever came to light. The park ended the organized search on February 23. Searchers returned to the area with bloodhounds after the summer thaw and made another unsuccessful attempt to find his body.

"There are a number of avalanche fields out there, and he could have been swept into deep forest," noted Carol Downing, administrator of the operations division of the Larimer County Sheriff's Office in Fort Collins, in response to an online posting in 2011 requesting information about the case. Another searcher in her office remembered "a large number of extremely deep crevasses where the snow never quite melts," which might be likely places for a body to remain hidden for decades.

With the lack of a body, however, it's conceivable that something else entirely took place in February 1983. Rumors circulated for years that Moder did not die at all, but instead staged his disappearance and left the area to begin a new life under a different identity. No one can prove this theory, of course, but speculation ran rampant after the formal search ended.

Still, for more than a decade after the event, rangers operated under a standing order: "Keep your eyes open for Rudi," ranger Jim Richardson told the Associated Press in January 1995. Richardson even once thought he might have found him, but the object that looked like a clothed skeleton turned out to be a rock formation with some peculiar coloration. "The myth and mystery surrounding Rudi Moder, an enduring figure in park folklore, was still intact," the news service said.

We may be on the verge of solving all of these mysteries, if the planet continues to warm and glaciers and snowfields melt completely for the first time in eons. Already glacial melt on Mount Everest has revealed the remains of several climbers who perished years ago while attempting to attain the summit. In the Swiss Alps, a couple who had gone out to feed their cattle in 1942—Marcelin and Francine Dumolin—disappeared without a trace. In 2017, their bodies emerged when a glacier melted away, revealing that they had fallen into a crevasse and died there. It's entirely possible that the bodies of Rudi Moder, Bruce Gerling, David Devitt, and Joe Halpern may come to the surface as well, when that surface lowers to whatever depth swallowed them so many years ago.

As of this writing, one more person is missing and presumed dead in the park.

On March 3, 2019, rangers discovered a vehicle parked at the Glacier Gorge trailhead that had clearly been there for several days. They determined the owner and contacted the family of James Pruitt, a 70-year-old man from Etowah, Tennessee, to see if they knew of his whereabouts. His family confirmed that they had not heard from him since February 28 at about ten a.m., and that he was indeed visiting Rocky Mountain National Park.

The rangers knew they had a difficult search ahead of them, as two feet of snow had fallen since the last time anyone had heard from James Pruitt. The only clue the family could provide was a description of his clothing: a blue jacket, a red or orange hat, and boots with microspikes.

The search began right away, involving drainage areas for Glacier Gorge, Loch Vale, and Glacier Creek. Larimer County Search and Rescue dog teams joined the park service's search-and-rescue operation, as did Diamond Peaks Ski Patrol, the Colorado Search and Rescue Board, and Rocky Mountain Rescue Group. As day after day produced no sign of the elderly man, the search area widened, and the State of Colorado sent a multi-mission aircraft to perform aerial reconnaissance.

After six days with no additional information, the park called an end to the full-scale search effort, with the commitment to continue on a more limited basis as new information arose. "Patrols will continue to occur in the search area, and further actions may be considered as conditions improve," park spokesperson Kyle Patterson told the *Estes Park Trail-Gazette* on March 15. "Reported clues will be investigated as appropriate."

Today James Pruitt is still missing in the park. What his plans may have been when he walked away from his vehicle on February 28 are anyone's guess.

CHAPTER 12

Strange Circumstances: Unusual Deaths

Not every death in a national park fits neatly into a specific category. Some people find themselves in precarious situations while participating in activities they've enjoyed hundreds of times before without incident. Others fall victim to accidents so startling that they might be considered "acts of God" by the pious. A select few did something completely silly and paid a terrible price. In this last chapter, you'll find a veritable potpourri of surprising, strange, and uncommon ways to die in Rocky Mountain National Park.

SLICKER SHOCK

Mrs. Emily Foster Russell, 40, of Webster Groves, Missouri, and her friend, Mrs. Roy Russell, chose to explore the route to Old Man Mountain on horseback during their visit to the park on July 28, 1938. Their day began pleasantly enough, but as they rode along the trail, the park's characteristic afternoon rain shower began to fall.

Emily pulled a slicker out of her pack and started to put it on. As she moved in her saddle and the slicker's surface caught the light, the combination of unfamiliar sensations startled the horse. The steed reared and jumped, throwing Emily to the ground, her back and head slamming against the rocks lining the trail.

Seeing the accident and finding Emily unconscious on the ground, Mrs. Roy Russell turned her horse around and rode back to the Elkhorn Hotel to get help. "Several men started from the hotel," the Associated Press reported the next day. "When they carried the victim half a mile down the trail, a ranger party, including Walter O'Brien, Leonard Volz and Ernest Field, arrived with a stretcher."

They were soon joined by CCC enrollees who took turns carrying the stretcher three miles to the road and directly to Estes Park Hospital. "Hospital doctors said Mrs. Russell suffered a basal skull fracture and her chances to recover are 'one in five,'" the AP reported bleakly. The doctors' prediction came to pass: Emily Russell died the following day.

Two other people died in the park when their horses threw them to the ground, though details are scant about these. Albert Furch, a 49-year-old visitor from Chicago, died on July 13, 1945, when he fell from his agitated horse on the trail from Loch Vale. A quarter of a century later, local business owner Herbert Kuhn, who was 42 at the time, was out for a morning ride when his horse threw him and pinned him against a tree on July 24, 1969, a position that essentially crushed him to death.

A TREE FALLS IN THE FOREST

Even the park calls this November 2007 incident "bizarre," according to reporter Trevor Hughes of the *Fort Collins Coloradoan*.

On November 28, 2007, William Hudson, 68, of Boulder and his friend Carl Cox, also 68, went for a hike along the Sandbeach Lake Trail in the Wild Basin section of the park. They were two miles down the trail when the wind gusted suddenly, blowing hard enough to break off and push over a dead Douglas fir tree with a weakened trunk. In an almost cartoonish moment of extraordinarily bad luck, the tree fell directly onto Hudson.

"It was very rotten and punky," Larry Frederick, a spokesperson for the park, told Hughes. "This is bizarre, a rare, rare incident."

Cox took a blow as well, stunning him momentarily, but he soon recovered and moved to help his friend. Hudson did not respond to Cox's attempts to revive him, so Cox, painfully aware that he had suffered a back injury, started hiking back to the trailhead to get help.

Rangers arrived on the scene soon after, and they completed the job of removing Hudson's body from the trail at about 8:15 p.m. Cox received treatment at Estes Park Hospital and went home the same night.

An investigation indicated that the tree stood about thirty feet from the trail and broke off roughly fifteen feet from the ground. "Frederick said the tree may have died as many as fifteen years ago, and was not likely killed by the ongoing pine bark beetle infestation, which strikes mostly lodgepole pine," Hughes continued. "The portion of the tree that struck the two men was about 10 inches in diameter."

DROPPING A LOADED GUN

Why Frank Stryker, a 24-year-old man from Cedar County, Iowa, felt he needed to carry a pistol on his ascent of Longs Peak in August of 1889 is anyone's guess. Perhaps he believed he might have a run-in with a wild animal—a black bear or a mountain lion, for example—or maybe he expected an altercation with Carlyle Lamb, the guide he and his two brothers had hired to take them to the summit. He may even have been suspicious of other climbers, if any were on the mountain that day, thinking that one of them could attempt to rob him of whatever else he might be carrying. Or perhaps carrying a gun was nothing more than habit.

Whatever his reasoning, Frank and his brothers climbed to the summit on August 28, spent about an hour on the level slab at the top, and started down. "Frank Stryker, taking his pistol from his pocket, placed it in his belt in front," an article later that week in the *Wichita Eagle* tells us. "But, stumbling over a ledge, the pistol went off, mortally wounding him. He walked 300 feet and fell."

Stryker clung to life for several hours as his brothers kept careful watch over him. As darkness fell on the mountain, however, the temperature dropped, and the three uninjured men, clad only in light clothing, shivered in the cold while they watched Frank's life ebb away. At about ten p.m., he breathed his last, and the others realized that they were stranded in place until first light, when they could begin to carry their brother down the mountain for burial at home in Iowa.

Now a snowstorm blew their way, making conditions on the mountain nothing short of miserable for the unprepared hikers. By morning, with fresh snow on the trail and miles to go, they picked up their brother's body and carried it between them, traipsing three miles until they arrived at the base of the mountain and could arrange for the use of a horse.

"It was on this peak, a few years ago, that Miss Carrie Welton, the New York heiress, lost her life and this same Lamb was acting as her guide," the news coverage reminded readers. Carlyle Lamb could not be blamed for this particular incident, but it's clear that the Welton death four years earlier had tarnished his reputation for the long term.

When a Lion Attacks
The park has recorded only one death from an animal attack in its century-long existence.

On July 17, 1997, 10-year-old Mark Miedema got ahead of his parents, Kathy and David Miedema, and his 6-year-old sister on their return hike along the North Inlet Trail, and it's no wonder he did. On this perfect hiking day, they had chosen a trail with a grazing area on one side, where it would be easy to see deer and elk. On the other side, thick foliage and tall trees hosted small animals that delighted children with their quick movements and curiosity about people. Birdsong filled the air. The family planned to enjoy a carefree day on this woodland trail.

As Mark ran to see if chipmunks and squirrels had eaten some nuts he'd placed there earlier that day, however, he caught the eye of a mountain lion in the forest.

"What we think may have happened—and this is pure theory —is that unfortunately Mark came along at the wrong time when the lion was in a hunting mood," park spokesperson Doug Caldwell told the Associated Press later that day. "Mountain lions don't distinguish between humans and deer and elk."

Maybe Mark stopped and bent over to tie his shoe, making him appear smaller and easy to catch, or maybe he did nothing at all to look like prey to the eighty-eight-pound lion. The animal came at him in a flash of speed and agility, grabbing the boy and dragging him off into the woods.

David and Kathy sprang into action. They ran at the big cat to fight for their son, scaring the lion enough that it let go of Mark and skulked away. Kathy, a registered nurse, set to work on Mark to stop the bleeding from the places the lion had penetrated with teeth and claws. Another hiker who had seen the altercation used a cell phone to call for help. Rangers with medical training arrived and did their best to revive the unconscious boy, but in the end, Mark died in the forest in his parents' arms.

Grand County coroner Dave Schoenfeld announced two days later that Mark did not die from the wounds he sustained, but from "respiratory failure brought on by massive asphyxiation." He had choked on his own vomit during the attack, and was probably dead before his parents had reached him and the lion. "The mountain lion didn't have that much time to cause that much trauma," he said. "Normally, he would have survived it."

"We are deeply mourning our loss of Mark," the Miedemas said in a statement. "We will miss his vibrant smile and his boundless energy, but we are a family of strong faith. We are certain Mark is safe in the arms of Jesus."

Park officials sent a team to the trail to find the lion and destroy it. "The lion, a female without cubs, eventually was tracked down and killed in the area of the attack," the AP reported. "Tests at Colorado State University will confirm whether the mountain lion is the one that attacked Mark." Caldwell told the media that the team found no other lions in the area, and that the deer in the grazing area showed no alarm, as they would have if they had known a predator was nearby. "We felt confident we had killed the animal responsible for the attack, and we reopened the trail for hiking."

The rare attack awakened pubic curiosity about mountain lions and their prevalence in Colorado's parks and open spaces. The media appeared only too happy to explore the topic, and to stoke the blaze of fear that the incident triggered—fear made even more urgent by a second attack that occurred in the state in the same week. In that event, a 4-year-old boy from France was mauled by a cougar at Mesa Verde National Park well south of Rocky Mountain, close to the border with Arizona.

"Mountain lions in Colorado are losing their fear of people as the parks become more crowded and people build more and more homes in the big cats' habitat," the AP began, in an article published the day after Mark Miedema's death. It went on to quote Todd Malmsbury of the Colorado Division of Wildlife, who said, "I'm not arguing in favor of hunting them, but when they were hunted regularly, they had a good reason to fear us. Now they don't."

This dire statement made it sound as if neighborhoods would soon be overrun by mountain lions looking for children to prey upon, but this did not become the case, said Don Hunter, science director of the Rocky Mountain Cat Conservancy, who has conducted extensive research on mountain lions in and around the park. "There have been maybe 18 or 20 mountain lion attacks in the last 100 years in the US and Canada," he said in an interview with me in August 2018. "It's not normal for lions to eat people. They don't think of us as prey. When the natural prey of big cats becomes diminished, they tend to seek out domestic livestock or sometimes small pets—not humans."

Lions have been in Colorado for about ten million years, Hunter said, and they evolved to eat a variety of prey, mostly small mammals and long-necked ungulates, including deer. When humans came along, lions feared them and learned to be secretive. "There's a lion within half a mile of us now," he said as we sat on the porch of the Fall River Visitor Center. "It's the most widely distributed mammal in the world, because it's in North and South America. They've lived with people for a very long time, and they don't like people. Lions here are no different than anywhere else."

The death of Mark Miedema triggered the park to engage Hunter, who spent much of his career researching snow leopards in Asia, to study mountain lions in the area. "Our study showed the population is healthy, especially in Estes Valley—there's lots and lots of food," he said. "We cataloged the first lion in 2003, and found it spends as much time outside of the park as inside the park. The deer and elk roam around the valley everywhere—we have tracked our lions right to the edges of town; they're around people all the time. So if the lions saw people as prey, they would be eating someone every day."

If someone is attacked by a lion, the defense is entirely different from a bear attack, Hunter said. "Do not play dead," he warned.

"Scream, yell, kick, punch. Many attacks have been thwarted. You fight, and the lion sometimes gives up."

DEATHS ON SKIS, TUBES, AND A TOBOGGAN

Not everyone climbs mountains in winter to make the most of the season. More traditional winter sports—from riding a toboggan down steep hills to skiing the packed powder on groomed slopes—come to life in Rocky Mountain National Park each year, with thousands of people visiting to embrace the short days and icy temperatures.

Considering the large numbers of people who make Rocky Mountain their snow-covered winter destination, it's truly remarkable that only four of them have not lived to see another spring.

The first death from winter sport came back in 1927—and it actually happened on a Sunday in late June, while snow still clung to many slopes in the Horseshoe Park area. Denver stenographer Flora Napier, 39, visiting with a larger group of friends and picnicking in the park, joined three other women for a toboggan ride down one of the Hidden Valley ski slopes. The sheer novelty of tobogganing in summer must have been an irresistible attraction to the happy group of women.

In an instant, however, the toboggan encountered some obstacle on the slope and rolled sideways, dumping the women into the more treacherous surrounding terrain. Flora struck her head on a boulder. "Miss Napier's skull was fractured and her body badly mangled against jagged masses of snow-covered rocks as she hurtled down the mountainside," the Associated Press reported. She died at the scene.

"The other three girls managed to save themselves by burrowing into the snow, but the heavy toboggan crashed into them," the AP continued. All three went to the hospital in Fort Collins for treatment and recovered from the ordeal.

Scott Thomas Anderson, a 21-year-old man from Mason City, Iowa, arrived in Rocky Mountain National Park in early February of 1985, ready to take on the Hidden Valley Ski Area. This popular skiing destination within the park operated from 1955 to 1991, offering a two-thousand-foot vertical rise and a base lodge with T-bars, Poma lifts, and a double chair to the top of the slopes.

On a busy Sunday, February 3, Scott and his brother Bill started down one of the runs meant for experts. Scott picked up too much speed on the way down, and instead of pulling up short at the bottom, he became airborne, flying over the embankment and the road and hitting a snowbank on the far side.

Many witnesses saw the accident and alerted the resort management, who came to his aid immediately and called for an ambulance to take him to Estes Park Medical Center. Scott died at 2:40 p.m. of a head injury sustained from the impact, becoming the only fatality in the history of Hidden Valley.

One other skier died in the park, but under very different circumstances. Forty-year-old Matthieu Chesaux of Boulder made the interesting choice to ski a glacier on his own on September 30, 2008. When he did not return home at the end of the day, friends who knew his plans called park rangers to investigate and then went out on their own to see if they could find him.

They discovered their friend's broken body on Taylor Glacier on Wednesday morning, October 1. "According to James A. Wilkerson IV, MD, Larimer County Deputy Coroner / Medical Examiner, Chesaux died of massive trauma from multiple blunt force injuries," a report on the ClimbingLife website said. He had clearly taken a fall at a significant rate of speed, ending with deadly impact on the ice and rocks at the end of the slide.

In the winter of 1988, Brenda Butrick, 30, and her family came to the park from their home in Longmont for an afternoon of snow-tubing down their favorite slope in the Beaver Meadows area. "They had used the same area before," said Glen Kaye, park spokesperson, to the media later that day. No two days in the park are alike, however, so perhaps the icy crust over the snow was thicker and frictionless that day, or perhaps the light or sun obscured the hazards ahead.

Whatever the reason, Brenda watched as her husband Chris took the first run or two down the hill, and then she "went down by herself headfirst," Kaye said.

Brenda hit a pine tree at top speed, with her head making first impact. She was pronounced dead at Estes Park Medical Center later in the day.

"We have a variety of hazards that we try to make people aware of," said Kaye. "Tubing is a dangerous sport." That being said, this was the first tubing death in the park's history, and there's only one other in park records.

On February 27, 2005, 17-year-old Omar Mehdawi and a group of friends from the Islamic Center of Fort Collins came to the park for a snow-tubing day. They chose a slope near Bear Lake and began riding their tubes down it. Mehdawi, who was known for his athletic prowess and excelled in indoor soccer and basketball, probably took the hill at as fast a speed as he could manage while staying in control.

On his last run, however, he hit a tree. The severe head trauma left him in a coma for a week, until he died on the following Saturday.

Science teacher Jeff Bibbey described Mehdawi as a student who was "always challenging himself," one who planned to pursue a degree in electrical engineering at Colorado State University after graduating from high school that spring.

"We strongly believe that Omar is in a better place," said his mother, Iman El Kiweri, to reporters Courtney Lingle and Kevin

Duggan at the *Fort Collins Coloradoan.* "This is a principle of our Islamic faith—we have to be patient when our beloved dies because this is the way to paradise . . . We miss him in this life, but we know we all die, and after that, we will meet again and be together in eternity."

The Monday after his death, Mehdawi's classmates wore terrycloth headbands embroidered with "Omar #1" in tribute to the friend they had lost. They gave the headbands away in exchange for donations to the Islamic Center in Omar's name, and held a fund-raising event the following Saturday as well. In May, at the Rocky Mountain High School graduation ceremony, students decorated an empty seat with flowers as a reminder of their absent friend.

EPILOGUE

How to Stay Alive in Rocky Mountain National Park

Are you ready to make the commitment to seeing all that is magnificent in Rocky Mountain National Park—its mountain peaks, snowfields, glaciers, forests, valleys, wildflowers, lakes, rivers, and scenic roads—and living to tell the tale?

It's easier than you may think after reading this book, so let me remind you again: More than four million people visit Rocky Mountain every year, and only five or six people per year actually die in the park. In some years, no one dies at all. By following a few simple rules and taking some entirely reasonable precautions, you can make the most of your visit and come home with plenty of photos and accounts of your adventures, and maybe some new summits obtained.

Here are the basic guidelines you need, based on the advice of the National Park Service, Rocky Mountain park management, and experts in hiking and climbing safety.

AROUND THE PARK

- **Stay on designated trails.** Most people are not prepared to venture off-trail into the backcountry, and you can see plenty of marvelous sights from the established trails throughout the park. Note the directions you'll see on trail signs, and pay attention to blazes and markers to be sure you're still on your intended trail.

- **Stay behind protective fences, guardrails, and barriers.**
  Barriers are placed for your protection, *not* to keep you from
  enjoying the park. The moment you step beyond a guardrail
  or boundary, you risk injury.

- **Watch out for traffic.** When you stop at a pull-off along
  the side of a road, keep an eye out for oncoming traffic and
  fast-moving vehicles, just as you would on any busy street.
  Drivers gazing out over a spectacular view may not see you
  on the road, so watch out for people who are not watching
  out for you.

- **If you're driving, watch the road.** It's easy to be distracted
  by everything there is to see in Rocky Mountain, so if
  you want more time to enjoy a view, pull over into an area
  designated for that purpose and stop. Pedestrians, bicyclists,
  and people on horseback are everywhere along the park's
  major roadways—so keep an eye out.

- **Enjoy wildlife from a safe distance.** While there has been
  only one death in the park because of an encounter with an
  animal, bighorn sheep, black bears, elk, mule deer, and moose
  all can feel threatened when humans get too close. Many of
  these animals will charge or attack you if you try to get in
  close for a photo. To get great photos, shoot with a telephoto
  lens from a safe distance away. If you're in your car and you
  spot wildlife from the road, pull over at the first available area
  and take your photos from inside your car. Above all, do not
  feed any wildlife in the park.

Hiking—Frontcountry or Backcountry

- **Don't hike or climb alone.** You've read in these pages about the many people who venture into the wilderness by themselves or break off from a group and are never seen alive again. I can't stress this enough: High mountain peaks and backcountry trails are not places to be enjoyed alone. The lure of solitude in the wild may be very attractive, but many lone hikers described in this book went missing for weeks, months, or even indefinitely. Hiking, climbing, and camping with at least one other person can make the difference between a great day on the trail and a misadventure that ends in tragedy.

- **File your plan with a ranger.** If you're planning a lengthy wilderness hike or climb, you will need a backcountry permit to camp—which means that you will file a hiking plan at a ranger station or visitor center. Even if you don't plan to camp, it's a good idea to let rangers know where you intend to go and when you plan to return. With a quarter of a million acres of land to search, the plan you file will allow rangers to narrow the field quickly if they need to locate you in a crisis.

- **Listen to rangers.** People who work in the park daily know which trails may be compromised by weather events, where avalanches and rockslides may be possible, where forest fires are burning within the park, what kind of weather is expected in the near term, and whether it's advisable to attempt the hike or climb you have in mind. If they warn you not to take a certain route, think very seriously about changing your plans. Likewise, more-experienced climbers and hikers also offer well-informed perspectives; if people coming down from a peak warn you not to go up, take their advice and turn back.

- **Acclimate to the elevation.** Most trails in Rocky Mountain begin at an elevation of 7,800 feet, and many involve hiking or climbing to elevations above 12,000 feet. If you're arriving from a home a good deal closer to sea level, give yourself at least three days—and longer if you're an older person—to adjust to the lowered oxygen content in the air. More than seventy-five people have died of heart attacks in this park, many of which can be attributed to individuals pushing themselves too hard in thinner air than they usually breathe.

- **Sign the trail register.** It may seem like a folksy tradition, but your signature in the trail and summit registers can save your life. It helps rangers discover exactly where you started your hike and when you planned to return, so they can narrow a search if you become lost in the wilderness. Hikers who took the same trail in the last few days also may make note of unusual obstacles like rockslides, washed-out stream crossings, icy areas, or weather hazards. Take heed of these warnings as you plan your route.

- **Pack for every possibility.** Any time you step out on a trail, you may encounter situations that require an abrupt change of plans. Maybe you miss a turn and find yourself lost in the wilderness. Perhaps a storm front moves in without warning, or someone in your party sustains an injury. Any of these circumstances can extend your time outdoors, turning a day hike into an overnight stay or forcing you to seek cover off-trail.

You're not the first to feel compromised in the backcountry—in fact, it happens often enough that there's a checklist of things you should have with you every time you hike. The list is known as the Ten Essentials—items that can help you take control of your situation and make it back home in one piece. The Ten were first developed by the Mountaineers, a club for hikers and climbers back in the 1930s, and they've since updated the list in their book, *Mountaineering: The Freedom of the Hills*, in which they group some individual items to provide a more thorough list. If you carry all of these things with you on every hike, you'll be ready for most of the things nature throws at you.

The Ten Essentials

- Navigation tools: a good map and compass (for backcountry hiking and climbing, consider adding a GPS beacon that you can use to alert rangers to your location if you become injured)

- Sun protection: sunscreen and sunglasses

- Insulation: extra clothing and a poncho

- Illumination: flashlight and/or headlamp

- First-aid kit

- Fire starter: a lighter and/or waterproof matches

- A repair kit and tools (I add a roll of duct tape to this one)

- Nutrition: more food than you think you will need

- Hydration: more water than you think you will need

- Emergency shelter: an emergency space blanket or ultralight tarp

In addition, Rocky Mountain National Park recommends that you carry an emergency whistle, so you have a way to alert others in the area if you or your hiking or climbing partner is injured and in need of assistance.

Keep in mind that while your smartphone may provide maps and a bright light, it will run out of power in the great outdoors, and you'll have nowhere to charge it. If you're going to bring a GPS device with you, choose one that relies on satellites, not on cellular—and bring extra batteries.

Additional Tips

- **Know your limits.** Many hikers and climbers come to Rocky Mountain National Park to take on a greater challenge than they have ever tried before. If you're one of these adventurers, be sure that you understand the kinds of skills required to complete the climb successfully. Hike or climb with someone who has the requisite experience to be sure your party gets home safely, and take all the necessary precautions, from carrying the right gear to recognizing that the challenge may be too great.

- **Watch your step on snowfields.** Even if you're not planning a technical climb across a glacier or snowfield, you may be fascinated by the opportunity to walk in snow in July. These snow-covered areas are not like your backyard, however: Snow can be crusted with thick, frictionless ice, and it can hide large crevasses in the ice below. A wrong step can send you plunging down several stories into a very cold place. Think twice before walking out onto open snow.

- **Watch out for loose scree and shale.** Rocky Mountain is not a granite park; these mountains are made of sedimentary and metamorphic rock, so ledges and slopes can be as flaky as piecrust and give way under your feet. Step carefully and gauge the stability of a surface before you tread there, especially if you're walking along narrow ledges.

Many climbing and hiking accidents result from unstable rock underfoot.

- **Check for avalanche advisories.** Check the Colorado Avalanche Information Center website at https://avalanche.state.co.us for updates about the potential for avalanches in specific areas of the park.

ON AND AROUND WATER

Drowning is not a leading cause of death in Rocky Mountain National Park, but seventeen people to date have lost their lives in the park's waterways. Take some basic precautions to enjoy Rocky's lakes, rivers, and streams without incident.

- **Understand that this water is very, very cold.** Fueled mostly by glacial meltwater and snowmelt, these waterways usually hover at just above the freezing point. A fall into water this cold can produce hypothermia, the condition that leads to freezing to death. Your best bet is to stay out of this water and enjoy it from the safety of the shore or riverbank.

- **Stay off of slippery or moss-covered rocks and logs.** It may look like fun to hop from one boulder to the next in the middle of a rushing stream, but you will be surprised at how slick these rocks become when they're wet. Many deaths result from people slipping and falling from these rocks into frigid water.

- **Don't wade in or ford swift streams.** The water is moving faster than you think, and it's deeper and colder than you realize. You can be swept away by the current, and the cold will take over very quickly once you're in the water.

- **Don't wade into a stream at the top of a waterfall.** It's hard to believe that this needs to be said, but people die in Rocky Mountain and other parks (most famously Yosemite) because they wade out into a rushing stream to get a photo of a waterfall from the top. Here's a lifesaving tip from my husband and me, the author and photographer of the book *Hiking Waterfalls in New York*: There's nothing to see up there at the top of the falls. You'll get a much better photo from the bottom—and from the shore.

- **If you fly-fish, choose a fairly calm stream.** It's no fun to fish if you're struggling against the current all morning, and it's less fun if the current wins. Talk to a ranger about the best and safest places to fish in the park on the day of your visit.

- **Carry water-filtration equipment.** If you are camping in the backcountry, you will need an approved filter if you plan to draw on the park's waterways. The parasite *Giardia lamblia* is found in the park's water; it causes giardiasis, a disease that gives you cramps, persistent diarrhea, and nausea. Your best defense against this is to carry water from one of the park's treated-water systems.

STAYING ALIVE ON LONGS PEAK

On average, fifteen thousand people attempt to summit Longs Peak every year, and all but a few of these make it home without injury. A total of seventy-three people to date have lost their lives on this mountain, however, making it one of the most hazardous in all of the national parks. The park recommends that you do these things to make certain that you are among the many people who have an amazingly positive experience on the peak.

- **This is a climb, not a hike.** The park's website calls Longs Peak's Keyhole Route the most popular and "easiest" route to the top, a "classic mountaineering route." It requires hiking, scrambling on all fours, crossing very thin ledges, and navigating snowfields at any time of year. In winter, it becomes a technical climbing route, requiring ropes and other equipment to complete safely. The elevation changes from 9,405 feet at the trailhead to 14,259 feet at the summit. Coming down the mountain can be even more difficult than going up. Be prepared for the kinds of conditions you will encounter.

- **Begin well before sunrise.** The fifteen-mile round-trip takes most parties ten to fifteen hours to complete. You need to be back below the timberline by midafternoon, before the late-day thunderstorms develop, as they do nearly every day in spring, summer, and fall, so you will be out of danger of a lightning strike.

- **Listen to rangers.** Rangers at the Longs Peak ranger station and trailhead can tell in a glance whether or not you are properly prepared for the climb. They also know what the weather conditions are on the mountain, the danger of avalanches in winter and spring or rockslides in other seasons, and the likelihood of other kinds of hazards. If a ranger tells you you're not properly prepared or that you don't have the skills for the route you've chosen, take heed. Longs Peak is not an entry-level hike; it's completely inappropriate for young children or for people who have never hiked in the Rockies before. Rangers give advice to help keep you safe.

- **If you get altitude sickness, turn around and come down.**
Whether you are in perfect physical condition or not, you
will be affected by the reduced oxygen at high altitude. If you
get altitude sickness—headache, nausea, vomiting, loss of
appetite, weakness, and dizziness—the only cure is to return
to an elevation with more oxygen.

- **Watch out for "summit fever."** People often get close to the
summit and feel they must reach it at all costs, even if the
weather has begun to change or the people in their party
are not faring well on the strenuous climb. If you're on the
Keyhole Route, stop when you reach the Keyhole formation
and check in with your fellow hikers. If you're not feeling
well enough to continue up the most challenging part of the
climb, or if high winds, rain, or snow have developed, this
may not be your day to reach the summit. The mountain will
be there for the rest of your life. Try it another day.

If you do get into trouble on the peak, call 911 and tell the
dispatcher you're in the national park. Provide this information to
the dispatcher:

- Your cell-phone number and carrier

- Your exact location, with GPS coordinates if you can get them

- Weather conditions

- Whether anyone in your party has a personal locator beacon
(PLB) or a satellite emergency notification device (SEND)
that can be activated

- Basic facts, including injuries or other conditions that caused
you to call

If you can't call 911, do this:

- Provide basic first aid to the injured person.

- Keep yourself and everyone in your party warm and dry.

- Blow your emergency whistle to get the attention of others nearby.

If you can't get anyone's attention or call 911, you may have to leave the injured person and go for help. Mark the area with anything you have in a bright color, so you can find it when you or a search team returns, and save the GPS coordinates to give to rescuers.

Follow these guidelines to make your visit to Rocky Mountain National Park the experience of a lifetime you hope it will be. Once again, I urge you to join the more than four million people who discover and explore this park every year, with the knowledge that a few simple precautions will help you make certain that your trip is memorable for all the right reasons: the outdoor adventures, the wildlife sightings, the spectacular landscapes, and the people you encounter here on the Continental Divide.

APPENDIX

List of Deaths in Rocky Mountain National Park by Date

Note: If you know of a death in the park that is not listed here, please contact me at author@minetor.com and I will be sure to add it to the list for the second edition of this book.

NAME	AGE	DATE	CAUSE	LOCATION
Carrie J. Welton	42	9/23/1884	Hypothermia	Longs Peak
Frank Stryker	24	8/28/1889	Gunshot	Longs Peak
Alexander MacGregor	50	6/17/1896	Lightning	Big Thompson
Louis Levings	20	8/2/1905	Fall	Ypsilon Mountain
William Edward Dillingham	35	8/20/1914	Lightning	Unspecified
Thornton R. Sampson	63	9/3/1915	Hypothermia	Odessa Lake cave
Eula Frost	19	8/2/1917	Fall	Fall River Canyon
Margaret Wood	n/a	8/22/1918	Auto accident	Fall River Road
Elizabeth Kimmelshue	4	8/22/1918	Auto accident	Fall River Road
Stinson Kimmelshue	18	8/22/1918	Auto accident	Fall River Road
Robert Kimmelshue	11	8/22/1918	Auto accident	Fall River Road
J. P. Chitwood	~60	9/9/1921	Hypothermia	Flattop Mountain
H. F. Targett	55	6/21/1921	Fall	Longs Peak
Gregory Aubuchon	18	7/20/1921	Fall	Longs Peak
Jesse Kitts	36	8/1/1922	Lightning	Longs Peak
Agnes Vaille	34	1/10/1925	Hypothermia	Longs Peak
Herbert Sortland	22	1/12/1925	Hypothermia	Longs Peak
Fred N. Selak	75	7/21/1926	Homicide	Grand Lake
Forrest Ketring	19	7/23/1926	Fall	Longs Peak
Charles Hupp	54	4/3/1926	Heart attack	n/a
Flora Napier	39	6/26/1927	Toboggan	Horseshoe Park
William N. Vaile	52	7/2/1927	Heart attack	Fall River Pass

NAME	AGE	DATE	CAUSE	LOCATION
Charles Thiemeyer	28	8/18/1929	Fall	Longs Peak
R. B. Key	45	9/13/1931	Fall	Longs Peak
Robert Smith	41	7/18/1932	Falling rock	Longs Peak
Mary S. Day	34	8/27/1932	Auto accident	Fall River Road
Lucille Day	10	8/27/1932	Auto accident	Fall River Road
Gray Secor Jr.	17	8/29/1932	Fall	Longs Peak
Joseph L. Halpern	22	8/15/1933	Lost, never found	Taylor Mountain
C. F. Peyton	n/a	7/30/1934	Auto accident	Grand Lake
Kenneth Meenan	22	8/13/1934	Motorcycle	Unspecified
A. B. Servey	46	7/1/1936	Heart attack	Horseshoe Park
James Fifer	32	7/2/1936	Auto accident	Bear Lake Road
Forrest Hein	16	9/6/1936	Fall	Mount McGregor
William S. Moore	75	7/4/1937	Heart attack	Onahu Creek
Nola Morris	n/a	1938	Auto accident	Trail Ridge Road
Alfred Beilhartz	4	7/3/1938	Lost, never found	Roaring River
Emily Foster Russell	40	7/28/1938	Fall from horse	Old Man Mountain
John Fuller	20	8/8/1938	Fall	Longs Peak
Gerald Clark	30	8/7/1939	Hypothermia	Longs Peak
Raymond Johnson	30	10/13/1939	Auto accident	Bear Lake Road
Hoyt White	33	9/6/1940	Fall	Twin Sisters
Wesley F. Diem	30	8/1/1941	Heart attack	Longs Peak
Albert W. Furch	49	7/13/1945	Fall from horse	Loch Vale Trail
Shelly Heimbichner	15	8/7/1945	Auto accident	Bear Lake Road
Thomas H. Evans	20	6/16/1946	Fall	Flattop Mountain
John E. Barney	41	7/22/1946	Heart attack	Wild Basin
Charles Grant	19	9/1/1946	Fall	Longs Peak
Robert Earl Briggs	6	7/17/1947	Drowned	N. St. Vrain Creek
Raymond J. Young	22	8/17/1947	Auto accident	Trail Ridge Road
Oscar Jacobson	n/a	8/17/1947	Auto accident	Trail Ridge Road
Wilmer S. Holley	30	9/14/1947	Drowned	N. St. Vrain Creek
L. C. Ingram	41	8/16/1948	Heart attack	Fall River Lodge
Lt. Cranston Dodd	23	8/27/1948	Plane crash	Fall River Canyon
Edward V. P. Schneiderhahn	73	9/1/1948	Heart attack	Fall River Lodge
David Devitt	21	10/9/1949	Lost, never found	Flattop Mountain
Bruce Gerling	20	10/9/1949	Lost, never found	Flattop Mountain

NAME	AGE	DATE	CAUSE	LOCATION
Kenneth Swisher	35	7/29/1950	Auto accident	Bear Lake Road
Lorena Pauley	39	7/29/1950	Suicide	Bear Lake
Earl S. Davis	n/a	9/8/1950	Heart attack	Sprague's Lodge
B. R. Schabarum	n/a	6/11/1952	Heart attack	Trail Ridge Road
John H. Tallmadge	21	7/11/1952	Fall	Hallet Peak
Wayne J. Kurtz	57	7/17/1952	Heart attack	Big Meadows
Ralph Corlew	n/a	9/26/1952	Heart attack	Poudre Lakes
Abe Brown	57	7/11/1953	Heart attack	Wild Basin
A. J. Canino	53	7/30/1953	Heart attack	Pear Lake area
Kathryn Rees	15	7/31/1953	Fall	Little Matterhorn
Sandra Miller	17	7/31/1953	Fall	Little Matterhorn
Robin Howarth	5	8/16/1953	Drowned	Glacier Creek area
Albert I. McPhillips	60	5/27/1954	Suicide	Longs Peak
Earl Harvey	19	6/5/1954	Fall	Longs Peak
Harold Grey	54	6/27/1954	Heart attack	Glacier Basin
Richard Williams	43	7/6/1954	Auto accident	Park road
Mrs. R. G. Van Blarican	34	7/13/1954	Medical	Lower Hidden Valley
Unidentified victim	n/a	9/6/1954	Suicide	Lumpy Ridge
Jack Roberts	43	6/2/1955	Heart attack	Grand Lake area
Irwin C. Oderkirk	22	7/17/1955	Auto accident	Bear Lake Road
Robert Salt	26	6/26/1956	Medical	Pear Lake
George Bloom	21	8/15/1956	Fall	Mount Craig
Rena Hoffman	33	8/15/1956	Lightning	Longs Peak
Cecil F. Hall	66	7/15/1957	Heart attack	Aspenglen camp
O. E. Kinnaman	71	7/3/1958	Heart attack	Bear Lake
Edwin V. Drake	68	7/17/1958	Heart attack	Glacier Basin
Bobby Bizup	10	8/15/1958	Hypothermia	Camp St. Malo
George F. Wellman	73	12/28/1958	Heart attack	Hidden Valley
Raymond Harrington	67	6/20/1959	Heart attack	Glacier Basin
Jeanne Gillett	31	8/21/1959	Fall	Tyndall Glacier
David Jones	18	4/20/1960	Fall	Longs Peak
Prince Willmon	23	4/20/1960	Hypothermia	Longs Peak
Charles Raidy	34	7/12/1960	Auto accident	Trail Ridge Road
Lester Reeble	45	7/31/1960	Fall	Spearhead Ridge
George W. Krah	65	8/24/1960	Heart attack	Glacier Basin

NAME	AGE	DATE	CAUSE	LOCATION
Myron M. Fritts	19	7/14/1961	Fall	Hallet Peak
Patricia L. Beatty	21	8/13/1962	Fall	Chaos Canyon
Gerald R. Noland Jr.	20	8/15/1962	Fall	Andrews Glacier
Kem Arnold Murphy	19	8/27/1962	Fall	Longs Peak
James O'Toole	20	9/30/1962	Fall	Longs Peak
Norris C. Livoni	50	5/27/1964	Suicide	Trail Ridge Road
James L. Keller	43	6/19/1964	Drowned	Chasm Falls
Leola H. Swain	46	8/6/1964	Lightning	Trail Ridge Road
Robert Emerson Brown	28	7/17/1965	Fall	Loch Vale Trail
Rev. Alvin Whittemore	61	7/24/1965	Heart attack	Eugenia Mine Trail
Jay DuPont	15	6/14/1966	Fall	Cliff, Mills Lake
Nathaniel R. Lacy	43	6/24/1966	Auto accident	Entrance Station Area
Ms. Xana Schurene	76	7/22/1966	Heart attack	Endovalley camp
Walter Stentzil	64	8/12/1966	Heart attack	Beaver Meadows
John Rapchak	n/a	8/22/1966	Heart attack	North Inlet Trail
C. Blake Heister Jr.	48	8/27/1966	Fall	Longs Peak
Jack D. Henander	28	4/9/1967	Plane crash	Signal Mountain
William P. Elrod	55	4/9/1967	Plane crash	Signal Mountain
Charles DeNovellis	54	4/9/1967	Plane crash	Signal Mountain
James B. Clifford	66	7/21/1967	Heart attack	Ouzel Lake
Marshal Wrubel	44	10/26/1968	Heart attack	Nymph Lake Trail
Jerry Paul Johnson	12	7/3/1969	Fall	Deer Mountain
Herbert D. Kuhn	42	7/24/1969	Fall from horse	Trail to Lost Lake
James D. Majors	50	9/20/1969	Heart attack	Trail Ridge Road
Walter G. Seabold	56	8/13/1971	Heart attack	Thatchtop Mountain
Roy C. Handshew	63	8/31/1971	Heart attack	Fall River Road
Rudolf Postweiler	48	9/11/1971	Heart attack	Chasm Lake Trail
William Frechtling	24	9/13/1971	Heart attack	Longs Peak camp
Fred Stone	20	1/23/1972	Hypothermia	Longs Peak
Joan Jardine	21	1/23/1972	Hypothermia	Longs Peak
Paul Russell	24	6/12/1972	Fall	Longs Peak
Steve Day	n/a	6/18/1972	Fall	Pagoda Peak
Gregory Holzer	22	6/18/1972	Medical	Wild Basin
Danny Saucier	12	7/30/1972	Drowned	N. St. Vrain Creek
Gerald Murphy	51	8/12/1972	Heart attack	Longs Peak

NAME	AGE	DATE	CAUSE	LOCATION
Lillie E. Brown	75	8/15/1972	Heart attack	Forest Canyon
John Kruppa	69	8/22/1972	Heart attack	Big Thompson River
Harry J. Sears	79	9/3/1972	Heart attack	Alpine Visitor Center
Jay Van Stavern	19	4/2/1973	Fall	Longs Peak
Lois Lee Matthews	19	5/27/1973	Drowned	Big Thompson River
Sherran Joy Haley	23	6/27/1973	Drowned	Big Thompson River
Kurtland Brandon Primosch	5	7/6/1973	Drowned	N. St. Vrain Creek
Michael Egan	20	8/1/1973	Drowned	Adams Falls
Joseph Holub	22	8/20/1973	Fall	Mount Meeker
Jonathan Andrew Williams	10	9/2/1973	Fall	Continental Divide
Robert Lewis Hritz	19	10/12/1973	Avalanche	Taylor Glacier
David Emerick	24	10/12/1973	Avalanche	Taylor Glacier
Barbara Gully	17	7/1/1974	Lightning	Trail Ridge Road
John Berger	11	8/15/1974	Fall	Twin Sisters
Richard Ankanbrandt	47	7/1/1975	Heart attack	Green Mountain Trail
Diana Hunter	26	7/2/1975	Fall	Cathedral Wall
Chris Rejeske	15	7/18/1975	Fall	Ypsilon Mountain
Allan Jacobs	21	8/4/1975	Fall	Elk Tooth
Domingo Alvarez	64	8/8/1975	Heart attack	Alpine Visitor Center
William Gizzie	45	8/24/1975	Heart attack	Longs Peak
Virgil Munsinger	68	9/5/1975	Heart attack	Sky Pond
Laurene S. Nuzzo	26	9/5/1975	Motorcycle	Trail Ridge Road
Don Mullett	57	9/16/1975	Heart attack	Hidden Valley
William A. Pistorio	18	10/1/1975	Fall	Longs Peak
James Boicourt	29	7/6/1976	Fall	Ypsilon Mountain
Asuncion Navarette	n/a	5/11/1977	Fall	Mount McGregor
Harold Holtzendorf	20	5/17/1977	Fall	Mount McGregor
Michael Neri	21	6/2/1977	Fall	Longs Peak
Sam Friedman	80	7/3/1977	Heart attack	Trail Ridge Road
Martin Ryan	23	8/16/1977	Plane crash	Fall River Road
Janet Bonneville	19	8/16/1977	Plane crash	Fall River Road
Jason E. Quest	20	9/1/1977	Auto accident	Trail Ridge Road
Eric Nolan Strahan	20	9/13/1977	Motorcycle	Trail Ridge Road
Eric Rumsey	25	9/19/1977	Suicide	Trail Ridge Road
Christopher Ermijo	6	5/14/1978	Drowned	Big Thompson River

NAME	AGE	DATE	CAUSE	LOCATION
John White-Lance	27	6/23/1978	Auto accident	Park road
Lawrence Berman	21	7/21/1978	Fall	Mount Ypsilon
Herman Milner	58	9/1/1978	Heart attack	Moraine Park camp
Grete E. Wignall	61	9/6/1978	Heart attack	Loch Vale Trail
Harvey Schneider	22	9/16/1978	Fall	Longs Peak
Denzel Baker	58	10/15/1978	Heart attack	Park staff housing
Andrew W. Paton	15	8/24/1979	Lightning	Twin Sisters
Coy Conley	37	9/1/1979	Fall	Ute Trail Crossing
Dr. Edward Sujansky	43	9/1/1979	Heart attack	Longs Peak
Charles Nesbit	31	10/6/1979	Fall	Longs Peak
Kris James Gedney	22	11/14/1979	Suicide	Longs Peak
Virginia Krieger	62	12/23/1979	Plane crash	Chippler Mountain
Ruth Magnuson	29	3/8/1980	Hypothermia	Mount Alice
Robert Silver	16	6/26/1980	Fall	Longs Peak
Bernard F. Conway	62	7/14/1980	Heart attack	Alpine Visitor Center
John Link	43	8/4/1980	Fall	The Cleaver
Christine Marie Ulbricht	12	8/24/1980	Fall	Twin Sisters
James S. Johnston	25	8/31/1980	Fall	Stone Man Pass
Robert Elliott	26	1/10/1981	Fall	Longs Peak
James Duffy III	24	12/14/1981	Hypothermia	Longs Peak
Robert Baldeshwiler	12	6/29/1982	Fall	Flattop Mountain
Terry W. Coates	36	7/15/1982	Drowned	Lawn Lake Flood
Bridget Dorris	20	7/15/1982	Drowned	Lawn Lake Flood
Steven See	21	7/15/1982	Drowned	Lawn Lake Flood
Audrey G. Daly	56	8/23/1982	Auto accident	Trail Ridge Road
John W. Daly	73	8/23/1982	Heart attack	Trail Ridge Road
Mark D. Frevert	28	2/6/1983	Rockslide	Notchtop Mountain
Samuel Mitchell III	19	2/6/1983	Rockslide	Notchtop Mountain
Rudi Moder	27	2/13/1983	Lost, never found	Box Canyon area
Edward Griess	14	8/17/1983	Fall	Unspecified
Cecelea Mulvihill	71	3/12/1984	Heart attack	Bear Lake Road
David P. Ormsby	23	6/12/1984	Fall	Mount McGregor
Lee S. Jamieson	19	7/1/1984	Fall	Notchtop Mountain
Gilbert Hana	60	9/22/1984	Heart attack	Moraine Park camp
Ruth L. Bruso	70	10/9/1984	Heart attack	Bear Lake

NAME	AGE	DATE	CAUSE	LOCATION
Scott Anderson	21	2/3/1985	Skiing accident	Hidden Valley
Nancy Garbs	27	8/3/1985	Medical	Never Summer Beach
Alice A. Philbrick	69	8/12/1985	Heart attack	Alpine Visitor Center
William Becker	21	9/11/1985	Suicide	Timber Creek camp
Edna M. Digman	44	9/21/1985	Suicide	Trail Ridge Road
Ellen Marx	13	7/13/1986	Drowned	N. St. Vrain Creek
Dr. Lawrence Farrell	33	9/12/1986	Fall	Longs Peak
Francis Murray	36	3/1/1987	Suicide	Wild Basin area
J. D. Burger	65	6/8/1987	Heart attack	Glacier Basin camp
Charles Housman	77	6/22/1987	Medical	Grand Lake
Rey Alexander Dermody	7	7/4/1987	Drowned	Roaring River
David Drea Felts	21	8/29/1987	Fall	Mount McGregor
John Schnakenberg	22	12/17/1987	Fall	Deer Mountain
Brenda K. Butrick	30	1/24/1988	Snow-tubing	Beaver Meadows
Kevin Hardwick	30	8/10/1988	Fall	Longs Peak
George C. Ogden	21	8/15/1988	Fall	Spearhead Mountain
Roger A. Boyce	44	10/8/1988	Suicide	Beaver Meadows
Terry Bentley	49	4/5/1989	Plane crash	Rowe Glacier
Evan Corbett	20	7/21/1989	Suicide	Longs Peak
Albert Fincham	52	8/25/1989	Heart attack	Longs Peak
Andrew Tufly	15	6/29/1990	Fall	Twin Sisters
Timothy Fromelt	27	7/29/1990	Fall	Longs Peak
William Wallace Carson	42	8/4/1990	Fall	Taylor Glacier
John R. Thomas	34	1/25/1991	Suicide	Trail Ridge Road
Joe Massari	45	4/22/1991	Avalanche	Longs Peak
Wilburn J. Parks	44	6/26/1991	Suicide	Trail Ridge Road
Lawrence Taylor	46	9/5/1991	Heart attack	Moraine Park camp
Kurt Witbeck	22	2/26/1992	Suicide	Park Entrance Road
Glenn McDonald	31	6/28/1992	Lightning	Hallet Peak
Lon L. Egbert	42	7/4/1992	Suicide	Trail Ridge Road
Sarah Wolenetz	11	7/11/1992	Fall	Flattop Trail
Gary Boyer	35	7/28/1992	Fall	Mount Meeker
Bruce Anderson	28	7/31/1992	Suicide	Flattop Mountain
Jon M. Hofstra	23	8/16/1992	Fall	Little Matterhorn
Todd Martin	24	11/1/1992	Avalanche	Flattop Mountain

NAME	AGE	DATE	CAUSE	LOCATION
Brad Farnan	30	11/1/1992	Avalanche	Flattop Mountain
Carl Siegel	30	2/3/1993	Fall	Longs Peak
Glenn M. Hays	17	7/3/1993	Drowned	N. St. Vrain Creek
Kelly Thomas	27	9/14/1993	Hypothermia	Longs Peak
Kip Lloyd	20	5/10/1994	Suicide	Bear Lake Road
Alison Bierma	18	5/19/1994	Suicide	Cub Lake Trail
Jack L. McConnell	59	5/23/1994	Fall	White Whale II
Robert Baker	70	6/14/1994	Heart attack	Trail Ridge Road
Noel Jarrell	49	7/3/1994	Heart attack	Alpine Visitor Center
Eugene Gomolka	50	7/17/1994	Heart attack	Trail Ridge Road
Jack E. Keene	47	9/1/1994	Heart attack	Sandbeach Lake
Richard Smith	45	10/4/1994	Suicide	Big Thompson River
Alan B. Farwell	19	6/8/1995	Auto accident	Trail Ridge Road
Forrest Sprague	19	6/8/1995	Auto accident	Trail Ridge Road
Jun Kamimura	33	8/25/1995	Fall	Longs Peak
Peter Smith	46	1/31/1996	Plane crash	Ypsilon Mountain
Robert C. Drury	50	5/15/1996	Heart attack	Trail Ridge Road
Francis W. Clyde	63	6/5/1997	Heart attack	Moraine Park camp
Todd Marshall	34	7/2/1997	Fall	Petit Grepon
Mark Miedema	10	7/17/1997	Mountain lion	North Inlet Trail
Hayes W. Reid	29	7/17/1997	Suicide	Alpine Visitor Center
Mona Barlow	65	8/12/1997	Heart attack	Alpine Visitor Center
Timothy Maron	26	9/9/1997	Fall	Longs Peak
William C. Heflin	70	7/7/1998	Heart attack	Gore Range Overlook
Raymond C. Barbknecht	47	8/14/1998	Heart attack	Twin Sisters Trail
Richard Ladue	37	11/15/1998	Fall	Thatchtop Mountain
Charlie Harrison	47	6/24/1999	Rockslide	Windy Gulch
Michael J. Fritzen	57	6/27/1999	Heart attack	Cub Lake Trail
John Retting	35	7/21/1999	Lightning	Alpine Visitor Center
Raymond Decker	75	8/3/1999	Fall	Longs Peak
James Page	56	8/4/1999	Fall	Gorrell's Traverse
Michael B. Hines	23	8/7/1999	Lightning	Bridal Veil Falls
Gregory Koczanski	42	8/14/1999	Fall	Longs Peak
Erin Colby Sharp	28	3/3/2000	Fall	Longs Peak
Rob Donoho	52	4/30/2000	Plane crash	Comanche Peak

NAME	AGE	DATE	CAUSE	LOCATION
Terri Donoho	47	4/30/2000	Plane crash	Comanche Peak
Cameron Tague	32	7/6/2000	Fall	Longs Peak
Andy Haberkorn	28	7/12/2000	Lightning	Longs Peak
Edward Calloway	53	8/26/2000	Heart attack	Cow Creek Trail
Melanie Wood	32	4/17/2001	Suicide	Gem Lake
Scott Johnson	9	5/12/2001	Drowned	Big Thompson River
Michael P. Carter	26	8/26/2001	Suicide	Upper High Drive
John C. Hodge	55	12/25/2001	Suicide	Lily Lake area
Robert Whittington	71	8/1/2002	Heart attack	Nymph Lake Trail
Robert Chu	n/a	5/24/2003	Heart attack	Fern Lake Road
Kurt Zollers	33	7/26/2003	Fall	Baker Mountain
Jonathan J. Rozecki	19	11/16/2003	Suicide	Moraine Park camp
Shannon Thomas	36	2/4/2004	Suicide	Kaley Cottage Road
Abigail Walter	13	6/23/2004	Fall	Cascade Falls
Marilyn Frongillo	71	6/23/2004	Heart attack	Lake Irene
Sudheer Averineni	26	9/4/2004	Hypothermia	Longs Peak
Omar Mehdawi	17	3/5/2005	Snow-tubing	Bear Lake area
Jeff Christensen (ranger)	31	7/29/2005	Fall	Mount Chiquita
John Whatmough	32	9/12/2005	Auto accident	Fall River Road
Clayton Smith	58	9/3/2006	Fall	Longs Peak
William N. Hudson	68	11/27/2007	Falling tree	Wild Basin area
Richard Frisbie	66	6/7/2008	Fall	Emerald Lake
Robert Bacon	70	6/12/2008	Heart attack	Alberta Falls
Matthieu Olivier Jacques Chesaux	40	9/30/2008	Skiing accident	Taylor Glacier
Albert Langemann	55	1/10/2009	Heart attack	Longs Peak
Connie Fanning	55	4/28/2009	Auto accident	US 34
Maynard Grant Brandsma	61	7/20/2009	Heart attack	Longs Peak
Carol Nicolaidis	62	9/4/2009	Hypothermia	Fern Lake Trail
John Bramley	55	9/10/2009	Fall	Longs Peak
Jeffrey Rosinski	29	7/15/2010	Fall	Longs Peak
Lacy Elliot Meadows	40	7/25/2010	Fall	Cony Lake
Benjamin Hebb	26	8/27/2010	Fall	Longs Peak
John M. Regan	57	9/25/2010	Fall	Longs Peak
James Charles Patrick	54	10/16/2010	Fall	Taylor Glacier
Christian Pruchnic	42	11/20/2010	Fall	Thatchtop Mountain

NAME	AGE	DATE	CAUSE	LOCATION
Name not released	n/a	0/0/2010	Suicide	Unnamed trailhead
"Man from Castle Rock"	47	7/12/2012	Fall	Andrews Glacier
Toni Henthorn	50	9/29/2012	Homicide	Deer Mountain
Troy Green	39	1/31/2013	Suicide	Flattop Trail
David Laurienti	43	3/17/2013	Avalanche	Ypsilon Mountain
Paul Nahon	20	8/15/2013	Fall	Longs Peak
Corey Stewart	22	8/22/2013	Fall	Lumpy Ridge
Tommy Cobb	55	10/21/2013	Heart attack	Moraine Park camp
Donald Belew	74	1/7/2014	Heart attack	Mills Lake
Matthew Burklow	25	6/9/2014	Fall	Longs Peak
Rebecca Telhet	42	7/11/2014	Lightning	Ute Crossing Trail
Gregory Cardwell	52	7/12/2014	Lightning	Trail Ridge Road
Patrician Briggs	67	7/15/2014	Heart attack	Trail Ridge Road
Nicholas Hellbusch	18	7/25/2014	Suicide	Longs Peak
Unnamed man	33	9/18/2014	Suicide	Glacier Creek area
Peter Anthony Jeffris	25	11/16/2014	Fall	Longs Peak
Spencer Veysey	26	10/3/2015	Fall (most likely)	Longs Peak
Ronald Webber	58	1/19/2016	Fall	Longs Peak
Christine James	38	2/27/2016	Unspecified	Deer Mountain Trail
David Grant	61	7/23/2016	Suicide	Trail Ridge Road
Scott Corliss	61	10/1/2016	Fall	Longs Peak
Pawel Abramczyk	39	3/18/2017	Fall	Longs Peak
Teresa Sajsa	59	8/22/2017	Unspecified	Tonahutu Creek
Ken Teselle	73	8/23/2017	Fall	Mt. Lady Washington
Michael McQuay	71	8/26/2017	Medical	Harbison Picnic area
Henry L. Gholz	65	9/30/2017	Fall	Lumpy Ridge
Brian Joseph Perri	38	6/30/2018	Fall	Mount Meeker
Jens "Jay" Yambert	60	8/26/2018	Fall	Longs Peak
Ryan Albert	30	10/4/2018	Fall	Longs Peak
Micah Tice	20	11/24/2018	Hypothermia	Longs Peak
James Pruitt	70	2/28/2019	Lost, still missing	Glacier Gorge

REFERENCES

CHAPTER 1

Associated Press. "Bizup Lad Wrote His Parents Happy Note before Vanishing." *Greeley Daily Tribune*, Colorado, August 27, 1958, p. 20. Accessed June 13, 2019. www .newspapers.com/image/25068187/?terms=Bobby%2BBizup.

———. "Bobby Bizup's Remains Found in High Ravine." *Greeley Daily Tribune*, Colorado, July 9, 1959, p. 5. Accessed June 13, 2019. www.newspapers.com/ image/25029984/?terms=Bobby%2BBizup.

———. "Bodies of Colorado Students Found on 14,255-Foot Peak." *News-Messenger*, Fremont, Ohio, April 22, 1960, p. 1. Accessed June 12, 2019. www.newspapers .com/image/304497460/?terms=David%2BJones%2BPrince%2BWilmot.

———. "Boy, 10, Still Missing in Estes Park." *Great Falls Tribune*, Montana, August 21, 1958, p. 2. Accessed June 13, 2019. www.newspapers.com/image/238761435/ ?terms=Bobby%2BBizup.

———. "CSU Skier's Body Found near Estes." *Fort Collins Coloradoan*, August 6, 1972, p. 3. Accessed June 13, 2019. www.newspapers.com/image/225542706/?terms= Fred%2BStone%2BJoan%2BJardine.

———. "Denver Boy Reported Missing in Mountains." *Greeley Daily Tribune*, August 16, 1958, p. 1. Accessed June 4, 2019. www.newspapers.com/image/25064554/ ?terms=Bobby%2BBizup.

———. "Denver Youth Still Missing." *Daily Sentinel*, Grand Junction, Colorado, August 24, 1958, p. 2. Accessed June 13, 2019. www.newspapers.com/image/537176139/ ?terms=Bobby%2BBizup.

———. "End Search for Boy." *Kansas City Times*, August 26, 1958, p. 1. Accessed June 4, 2019. www.newspapers.com/image/51157746/?terms=Bobby%2BBizup.

———. "Hiker's Body Found in Rockies." *Anderson Herald Bulletin*, Anderson, Indiana, September 16, 1993, p. 3. Accessed June 15, 2019. https://newspaperarchive.com/ anderson-herald-bulletin-sep-16-1993-p-3.

———. "Hunt for Lost Boy Halted." *Great Falls Tribune*, Montana, August 26, 1958, p. 2. Accessed June 13, 2019. www.newspapers.com/image/238762306/?terms =Bobby%2BBizup.

———. "Indian Tracker Fails in Search for Missing Lad." *Daily Sentinel*, Grand Junction, Colorado, August 23, 1958, p. 4. Accessed June 13, 2019. www.newspapers .com/image/537176133/?terms=Bobby%2BBizup.

———. "Missing Youth Thought to Be in Estes Park." *Greeley Daily Tribune*, Colorado, August 19, 1958, p. 1 Accessed June 13, 2019. www.newspapers.com/image/ 25065095/?terms=Bobby%2BBizup.

———. "Miss Jardine Died Early on Ski Hike." *Greeley Daily Tribune*, February 1, 1972, p. 6. Accessed June 13, 2019. www.newspapers.com/image/25070908/?terms=Fred%2BStone%2BJoan%2BJardine.

———. "Mountain Climber Dies from Injury, Exposure." *Daily Sentinel*, Grand Junction, Colorado, August 8, 1939, pp. 1 and 8. Accessed June 12, 2019. www.newspapers.com/image/537360721.

———. "No Word of Missing Man." *Oshkosh Northwestern*, September 20, 1915, p. 9. Accessed June 16, 2019. www.newspapers.com/image/248751137/?terms=Thornton%2BSampson.

———. "1 Climber Dies, 1 Injured after Being Trapped by Snowstorm." *Daily Sentinel*, Grand Junction, Colorado, September 15, 1993, p. 3. Accessed June 15, 2019. www.newspapers.com/image/540495982/?terms=Kelly%2BThomas.

———. "Report Lost Boy Seen Turns Out to Be False Alarm." *Daily Sentinel*, Grand Junction, Colorado, September 5, 1958, p. 7. Accessed June 13, 2019. www.newspapers.com/image/537135093/?terms=Bobby%2BBizup.

———. "Rescue Team Finds Body near Longs Peak Shelter." *Daily Sentinel*, Grand Junction, Colorado, December 18, 1981, p. 3. Accessed June 15, 2019. www.newspapers.com/image/537729350/?terms=Longs%2BPeak.

———. "Search Continues for Missing Skier." *Daily Sentinel*, Grand Junction, Colorado, January 30, 1972, p. 6. Accessed June 13, 2019. www.newspapers.com/image/535852495/?terms=Fred%2BStone%2BJoan%2BJardine.

———. "Searchers Find Climber's Body." *Daily Sentinel*, Grand Junction, Colorado, March 11, 1980, p. 19. Accessed June 14, 2019. www.newspapers.com/image/537588815/?terms=death%2BRocky%2BMountain%2BNational%2BPark.

———. "Search Goes On for Missing 10-Year-Old." *Daily Sentinel*, Grand Junction, Colorado, August 17, 1958, p. 1. Accessed June 13, 2019. www.newspapers.com/image/537176018/?terms=Bobby%2BBizup.

———. "Shift Quest for Boy." *Kansas City Ties*, Missouri, August 20, 1958, p. 10. Accessed June 13, 2019. www.newspapers.com/image/53018319/?terms=Bobby%2BBizup.

———. "Skiers' Gear Discovered." *Greeley Daily Tribune*, January 27, 1972, p. 6. Accessed June 13, 2019. www.newspapers.com/image/25068315/?terms=Fred%2BStone%2BJoan%2BJardine.

———. "Skiers Remain Missing." *Greeley Daily Tribune*, January 26, 1972, p. 2. Accessed June 13, 2019. www.newspapers.com/image/25067278/?terms=Fred%2BStone%2BJoan%2BJardine.

———. "Skiers Still Missing." *Colorado Springs Gazette Telegraph*, January 28, 1972, p. 1. Accessed June 13, 2019. www.newspapers.com/image/58324615/?terms=Fred%2BStone%2BJoan%2BJardine.

———. "Small Party to Continue Skier Search." *Greeley Daily Tribune*, January 31, 1972, p. 6. Accessed June 13, 2019. www.newspapers.com/image/25070252/?terms=Fred%2BStone%2BJoan%2BJardine.

———. "Still No Trace of Lost Skier." *Greeley Daily Tribune*, February 22, 1972, p. 6. Accessed June 13, 2019. www.newspapers.com/image/25083062/?terms=Fred%2BStone%2BJoan%2BJardine.

————. "Trapped on Peak 20 Hours, Dies." *Morning Call*, Allentown, Pennsylvania, August 8, 1939, pp. 1 and 15. Accessed June 12, 2019. https://www.newspapers .com/image/274015807/?terms=Gerald%2BClark.

"Body Discovered after 17 Years." *Gaffney Ledger*, South Carolina, July 28, 1932, p. 1. Accessed June 16, 2019. www.newspapers.com/image/78340096/?terms=%22 Thornton%2BSampson%22.

Burdick, Chuck. "ART Mission 7203, January 25–30." *Alpine Rescue Team News*, April 1972, Vol. 3, Issue 2, pp. 13–16. Accessed June 13, 2019. www.alpinerescueteam .org/wp-content/uploads/2012/02/ART_newsletter_apr1972.pdf.

"Climber Dies after Being Lowered to Chasm Lake." *Greeley Daily Tribune*, Colorado, August 7, 1939, p. 1. Accessed June 12, 2019. www.newspapers.com/image/ 24982255/?terms=Gerald%2BClark.

"Cursed and Haunted: An Old Waterbury Mansion Which Cannot Be Sold." *Boston Globe*, September 30, 1884, p. 4. Accessed June 12, 2019. www.newspapers.com/ image/430652711/?terms=Carrie%2BWelton.

Detterline, Jim. "Stranded, Unable to Find Route, Weather, Inadequate Equipment, Exhaustion, Hypothermia, Etc., Colorado, Rocky Mountain National Park, Longs Peak." American Alpine Club Accident Report, 1994. Accessed June 15, 2019. http://publications.americanalpineclub.org/articles/13199404202/ Stranded-Unable-to-Find-Route-Weather-Inadequate-Equipment -Exhaustion-Hypothermia-Etc-Colorado-Rocky-Mountain-National -Park-Longs-Peak.

"Dogs Trail Missing Deaf Boy in Wilds." *Oakland Tribune*, California, August 18, 1958, p. 1. Accessed June 13, 2019. www.newspapers.com/image/331931671/?terms= Bobby%2BBizup.

"Dr. Sampson's Body Found." *Gastonia Gazette*, North Carolina, October 5, 1915, p. 7. Accessed June 16, 2019. www.newspapers.com/image/73938162/?terms=Thornton %2BSampson.

"Ep #3: Bobby Bizup: Rocky Mountain National Park." *Locations Unknown* podcast, January 17, 2019. Accessed June 13, 2019. www.stitcher.com/podcast/locations -unknown/e/58258786.

"Fatality near Odessa Lake at Rocky Mountain National Park." National Park Service news release, September 4, 2009. Accessed June 15, 2019. www.nps.gov/romo/ learn/news/pr_fatality_september09.htm.

"Frozen to Death: A Wealthy New York Girl's Fatal Ascent of Longs Peak." *Sunday News-Dealer*, Wilkes-Barre, Pennsylvania, October 5, 1884, p. 3. Accessed June 12, 2019. www.newspapers.com/image/425726780/?terms=Carrie%2BWelton.

"Greeley CAP Assigned to Search for Youth." *Greeley Daily Tribune*, August 18, 1958, p. 1. Accessed June 4, 2019. www.newspapers.com/image/25064738/?terms= Bobby%2BBizup.

"Hiker Who Died on Longs Peak ID'd as HP Engineer from India." *Fort Collins Coloradoan*, September 8, 2004, p. 12. Accessed June 15, 2019. https://coloradoan .newspapers.com/image/227238512/?terms=death%2BRocky%2BMountain%2B National%2BPark.

"Man Survives Mountain Storm Using Metal Footlocker as Shield." *Chillicothe Gazette*, Ohio, December 16, 1981, p. 2. Accessed June 15, 2019. www.newspapers.com/image/292504567/?terms=Longs%2BPeak.

"May Be Body of Missing Man." *Lincoln Journal Star*, Nebraska, October 2, 1915, p. 7. Accessed June 16, 2019. www.newspapers.com/image/298199315/?terms=Thornton%2BSampson.

"Miss Carrie Welton's Legacy." *Pittsburgh Post-Gazette*, December 1, 1884, p. 1. Accessed June 12, 2019. www.newspapers.com/image/85450141/?terms=Carrie%2BWelton.

"Miss Welton's Will: Disappointed Relatives to Contest It in Court." *New York Times*, November 29, 1884, p. 1. Accessed June 12, 2019. www.newspapers.com/image/20350310/?terms=Carrie%2BWelton.

"Only Hope Now to Find Body of Sampson." *South Bend Tribune*, Indiana, November 6, 1915, p. 13. Accessed June 16, 2019. www.newspapers.com/image/513933947/?terms=Thornton%2BSampson.

"Perishes in the Rockies." *Ottawa Evening Journal*, Kansas, November 18, 1915, p. 2. Accessed June 16, 2019. www.newspapers.com/image/365704002/?terms=Thornton%2BSampson.

Perry, Phyllis J. *It Happened in Rocky Mountain National Park: Stories of Events and People That Shaped a National Park*. Guilford, CT: TwoDot, 2018, pp. 170–71.

"Rev. Dr. T. R. Sampson Is Strangely Missing." *Asheville Gazette-News*, North Carolina, September 27, 1915, p. 7. Accessed June 16, 2019. www.newspapers.com/image/59383950/?terms=Thornton%2BSampson.

"Rev. Thornton R. Sampson, D.D." *Presbyterian of the South*, October 6, 1915, pp. 16–17. Accessed June 16, 2019. www.newspapers.com/image/465127916.

"Rotarians at Denver Offer $500 Reward to Find Dr. Sampson." *Austin American*, September 16, 1915, pp. 1 and 7. Accessed June 16, 2019. www.newspapers.com/image/385042082.

"Searchers Never May Find Sampson's Body, Dr. R. E. Vinson Says." *Austin American*, September 23, 1915, p. 2. Accessed June 16, 2019. www.newspapers.com/image/385043046/?terms=Thornton%2BSampson.

"Spoiled by Spooks." *St. Louis Post-Dispatch*, September 30, 1884, p. 1. Accessed June 12, 2019. www.newspapers.com/image/138076037/?terms=Carrie%2BWelton.

"Thornton Rogers Sampson." *Presbyterian of the South*, October 27, 1915, p. 4. Accessed June 16, 2019. www.newspapers.com/image/465128293/?terms=Thornton%2BSampson.

United Press International. "Boy's Picture Printed as Search Aid." *Indianapolis Star*, August 20, 1958, p. 36. Accessed June 13, 2019. www.newspapers.com/image/105711077/?terms=Bobby%2BBizup.

———. "Climber Describes Crawl in Blizzard Down Longs Peak." *The Herald*, Provo, Utah, December 17, 1981, p. 20. Accessed June 15, 2019. www.newspapers.com/image/469209275/?terms=Longs%2BPeak.

————. "Colorado Search for Boy Continues." *Idaho State Journal*, August 19, 1958, p. 11. Accessed June 13, 2019. www.newspapers.com/image/16113303/?terms= Bobby%2BBizup.

————. "Deaf Boy Thought Hiding in Rockies." *Press Democrat*, Santa Rosa, California, August 21, 1958, p. 5. Accessed June 13, 2019. www.newspapers.com/ image/348307806/?terms=Bobby%2BBizup.

————. "Search Continues for Lost Boy." *Daily Courier*, Connellsville, Pennsylvania, August 18, 1958, p. 4. Accessed June 13, 2019. www.newspapers.com/ image/42451531/?terms=Bobby%2BBizup.

————. "Search Given Up for Lost Boy, 10." *Bridgeport Post*, Connecticut, August 25, 1958, p. 40. Accessed June 13, 2019. www.newspapers.com/image/60228328/ ?terms=Bobby%2BBizup.

————. "A 20-Member Mountain Rescue Team Include Its Way Up . . ." UPI Archives, December 17, 1981. Accessed June 15, 2019. www.upi.com/Archives/1981/12/17/ A-20-member-mountain-rescue-team-inched-its-way-up/4987377413200.

"Winds, Cold Slow Search for Missing CSU Student." *Fort Collins Coloradoan*, February 2, 1972, p. 1. Accessed June 13, 2019. www.newspapers.com/ image/225538994/?terms=Fred%2BStone%2BJoan%2BJardine.

CHAPTER 2

"Are Afraid Son Is Dead in Mountains." *Salt Lake Telegram*, August 3, 1921, p. 1. Accessed June 3, 2019. www.newspapers.com/image/288668810/?terms= Gregory%2BAubuchon.

Associated Press. "Body Removed off Steep Face of Long's Peak." *Greeley Daily Tribune*, June 7, 1954, p. 7. Accessed June 4, 2019. www.newspapers.com/ image/25007526/?terms=Earl%2BHarvey.

————. "Gray Secor's Son Killed on Longs Peak." *Greeley Daily Tribune*, August 30, 1932, p. 1. Accessed June 4, 2019. www.newspapers.com/image/24987613/ ?terms=Secor.

————. "Iowa College Student Falls to Death." *Clovis News-Journal*, New Mexico, August 9, 1938, p. 1. Accessed June 4, 2019. www.newspapers.com/image/ 2996359/?terms=death%2BRocky%2BMountain%2BNational%2BPark.

————. "Search Teams Recover Body on Longs Peak." *Fort Collins Coloradoan*, April 4, 1973, p. 3. Accessed June 5, 2019. https://coloradoan.newspapers.com/image/ 225542316/?terms=Jay%2BVan%2BStavern.

————. "Student Falls 500 Feet to Death on Mountain." *Daily Sentinel*, Grand Junction, Colorado, June 7, 1954, p. 1. Accessed June 4, 2019. www.newspapers.com/ image/537565387.

————. "Three Dozen Motorists Trapped by Blizzard Rescued in Mountains." *Daily Sentinel*, Grand Junction, Colorado, June 7, 1954, p. 1. Accessed June 4, 2019. www.newspapers.com/image/537565387.

Blumhardt, Miles. "How Rocky Mountain National Park Rangers Found Body of Ryan Albert on Longs Peak." *Fort Collins Coloradoan*, June 11, 2019. Accessed June 11,

2019. www.coloradoan.com/story/news/2019/06/11/rocky-mountain-national
-park-rangers-find-hikers-buried-body-unlikely-way/1420035001.

"Body of Missing Man Recovered." National Park Service news release, November 20,
2014. Accessed June 7, 2019. www.nps.gov/romo/learn/news/pr_body_of_missing
_man_recovered.htm.

"Body of Missing Man Recovered near Peacock Pool in Rocky Mountain National
Park." National Park Service news release, January 22, 2016. Accessed June 7,
2019. www.nps.gov/romo/learn/news/pr_body_of_missing_man_recovered_near
_peacock_pool.htm.

"Boulder Climber Dies in Fall." *Farmington Daily Times*, New Mexico, March 8, 2000,
p. 17. Accessed June 6, 2019. https://newspaperarchive.com/farmington-daily
-times-mar-08-2000-p-17.

"Clinton County Youth Missing." *Journal and Courier*, Lafayette, Indiana, August 1,
1921, p. 1. Accessed June 3, 2019. www.newspapers.com/image/261699078/
?terms=Gregory%2BAubuchon.

Coltrain, Nick. "RMNP Rangers Locate Missing Texas Hiker." *Fort Collins Coloradoan*,
August 13, 2017, p. A2. Accessed June 7, 2019. https://coloradoan.newspapers
.com/image/328638475/?terms=Steve%2BElliott%2BLongs%2BPeak.

"DC Lobbyist Dies Climbing Longs Peak." Bloomberg News, located in *Rocky Mountain News*, August 30, 1999, p. 19A. Accessed June 5, 2019. www.ancestry.com/
boards/localities.northam.usa.states.colorado.counties.larimer/880/mb.ashx.

Detterline, Jim. "Fall on Snow, Unable to Self-Arrest, No Hard Hat, Colorado, Rocky
Mountain National Park, Longs Peak." American Alpine Club Accident Report,
1994. Accessed June 5, 2019. http://publications.americanalpineclub.org/articles/
13199403902/Fall-on-Snow-Unable-to-Self-Arrest-No-Hard-Hat-Colorado
-Rocky-Mountain-National-Park-Longs-Peak.

"Fall Victim's Body Found." *Daily Oklahoman*, August 29, 1962, p. 43. Accessed June 4,
2019. www.newspapers.com/image/453365596/?terms=Ken%2BMurphy.

"Fall Victim's Rites Friday." *Daily Oklahoman*, Oklahoma City, August 30, 1962, p. 47.
Accessed June 4, 2019. www.newspapers.com/image/453367642/?terms=Ken
%2BMurphy.

"Fatality on Longs Peak at RMNP." National Park Service news release, September 11,
2009. Accessed June 7, 2019. www.nps.gov/romo/learn/news/pr_longs_peak
_fatality.htm.

"Fatality on the Keyhole Route of Longs Peak in Rocky Mountain National Park."
National Park Service news release, September 25, 2010. Accessed June 5, 2019.
www.nps.gov/romo/learn/news/fatality-on-the-keyhole-route-of-longs-peak.htm.

"Fatality on the Narrows Section on Longs Peak." National Park Service news release,
October 2, 2016. Accessed June 7, 2019. www.nps.gov/romo/learn/news/fatality
-on-the-narrows-section-on-longs-peak.htm.

"Favorable Weather Allows Aerial Search Efforts for Missing Man." National Park
Service news release, November 20, 2014. Accessed June 7, 2019. www.nps.gov/
romo/learn/news/pr_favorable_weather_allows_aerial_search_efforts_for_missing
_man.htm.

"Gregory Koczanski, 42, Dies." *Washington Post*, August 20, 1999. Accessed June 5, 2019. www.washingtonpost.com/archive/local/1999/08/20/gregory-koczanski -42-dies/9ed9da01-5924-426c-9d06-d18ca40c698a/?utm_term=.8800685 c4ded.

Hefty, Jennifer. "Parents of Hiker Missing on Longs Peak: Suspending Search for Micah Tice 'Wrong' Call by National Park Service." *Fort Collins Coloradoan*, December 10, 2018. Accessed September 10, 2019. https://www.coloradoan.com/ story/news/2018/12/10/parents-hiker-missing-longs-peak-suspending-search -micah-tice-wrong-call-national-park-service/2265759002.

"Hiker Who Died on Longs Peak Was N.H. Pastor." 9news.com, reprinted in *Fort Collins Coloradoan*, July 18, 2010, p. 3. Accessed June 7, 2019. https://coloradoan .newspapers.com/image/227049873/?terms=Jeffrey%2BRosinski.

Hindl, Saja. "RMNP Calls Off Search for NJ Hiker until Weather Improves." *Fort Collins Coloradoan*, November 4, 2018, p. A2. Accessed June 7, 2019. https:// coloradoan.newspapers.com/image/505132142/?terms=Ryan%2BAlbert.

———. "RMNP Crews Search for Missing Hiker in Longs Peak Area." *Fort Collins Coloradoan*, October 7, 2019, p. A2. Accessed June 7, 2019. https://coloradoan .newspapers.com/image/492998742/?terms=Ryan%2BAlbert.

"Jeffris, Peter Anthony." *Wisconsin State Journal*, November 27, 2014, p. 18. Accessed June 7, 2019. https://newspaperarchive.com/madison-wisconsin-state-journal -nov-27-2014-p-18.

"John A. Bramley." Legacy.com, September 11, 2009. Accessed June 7, 2019. www .legacy.com/obituaries/name/john-bramley-obituary?pid=132890717&affiliateid =1790&page=4.

Kahn, Ric. "Boston Man Falls to Death in Colorado National Park." *Boston Globe*, August 27, 1995, p. 30. Accessed June 5, 2019. www.newspapers.com/image/ 441120073/?terms=Jun%2BKamimura.

"Kem Arnold Murphy." Find a Grave, accessed June 4, 2019. www.findagrave.com/ memorial/70952195/kem-arnold-murphy.

Kurtz, Edward J. "Colorado, Rocky Mountain National Park." American Alpine Club Accident Report, 1955. Accessed June 4, 2019. http://publications.american alpineclub.org/articles/13195500900/Colorado-Rocky-Mountain-National -Park-1.

Kyle, Sarah. "Missing Hiker's Body Recovered from RMNP." *Fort Collins Coloradoan*, September 4, 2018, p. A2. Accessed June 6, 2019. www.newspapers.com/image/ 480210951/?terms=death%2BRocky%2BMountain%2BNational%2BPark.

"Longs Peak Hiking and Climbing." American Alpine Institute, accessed June 3, 2019. www.alpineinstitute.com/catalog/longs-peak-hiking-climbing.

"Massachusetts Hiker Killed with Descending Longs Peak." *Daily Sentinel*, Grand Junction, Colorado, August 27, 1995, p. 23. Accessed June 5, 2019. www.newspapers .com/image/538658349/?terms=Jun%2BKamimura.

Meyers, Stephen. "Body of Hiker Removed from Mountain." *Fort Collins Coloradoan*, June 13, 2014, p. A1. Accessed June 5, 2019. https://coloradoan.newspapers.com/ image/113874496/?terms=Matthew%2BBurklow.

———. " 'Every Step Counts' on Longs." *Fort Collins Coloradoan*, June 29, 2014, pp. A13–14. Accessed June 5, 2019. www.newspapers.com/image/113881452.

"Michigan Man Killed in Fall on Longs Peak." *Daily Sentinel*, Grand Junction, Colorado, June 13, 1972, p. 8. Accessed June 4, 2019. www.newspapers.com/image/536412197/?terms=Paul%2BRussell.

"Missing Man's Body Discovered in Longs Peak Area." National Park Service news release, March 19, 2017. Accessed June 29, 2019. www.nps.gov/romo/learn/news/pr_body_of_missing_man_discovered_in_longs_peak_area.htm.

"News of a Week in Condensed Form." *Davis County Clipper*, Bountiful, Utah, August 5, 1921, p. 3. Accessed June 3, 2019. www.newspapers.com/image/285953420/?terms=Gregory%2BAubuchon.

"No Clue to Fate of Missing Man Is Found." *Estes Park Trail-Gazette*, Colorado, June 24, 1921. Accessed via the Estes Park History Rescue Project, June 4, 2019. https://studylib.net/doc/18621658/1921-eptrail---estes-park-history-rescue-project.

"Obituary: Scott Alan Corliss." Dignity Memorial, October 1, 2016. Accessed June 7, 2019. www.dignitymemorial.com/obituaries/greeley-co/scott-corliss-7112536.

"Oklahoma Correspondence." *Catholic Advance*, August 27, 1921, p. 9. Accessed June 3, 2019. www.newspapers.com/image/183636019/?terms=Gregory%2BAubuchon.

———. *Catholic Advance*, September 17, 1921, p. 9. Accessed June 3, 2019. www.newspapers.com/image/183636175/?terms=Gregory%2BAubuchon.

———. *Catholic Advance*, October 1, 1921, p. 9. Accessed June 3, 2019. www.newspapers.com/image/183636270/?terms=Gregory%2BAubuchon.

"Paul G. Nahon III." *Springfield News-Leader*, August 15, 2013. Accessed June 7, 2019. www.legacy.com/obituaries/news-leader/obituary.aspx?n=paul-g-nahon&pid=166472973&fhid=12405.

Pialet, Tyler. "Coroner Identifies Remains Found in RMNP as 20-Year-Old Micah Tice." *Estes Park Trail-Gazette*, July 10, 2019. Accessed September 10, 2019. https://www.eptrail.com/2019/07/10/coroner-identifies-remains-found-in-rmnp-as-20-year-old-micah-tice.

Pohl, Jason. "Missing Man's Body Found by Longs Peak." *Fort Collins Coloradoan*, January 23, 2016, p. A2. Accessed June 7, 2019. www.newspapers.com/image/149505445/?terms=death%2BRocky%2BMountain%2BNational%2BPark.

"Publisher of Legion Paper Meets Death." *Jacksonville Daily Journal*, Illinois, July 19, 1932, p. 1. Accessed June 4, 2019. www.newspapers.com/image/32819661/?terms=Robert%2BSmith%2BLongs%2BPeak.

"Rangers Recover Body of Climber near Longs Peak." *Fort Collins Coloradoan*, June 13, 1972, p. 1. Accessed June 4, 2019. www.newspapers.com/image/225549519/?terms=Paul%2BRussell.

"Recovery Efforts Completed for Jens 'Jay' Yambert." National Park Service news release, September 2, 2018. Accessed June 6, 2018. www.nps.gov/romo/learn/news/recovery-efforts-completed-for-jens-jay-yambert.htm.

"Recovery of Body Delayed by Second Fall." *Fort Collins Coloradoan*, August 17, 2013, p. A4. Accessed June 7, 2019. https://coloradoan.newspapers.com/image/113855893/?terms=Paul%2BNahon.

"Recovery Operations for Micah Tice—Missing since November." National Park Service news release, July 5, 2019. Accessed September 10, 2019. https://www.nps.gov/romo/learn/news/recovery-operations-for-micah-tice-missing-since-november.htm.

"Rockies Claim Hoosier Youth Climbing Peak." *Journal and Courier*, Lafayette, Indiana, September 19, 1921. Accessed June 3, 2019. www.newspapers.com/image/261728213/?terms=Gregory%2BAubuchon.

"Ronald Graham Webber." Legacy.com, January 28, 2016, accessed June 7, 2019. www.legacy.com/obituaries/timesunion/obituary.aspx?pid=177485788.

"Search Efforts Continue Today for Missing Man." National Park Service news release, November 19, 2014. Accessed June 7, 2019. www.nps.gov/romo/learn/news/pr_search_efforts_continue_today_for_missing_man.htm.

"Search for Ryan Albert in Rocky Mountain National Park." National Park Service news release, October 9, 2018. Accessed June 6, 2019. www.nps.gov/romo/learn/news/search-for-ryan-albert-in-rocky-mountain-national-park.htm.

"Search in Longs Peak and Mount Meeker Area." National Park Service news release, July 28, 2014. Accessed June 6, 2019. www.nps.gov/romo/learn/news/pr_search_in_longs_peak_and_mount_meeker_area.htm.

"Search in Longs Peak Area Continues for Ryan Albert." National Park Service news release, October 7, 2018. Accessed June 7, 2019. www.nps.gov/romo/learn/news/search-in-longs-peak-area-continues-for-ryan-albert.htm.

"Search in Longs Peak Area Continues for Yambert; Separate Rescue Effort Takes Place in Search Area." National Park Service news release, August 30, 2018. Accessed June 6, 2019. www.nps.gov/romo/learn/news/search-in-longs-peak-area-continues-for-yambert-separate-rescue-effort-takes-place-in-search-area.htm.

"Search in Longs Peak Area for Overdue Man." National Park Service news release, August 29, 2018. Accessed June 6, 2019. www.nps.gov/romo/learn/news/search-in-longs-peak-area-for-overdue-man.htm.

"Searching Parties Out after Tourist." *Ogden Standard*, Utah, June 23, 1921, p. 8. Accessed June 4, 2019. www.newspapers.com/image/533575932/?terms=H.F.%2BTargett.

"Search Underway in Longs Peak Area." National Park Service news release, January 21, 2016. Accessed June 7, 2019. www.nps.gov/romo/learn/news/pr_search_underway_in_longs_peak_area.htm.

"Search Underway on Longs Peak." National Park Service news release, November 18, 2014. Accessed June 7, 2019. www.nps.gov/romo/learn/news/pr_search_underway_on_longs_peak.htm.

"Service Honors Victim." *Daily Oklahoman*, August 29, 1962, p. 13. Accessed June 4, 2019. www.newspapers.com/image/453364986/?terms=Ken%2BMurphy.

"Skull Discovery Offers Clue to Fate of Los Angeles Man." *Los Angeles Times*, September 21, 1940, p. 21. Accessed June 4, 2019. www.newspapers.com/image/385518832/?terms=Targett%2Bskull.

Swanson, Sady. "Cause of Death Released for New Jersey Hiker Missing since October in Longs Peak Area." *Fort Collins Coloradoan*, July 28, 2019. Accessed Sepember

10, 2019. https://www.coloradoan.com/story/news/2019/07/28/new-jersey-hiker
-ryan-albert-died-hypothermia-blunt-force-trauma/1851931001.

———. "Hiking's Deadly Allure." *Windsor Beacon*, Colorado, November 25, 2018,
pp. 1W, 3W, 4W. Accessed June 7, 2019. https://coloradoan.newspapers.com/
image/508668412.

———. "NJ Man Still Missing after Leaving for Longs Peak Last Week." *Fort Collins
Coloradoan*, October 10, 2018, pp. A1, A3. Accessed June 7, 2019. https://
coloradoan.newspapers.com/image/494497321/?terms=Ryan%2BAlbert.

———. "Remains Found on Longs Peak Confirmed to Be Micah Tice, Coroner
Releases Cause of Death." *Fort Collins Coloradoan*, July 8, 2019. Accessed September 10, 2019. https://www.coloradoan.com/story/news/2019/07/08/coroner
-remains-found-longs-peak-micah-tice-las-vegas/1673117001.

———. "Rocky Mountain National Park Search Crews Find Remains Believed to Be
Missing Air Force Cadet Micah Tice." *Fort Collins Coloradoan*, July 5, 2019.
Accessed September 10, 2019. https://www.coloradoan.com/story/news/2019/
07/05/rmnp-search-crews-find-remains-believed-to-be-missing-air-force-cadet
-micah-tice/1661503001.

"Teams Continue Efforts in the Search for Ryan Albert in Rocky Mountain National
Park." National Park Service news release, October 11, 2018. Accessed June 7,
2019. www.nps.gov/romo/learn/news/teams-continue-efforts-in-the-search-for
-ryan-albert-in-rocky-mountain-national-park.htm.

United Press. "Body of Boy, Long Missing, Is Discovered," located in *Visalia Daily
Times*, California, September 17, 1921. Accessed June 3, 2019. www.newspapers
.com/image/531414570/?terms=Gregory%2BAubuchon.

United Press International. "Team Recovers Body of Climber." *Albuquerque Journal*,
April 6, 1973, p. 12. Accessed June 5, 2019. www.newspapers.com/image/
156200918/?terms=Jay%2BVan%2BStavern.

Van Slyke, Larry. "Fall on Rock, Exceeding Abilities, Failure to Follow Route, Party
Separated, Inadequate Equipment, Colorado, Longs Peak." American Alpine Club
Accident Reports, 1981. Accessed June 4, 2019. http://publications.americanalpine
club.org/articles/13198103400/Fall-on-Rock-Exceeding-Abilities-Failure-to-Follow
-Route-Party-Separated-Inadequate-Equipment-Colorado-Longs-Peak.

"Wichitan Dies in Fall in Colorado Park." *Salina Journal*, Kansas, September 27, 2010,
p. 5. Accessed June 5, 2019. https://newspaperarchive.com/salina-journal-sep-27
-2010-p-5.

"Winter Weather Conditions since Early October Hamper Search Efforts for Ryan
Albert." National Park Service news release, November 2, 2018. Accessed June 6,
2019. www.nps.gov/romo/learn/news/winter-weather-conditions-since-early
-october-hamper-search-efforts-for-ryan-albert.htm.

CHAPTER 3

Associated Press. "Chicagoan, 18, Falls 600 Ft to Death on Peak." *Chicago Tribune*,
September 2, 1946, p. 16. Accessed June 8, 2019. www.newspapers.com/image/
370304575/?terms=%22Charles%2BGrant%22.

————. "Falls to Death off Longs Peak." *El Paso Herald*, August 19, 1929, p. 1. Accessed June 8, 2019. www.newspapers.com/image/41283675/?terms=Charles%2BThiemeyer.

————. "Mountain Plunge to Death Ends Scaling Contest." *Nevada State Journal*, August 20, 1929, p. 2. Accessed June 8, 2019. www.newspapers.com/image/78814175/?terms=Charles%2BThiemeyer.

Bachman, Don. "Colorado, Rocky Mountain National Park, Longs Peak." American Alpine Club Accident Reports, 1967. Accessed June 9, 2019. http://publications.americanalpineclub.org/articles/13196701002/Colorado-Rocky-Mountain-National-Park-Longs-Peak.

Briggeman, Kim. "Climbing Death Casts Pall over Montana Innocence Project, Others." *Missoulian*, October 5, 2015. Accessed June 11, 2019. https://missoulian.com/news/local/climbing-death-casts-pall-over-montana-innocence-project-others/article_f7e78d4b-4662-5257-813c-e36f734211bd.html.

Briggs, Roger. "The Diamond." *The Alpinist*, March 1, 2007. Accessed June 11, 2019. www.alpinist.com/doc/_print/ALP19/mountain-profile-longs-diamond.

Browne, Rich. "Fall on Rock—Loose Rock, Climbing Unroped, Climbing Alone, Colorado, Rocky Mountain National Park, Longs Peak, the Diamond." *American Alpine Journal Accident Report*, 2011. Accessed June 11, 2019. http://publications.americanalpineclub.org/articles/13201105202/Fall-on-Rock-Loose-Rock-Climbing-Unroped-Climbing-Alone-Colorado-Rocky-Mountain-National-Park-Longs-Peak-The-Diamond.

"'Chuck' Grant Loses Life in Longs Peak Fall This Sunday." *Lafayette Leader*, September 6, 1946.

"Climber Killed in Rocky Mountain Park." *Fort Collins Coloradoan*, June 3, 1977, p. 25. Accessed June 9, 2019. https://coloradoan.newspapers.com/image/226806113/?terms=Michael%2BNeri.

"Climber Who Died Was from Broomfield." *Fort Collins Coloradoan*, August 29, 2010, p. 3. Accessed June 11, 2019. https://coloradoan.newspapers.com/image/227219922/?terms=Benjamin%2BHebb.

Collins, Jim. "Leadership Lessons of a Rock Climber." *Fast Company*, December 1, 2003. Accessed June 11, 2019. www.fastcompany.com/47527/leadership-lessons-rock-climber.

Cordes, Kelly. "North American 2000." *American Alpine Journal*, UK edition, 2001. Accessed June 11, 2019. www.alpinejournal.org.uk/Contents/Contents_2001_files/AJ%202001%20279-283%20North%20America.pdf.

Covington, Michael M. "North America, United States, Colorado 1977." American Alpine Club Accident Report, 1978. Accessed June 9, 2019. http://publications.americanalpineclub.org/articles/12197853403/North-America-United-States-Colorado-1977.

"Dangerous Longs Peak Claims Sixth Victim." *Huntington Press*, Indiana, July 24, 1926, p. 1. Accessed June 8, 2019. www.newspapers.com/image/39973551/?terms=Forrest%2BKetring.

"Denver Man Is Dead after Dive." *Clarion-Ledger*, Jackson, Mississippi, August 19, 1929. Accessed June 8, 2019. www.newspapers.com/image/202673959/?terms=Charles%2BThiemeyer.

Detterline, Jim, and Mark Magnuson. "Fall on Rock, Climbing Unroped—Trying to Save Time, Colorado, Rocky Mountain National Park, Longs Peak." American Alpine Club Accident Reports, 2001. Accessed June 11, 2019. http://publications.americanalpineclub.org/articles/13200106302/Fall-on-Rock-Climbing-UnropedTrying-to-Save-Time-Colorado-Rocky-Mountain-National-Park-Longs-Peak.

Evans, Joseph R. *Death, Despair, and Second Chances in Rocky Mountain National Park.* Boulder, CO: Johnson Books, 2010, pp. 165–69.

"Fall on Ice, Crampon Problem, Unable to Self-Arrest, Climbing Unroped." In *Accidents in North American Mountaineering.* Seattle, WA: Mountaineers Books, 1989, pp. 56–57. Accessed June 10, 2019. https://books.google.com/books?id=0LySqJli9coC&pg=PA56&lpg=PA56&dq=1988+Kevin+Hardwick+Longs+Peak&source=bl&ots=yZP4u2O9KT&sig=ACfU3U16jkKVj_7yfyva7SERUi4ZHUNl-A&hl=en&sa=X&ved=2ahUKEwjI2POX3cbhAhVqZN8KHYxwB-EQ6AEwAXoECAcQAQ#v=onepage&q=1988%20Kevin%20Hardwick%20Longs%20Peak&f=false.

"Fatality on Longs Peak Recovery Efforts Complete." National Park Service news release, October 4, 2015. Accessed June 11, 2019. www.nps.gov/romo/learn/news/pr_fatality_on_longs_peak_recovery_efforts_complete.htm.

"Girl Victim of Blizzard." *Nebraska State Journal,* Lincoln, Neb., January 14, 1925, p. 2. Accessed December 9, 2018. www.newspapers.com/image/314077592/?terms=Agnes%2BVaille.

Hebb, Mike. "Climbing with Ben." *TimeToFiddle,* accessed June 11, 2019. http://timetofiddle.yolasite.com/bens-page.php.

"Kiener, Walter, 1894–1959." From the Description of Papers, 1848–1959 (University of Nebraska–Lincoln, found on Social Networks and Archival Context Cooperative). Accessed December 9, 2018. http://snaccooperative.org/ark:/99166/w6wd8nwk.

"Longs Peak Exacts Its Penalty." *St. Louis Post-Dispatch,* located in *Biddeford Daily Journal,* September 1, 1926, p. 11. Accessed June 8, 2019. https://newspaperarchive.com/biddeford-daily-journal-sep-01-1926-p-11.

"Man Falls to Death from Longs Peak." *Greeley Daily Tribune,* September 14, 1931, p. 1. Accessed June 8, 2019. https://www.newspapers.com/image/27261245/?terms=R.B.%2BKey.

McClannan, Kent. "Cameron Tague, 1967–2000." In *Accidents in North American Mountaineering.* Golden, CO: American Alpine Club, 2001. Accessed June 11, 2019. http://publications.americanalpineclub.org/articles/12200146900/Cameron-Tague-1967-2000#.

"North America, United States, Colorado, Longs Peak." American Alpine Club Accident Report, 1930. Accessed June 8, 2019. http://publications.americanalpineclub.org/articles/12193024101/North-America-United-States-Colorado-Longs-Peak.

"Patrolman Dies during Climb." *Times-Leader,* Wilkes-Barre, Pennsylvania, October 8, 1979, p. 3. Accessed June 9, 2019. www.newspapers.com/image/415826159/?terms=Charles%2BNesbit.

Payne, Matt. "Benjamin Russell Hebb-Longs Peak-Diamond-Dunn-Westbay Route -Broadway Ledge-8/27/2010." 100Summits.com. Accessed June 11, 2019. www .100summits.com/itemlist/tag/Benjamin%20Russell%20Hebb#ben.

Reveley, Chris. "Loss of Control, Voluntary Glissade, Faulty Use of Crampons, Colorado, Longs Peak." American Alpine Club Accident Report, 1980. Accessed June 9, 2019. http://publications.americanalpineclub.org/articles/13198003402/Loss -of-Control-Voluntary-Glissade-Faulty-Use-of-Crampons-Colorado-Longs-Peak.

Robertson, Janet. *The Magnificent Mountain Women: Adventures in the Colorado Rockies*, Lincoln, NE: Bison Books, 2003, pp. 47–56.

Sherman, John Dickinson. "Kiener's Lookout." *Waterville Telegraph*, Kansas, September 11, 1925, p. 7. Accessed December 9, 2018. www.newspapers.com/image/ 424465672/?terms=Agnes%2BVaille.

"Spencer Veysey June 14, 1989–October 2, 2015." *Ames Tribune*, Iowa, October 15, 2015. Accessed June 11, 2019. www.amestrib.com/article/20151015/ OBITUARIES/310159972.

Sunnysummit. "Kiener's Route." Summitpost.org. Accessed December 9, 2018. www .summitpost.org/kiener-s-route/155570.

Tague, Cameron, and Michael Pennings. "Chilean Patagonia, Various Ascents." *American Alpine Journal*, 1997, pp. 263–65. Accessed June 11, 2019. http://aac-publications .s3.amazonaws.com/documents/aaj/1997/PDF/AAJ_1997_39_71_263.pdf.

Taylor, Carol, and Silvia Pettem. "A Fatal Winter Climb in 1925." *Daily Camera*, January 11, 2013. Accessed December 9, 2018. www.dailycamera.com/ci_22355341/ agnes-vailles-longs-peak-fatal-winter-climb-1925.

United Press. "Rangers Hunt Peak's Victim." *Billings Gazette*, August 20, 1929, p. 14. Accessed June 8, 2019. www.newspapers.com/image/411309694/?terms=Charles %2BThiemeyer.

Weidner, Chris. "Colorado Climbers' Legacy of First Ascents of North Howser Tower." *Daily Camera*, September 20, 2016. Accessed June 11, 2019. www.dailycamera .com/2016/09/20/chris-weidner-colorado-climbers-legacy-of-first-ascents-of -north-howser-tower.

CHAPTER 4

Allen, Robert. "Park Rangers Protect Fallen in Body Recovery Efforts." *Fort Collins Coloradoan*, September 12, 2013, p. A1–2. Accessed June 29, 2019. www.newspapers .com/image/113856559.

Associated Press. "Body of Lost Soldier Discovered." *The Missoulian*, Montana, July 8, 1946, p. 1. Accessed June 18, 2019. www.newspapers.com/image/349176086/ ?terms=%22Thomas%2BH.%2BEvans%22.

———. "Body of Missing Boy, 12, Found on Mountainside." *Southern Illinoisian*, Carbondale, Illinois, July 12, 1982, p. 12. Accessed June 28, 2019. www.newspapers .com/image/82579947/?terms=Robert%2BBaldeshwiler

———. "Body of Missouri Youth Found after Fall Down Cliff." *Daily Sentinel*, Grand Junction, Colorado, August 17, 1956, p. 3. Accessed June 28, 2019. www.newspapers .com/image/537665297/?terms=George%2BBloom.

———. "Climber with One Arm Falls 600 Feet to Death." *Albuquerque Journal*, May 16, 1977, p. 71. Accessed June 18, 2019. https://newspaperarchive.com/albuquerque-journal-may-16-1977-p-71.

———. "Continue Search for Missing Man." *Montana Standard*, Butte, Montana, June 23, 1946, p. 6. Accessed June 18, 2019. www.newspapers.com/image/350456052/?terms=%22Thomas%2BH.%2BEvans%22.

———. "Continue Search for Woodson Attorney." *Emporia Gazette*, September 18, 1940, p. 1. Accessed June 18, 2019. www.newspapers.com/image/11347640/?terms=%22Hoyt%2BWhite%22.

———. "Find Body of Missing Attorney." *Iola Register*, September 20, 1940, p. 1. Accessed June 18, 2019. www.newspapers.com/image/4810477/?terms=%22Hoyt%2BWhite%22.

———. "Find Body of Youth." *Lansing State Journal*, Michigan, July 17, 1961, p. 6. Accessed June 29, 2019. www.newspapers.com/image/207841536/?terms=Myron%2BFritts.

———. "Iowan Dies while Climbing." *Iowa City Press-Citizen*, June 13, 1984, p. 2. Accessed June 18, 2019. www.newspapers.com/image/204830346/?terms=David%2BOrmsby.

———. "Labor Day in Colorado Is Uneventful." *Greeley Daily Tribune*, September 8, 1936, p. 12. Accessed June 18, 2019. www.newspapers.com/image/24984711/?terms=Forrest%2BHein.

———. "Lincoln Scout's Body Is Recovered." *Beatrice Daily Sun*, June 16, 1966, p. 1. Accessed June 28, 2019. www.newspapers.com/image/507389932/?terms=Jay%2BDuPont.

———. "Nebraska Teen Falls to Death in Park." *Daily Sentinel*, Grand Junction, Colorado, July 1, 1990, p. 13. Accessed June 29, 2019. www.newspapers.com/image/539720059/?terms=Andrew%2BTufly.

———. "Schoolboy Killed Trying to Scale 9,500-Foot Peak." *Chicago Tribune*, September 7, 1936, p. 7. Accessed June 18, 2019. www.newspapers.com/image/355098398/?terms=Forrest%2BHein.

———. "State Hiking, Climbing Death Toll Up." *Daily Sentinel*, Grand Junction, Colorado, August 25, 1980, p. 3. Accessed June 18, 2019. www.newspapers.com/image/537702150/?terms=death%2BRocky%2BMountain%2BNational%2BPark.

———. "Youth Is Killed Climbing Peak." *Arizona Republic*, September 7, 1936, p. 4. Accessed June 18, 2019. www.newspapers.com/image/117215990/?terms=Forrest%2BHein.

Associated Press/Staff Reports. "New Angle on White." *Iola Register*, September 19, 1940, pp. 1 and 5. Accessed June 18, 2019. www.newspapers.com/image/4810427.

"Await Mountain Victim." *Inter Ocean*, Chicago, Illinois, August 6, 1905, p. 3. Accessed June 16, 2019. www.newspapers.com/image/34535038/?terms=Louis%2BLevings.

"Body Found Believed to Be That of Brian Perri." National Park Service news release, July 28, 2018. Accessed June 29, 2019. www.nps.gov/romo/learn/news/body-found-believed-to-be-that-of-brian-perri.htm.

"Body Recovery of Climber Occurring in Rocky Mountain National Park." National Park Service news release, November 21, 2010. Accessed June 29, 2019. www.nps .gov/romo/learn/news/pr_climbing_fatality_allmixedup.htm.

Brown, Joye. "Lansing Boy Missing on 1st Mountain Trek." *Chicago Tribune*, July 2, 1982, p. 40. Accessed June 28, 2019. www.newspapers.com/image/387769301/ ?terms=Robert%2BBaldeshwiler.

Bruce, Kaitlyn. "Officials ID Man Killed in Fall at RMNP." *Fort Collins Coloradoan*, October 18, 2010, p. 1. Accessed June 29, 2019. https://coloradoan.newspapers .com/image/227059740/?terms=James%2BCharles%2BPatrick.

"Canyon Holds Chicago Dead." *Chicago Tribune*, August 7, 1905, p. 5. Accessed June 16, 2019. www.newspapers.com/image/350209417/?terms=Louis%2BLevings.

"Colorado News Items." *Telluride San Miguel Examiner*, Colorado, October 14, 1905, p. 7. Accessed June 16, 2019. https://newspaperarchive.com/telluride-san-miguel -examiner-oct-14-1905-p-7.

"Colorado–Rocky Mountain National Park (1)." American Alpine Club Accident Report, 1954. Accessed June 28, 2019. http://publications.americanalpineclub .org/articles/13195400801/ColoradoRocky-Mountain-National-Park-1.

"CSU Researcher Dies in RMNP." *Fort Collins Coloradoan*, July 29, 2003, p. 9. Accessed June 29, 2019. www.newspapers.com/image/227096872/?terms=Kurt%2BZollers.

Darst, Kevin. "Ranger's Death Prompts Change." *Fort Collins Coloradoan*, February 3, 2006, pp. 1–2. Accessed June 29, 2019. https://coloradoan.newspapers.com/ image/226997743.

Detterline, Jim. "Fall on Ice, Climbing Alone, Inadequate Protection, Colorado, Rocky Mountain National Park, Thatchtop." American Alpine Club Accident Report, 1999. Accessed June 29, 2019. http://publications.americanalpineclub.org/ articles/13199904901/Fall-on-Ice-Climbing-Alone-Inadequate-Protection -Colorado-Rocky-Mountain-National-Park-Thatchtop.

———. "Fall on Rock—Blown Off by Wind Gust, Inadequate Protection, Partner Stranded, Inexperience." American Alpine Club Accident Report, 1998. Accessed June 29, 2019. http://publications.americanalpineclub.org/articles/13199804300/ Fall-on-Rock-Blown-Off-by-Wind-Gust-Inadequate-Protection-Partner -Stranded-Inexeperience.

———. "Fall on Rock, Climbing Alone and Unroped, Exceeding Abilities, Colorado, Rocky Mountain National Park, Mount Meeker." American Alpine Club Accident Report, 1993. Accessed June 29, 2019. http://publications.american alpineclub.org/articles/13199305501/Fall-on-Rock-Climbing-Alone-and -Unroped-Exceeding-Abilities-Colorado-Rocky-Mountain-National-Park -Mount-Meeker.

"Dies in Snow, East Swelters." *Los Angeles Times*, August 4, 1917, p. 2. Accessed June 28, 2019. www.newspapers.com/image/380408264/?terms=Eula%2BFrost.

Erskine, Doug. "Colorado, Rocky Mountain National Park." American Alpine Club Accident Report, 1967. Accessed June 28, 2019. http://publications.american alpineclub.org/articles/13196701001/Colorado-Rocky-Mountain-National -Park.

"Falling Fatality in Rocky Mountain National Park." National Park Service news release, August 22, 2013. Accessed June 29, 2019. www.nps.gov/romo/learn/news/pr_falling_fatality_in_rocky_mountain_national_park.htm.

"Fall Kills Austinite in Colorado." *Austin American-Statesman*, May 20, 1977, p. 12. Accessed June 18, 2019. www.newspapers.com/image/378936188/?terms=Harold%2BHoltzendorf.

"Falls on Rock and Snow, Stranded, Falling Rocks, etc., Colorado, Various Locations." American Alpine Club Accident Report, 1988 Accessed June 18, 2019. http://publications.americanalpineclub.org/articles/13198803900/Falls-on-Rock-and-Snow-Stranded-Falling-Rocks-etc-Colorado-Various-Locations.

"Fatality above Chasm Lake in Rocky Mountain National Park." National Park Service news release, August 23, 2017. Accessed June 29, 2019. www.nps.gov/romo/learn/news/pr_fatality_above_chasm_lake.htm.

"Fatality in Lumpy Ridge Area of Rocky Mountain National Park." National Park Service news release, October 1, 2017. Accessed June 29, 2019. www.nps.gov/romo/learn/news/pr_fatality_in_lumpy_ridge_area.htm.

"Fatality near Emerald Lake in Rocky Mountain National Park." National Park Service news release, June 8, 2008. Accessed June 29, 2019. www.nps.gov/romo/learn/news/pr_emerald_fatality.htm.

Fuson, Ken. "Marshalltown Man Dies in Fall from Mountain." *Des Moines Register*, July 14, 1984, p. 3. Accessed June 18, 2019. www.newspapers.com/image/131769057/?terms=David%2BOrmsby.

"Greenfield Girl Killed in Fall in Colorado Canyon." *Press-Gazette*, Hillsboro, Ohio, August 17, 1962, p. 12. Accessed June 28, 2019. www.newspapers.com/image/10032337/?terms=Patricia%2BBeatty.

Hartzog, George B. "Colorado, Rocky Mountain National Park (4)." American Alpine Club Accident Report, 1957. Accessed June 28, 2019. http://publications.americanalpineclub.org/articles/13195700802/Colorado-Rocky-Mountain-National-Park-4.

"Henry L. Gholz." *Fort Collins Coloradoan*, October 22, 2017, p. W9. Accessed June 29, 2019. www.newspapers.com/image/349461974/?terms=death%2BRocky%2BMountain%2BNational%2BPark.

"In Mountain Tomb." *Topeka Daily Herald*, Kansas, August 8, 1905, p. 3. Accessed June 16, 2019. www.newspapers.com/image/387508332/?terms=Louis%2BLevings.

International News Service. "Missing Soldier Found Dead in Colorado Park." *Lincoln Journal Star*, Nebraska, July 8, 1946, p. 7. Accessed June 18, 2019. www.newspapers.com/image/61012802/?terms=%22Thomas%2BH.%2BEvans%22.

"Killed by Awful Fall." *Salt Lake Telegram*, Utah, August 5, 1905, p. 8. Accessed June 16, 2019. www.newspapers.com/image/289771286/?terms=Louis%2BLevings.

Landgraf, Amel. "Colorado, Rocky Mountain National Park." American Alpine Club Accident Report, 1961. Accessed June 29, 2019. http://publications.americanalpineclub.org/articles/13196102901/Colorado-Rocky-Mountain-National-Park.

"Lincoln Scout Dies in Fall." *Lincoln Journal Star*, Nebraska, June 15, 1966, p. 1. Accessed June 28, 2019. www.newspapers.com/image/313586504/?terms=Jay%2BDuPont.

Mahany, Barbara. "220 End 6th Day Hunting Lost Boy." *Chicago Tribune*, July 5, 1982, p. 12. Accessed June 28, 2019. www.newspapers.com/image/387872925/?terms =Robert%2BBaldeshwiler.

"Miscellaneous." *Iola Register*, Kansas, September 23, 1940, p. 1. Accessed June 18, 2019. www.newspapers.com/image/4810550/?terms=%22Hoyt%2BWhite%22.

"Monday's Search Efforts for Missing Man Last Seen on Mount Meeker." National Park Service news release, July 9, 2018. Accessed June 29, 2019. www.nps.gov/ romo/learn/news/monday-s-search-efforts-for-missing-man-last-seen-on -mount-meeker.htm.

"N.D. Student Dies in Fall from Colorado Mountain." *South Bend Tribune*, Indiana, July 17, 1961, p. 13. Accessed June 29, 2019. www.newspapers.com/image/ 515113601/?terms=Myron%2BFritts.

Nguyen, Kim. "Rangers Better Prepared Than Most Visitors." Associated Press, located in *Daily Herald*, Provo, Utah, August 12, 2005. Accessed June 29, 2019. www .newspapers.com/image/472473836/?terms=Jeff%2BChristensen.

"Obituaries: David Drea Felts." *Colorado Springs Gazette Telegraph*, September 3, 1987, p. 23. Accessed June 18, 2019. https://newspaperarchive.com/colorado-springs -gazette-telegraph-sep-03-1987-p-23.

"Recovery Efforts Completed for Brian Perri." National Park Service news release, July 31, 2018. Accessed June 29, 2019. www.nps.gov/romo/learn/news/recovery -efforts-completed-for-brian-perri.htm.

"Richard Thomas Frisbee." *Fort Collins Coloradoan*, June 13, 2008, p. 21. Accessed June 29, 2018. https://coloradoan.newspapers.com/image/227001536/?terms=Richard %2BFrisbie.

"Rocky Mountain Printmaker: Estes Park Artist Dean Babcock." Birger Sander Memorial Gallery, Lindsborg, Kansas, August 2017. Accessed June 16, 2019. http://sandzen.org/wp-content/uploads/2013/05/2017-Dean-Babcock -BROCHURE-1.pdf.

"Saturday's Search Efforts for Missing Man Last Seen on Mount Meeker." National Park Service news release, July 7, 2018. Accessed June 29, 2019. www.nps.gov/ romo/learn/news/saturday-s-search-efforts-for-missing-man-last-seen-on -mount-meeker.htm.

"Search Efforts Continue for Missing Man." National Park Service news release, July 10, 2018. Accessed June 29, 2019. www.nps.gov/romo/learn/news/search-efforts -continue-for-missing-man.htm.

"Searchers Give Up on Lost Lad." *The Record*, Hackensack, New Jersey, July 6, 1982, p. 7. Accessed June 28, 2019. www.newspapers.com/image/493362387/?terms =Robert%2BBaldeshwiler.

"Search Underway in Mount Meeker Area Rocky Mountain National Park." National Park Service news release, July 6, 2018. Accessed June 29, 2019. www.nps.gov/ romo/learn/news/search-underway-in-mount-meeker-area-rocky-mountain -national-park.htm.

"Sunday's Search Efforts for Missing Man Last Seen on Mount Meeker." National Park Service news release, July 8, 2018. Accessed June 29, 2019. www.nps.gov/romo/learn/ news/sunday-s-search-efforts-for-missing-man-last-seen-on-mount-meeker.htm.

Swanson, Sady. "Officials Believe Missing Local Hiker Fell." *Windsor Beacon*, Colorado, August 5, 2018, p. W3. Accessed June 29, 2019. www.newspapers.com/image/469 101193/?terms=death%2BRocky%2BMountain%2BNational%2BPark.

United Press International. "Climber Falls to His Death." *Greeley Daily Tribune*, May 13, 1977, p. 8. Accessed June 18, 2019. www.newspapers.com/image/25103091/ ?terms=Asuncion%2BNavarette.

———. "Hunt Abandoned for Akron GI." *News-Messenger*, Fremont, Ohio, July 6, 1946, p. 1. Accessed June 18, 2019. www.newspapers.com/image/304970272/ ?terms=%22Thomas%2BH.%2BEvans%22.

———. "Mountain Troops Seeking Lost GI." *Statesville Daily Record*, North Carolina, June 21, 1946, p. 8. Accessed June 18, 2019. www.newspapers.com/image/ 38492350/?terms=%22Thomas%2BH.%2BEvans%22.

———. "Scout Falls to Death in Colorado Mountains." *Albuquerque Journal*, June 16, 1966, p. 25. Accessed June 28, 2019. www.newspapers.com/image/157011557/ ?terms=Jay%2BDuPont.

———. "Texan Falls to Death from Rock." *Waxahachie Daily Light*, Texas, May 20, 1977, p. 10. Accessed June 18, 2019. www.newspapers.com/image/84898934/?terms= Harold%2BHoltzendorf.

———. "29 Experts Seek GI Lost in Snowy Rockies." *Boston Globe*, June 21, 1946, p. 5. Accessed June 18, 2019. www.newspapers.com/image/434037450/?terms= %22Thomas%2BH.%2BEvans%22.

———. "A Young Climber from Kentucky . . ." *Democrat & Chronicle*, Rochester, New York, July 22, 1978, p. 3. Accessed June 16, 2019. www .newspapers.com/ image/137337675/?terms=Lawrence%2BBerman.

Van Slyke, Larry. "Fall on Snow, Climbing Unroped, Placed No Protection, Colorado, Mt. Ypsilon." American Alpine Club Accident Report, 1979. Accessed June 16, 2019. http://publications.americanalpineclub.org/articles/13197903800/Fall-on -Snow-Climbing-Unroped-Placed-No-Protection-Colorado-Mt-Ypsilon.

Whiteman, Dave. "Colorado, Rocky Mountain National Park, Pagoda Peak." American Alpine Club Accident Report, 1973. Accessed June 29, 2019. http://publications .americanalpineclub.org/articles/13197302000/Colorado-Rocky-Mountain -National-Park-Pagoda-Peak.

CHAPTER 5

Associated Press. "Avalanches Slow Search for Climber." *Daily Sentinel*, Grand Junction, Colorado, April 25, 1991, p. 15. Accessed June 24, 2019. www.newspapers.com/ image/538354415/?terms=Joe%2BMassari.

———. "Body Found 2 Years after Avalanche." *Daily Sentinel*, Grand Junction, Colorado, August 14, 1994, p. 3. Accessed June 24, 2019. www.newspapers.com/ image/538627596/?terms=Brad%2BFarnan.

———. "Bucks Couple's Son Found Dead in Colo.," *Morning Call*, Allentown, Pennsylvania, June 20, 1991, p. 22. Accessed June 24, 2019. www.newspapers.com/ image/284556063/?terms=Joe%2BMassari.

———. "Climber's Body Found." *Sandusky Register*, Ohio, August 14, 1994, p. 3. Accessed June 24, 2019. https://newspaperarchive.com/sandusky-register-aug -14-1994-p-3.

———. "Mitchell Death Was Caused by Rockslide." *Daily Advertiser*, Lafayette, Louisiana, February 26, 1983, p. 3. Accessed June 24, 2019. www.newspapers.com/ image/537121349/?terms=Mark%2BFrevert.

———. "Pastor Dies in Hiking Accident." *Beatrice Daily Sun*, Nebraska, June 28, 1999, p. 2. Accessed June 24, 2019. www.newspapers.com/image/506736743/?terms= %22Charlie%2BHarrison%22.

———. "Searchers Account for All Stranded Hunters Except One." *Colorado Springs Gazette Telegraph*, November 6, 1992, p. B8. Accessed June 24, 2019. https:// newspaperarchive.com/colorado-springs-gazette-nov-06-1992-p-24.

———. "Second Man Found Dead in Park Climbing Accident." *Daily Sentinel*, Grand Junction, Colorado, February 7, 1983, p. 3. Accessed June 24, 2019. www.newspapers .com/image/538234424/?terms=Mark%2BFrevert.

———. "Two Climbers Found Dead." *Daily Sentinel*, Grand Junction, Colorado, October 15, 1973, p. 2. Accessed June 24, 2019. www.newspapers.com/image/ 536301761/?terms=%22David%2BEmerick%22.

Blumhardt, Miles. "Searchers Find Body of Man Killed in RMNP Avalanche." *Fort Collins Coloradoan*, March 20, 2013, p. A1–2. Accessed June 24, 2019. https:// coloradoan.newspapers.com/image/113850655.

"Body of Victim Found." National Park Service news release, March 19, 2013. Accessed June 24, 2019. www.nps.gov/romo/learn/news/pr_body_of_victim_found.htm.

"David Paul Laurienti." *Estes Park Trail-Gazette*, March 28, 2013. Accessed June 22, 2019. www.legacy.com/obituaries/eptrail/obituary.aspx?n=david-paul-laurienti &pid=163888611.

Detterline, Jim. "Avalanche, Weather, Colorado, Rocky Mountain National Park, Flattop Mountain." American Alpine Club Accident Report, 1993. Accessed June 24, 2019. http://publications.americanalpineclub.org/articles/13199305702/Avalanche -Weather-Colorado-Rocky-Mountain-National-Park-Flattop-Mountain.

———. "Fall on Snow, Climbing Alone and Unroped, Possible Avalanche, Exceeding Abilities." American Alpine Club Accident Report, 1992. Accessed June 24, 2019. http://publications.americanalpineclub.org/articles/13199202902/Fall-on-Snow -Climbing-Alone-and-Unroped-Possible-Avalanche-Exceeding-Abilities -Colorado-Rocky-Mountain-National-Park-Longs-Park.

"Fatality in Rocky Mountain National Park on Ypsilon Mountain." National Park Service news release, March 18, 2013. Accessed June 24, 2019. www.nps.gov/romo/ learn/news/pr_fatality_on_ypsilon_mountain.htm.

"Follow Up from Yesterday's Fatality near Ypsilon Mountain in Rocky Mountain National Park." National Park Service news release, March 19, 2013. Accessed June 24, 2019. www.nps.gov/romo/learn/news/pr_follow_up_fatality_near _ypsilon_mountain.htm.

Forrester, Joe. "Avalanche, Hypothermia–Fatigue, Exceeding Abilities, Failure to Follow Route." American Alpine Club Accident Report, 2014. Accessed June 22, 2019.

http://publications.americanalpineclub.org/articles/13201213012/Avalanche
-Hypothermia-Fatigue-Exceeding-Abilities-Failure-to-Follow-Route.

Hughes, Trevor. "Estes Park Man Killed in Avalanche Died from Hypothermia,
Coroner Says." *Fort Collins Coloradoan*, March 26, 2013, p. A4. Accessed June
24, 2019. https://coloradoan.newspapers.com/image/113851773/?terms=David
%2BLaurienti.

Lawson, Fred, and Anna Cearley. "Snow Stalls Search for Missing Man." *Dayton Daily
News*, Ohio, November 11, 1992, p. 13. Accessed June 24, 2019. www.newspapers
.com/image/412123418/?terms=Todd%2BMartin%2BBrad%2BFarnan.

"Lisa Foster Sets New Longs Peak Record!" *Estes Park News*, August 21, 2015. Accessed
June 24, 2019. www.estesparknews.com/featured_articles/article_acd9974e-46b6
-11e5-830f-b7212af15eec.html.

"One for the Record Books, New Longs Peak Record: Lisa Foster Becomes the
First Woman on Record to Climb the Mountain in Every Month of the Year."
Estes Park Trail-Gazette, April 25, 2012. Accessed June 24, 2019. www.eptrail.
com/2012/04/25/one-for-the-record-books-new-longs-peak-record-lisa-foster
-becomes-the-first-woman-on-record-to-climb-the-mountain-in-every-month
-of-the-year.

"Recovery Efforts Began This Morning for David Laurienti." National Park Service
news release, March 21, 2013. Accessed June 24, 2019. www.nps.gov/romo/learn/
news/pr_recover_efforts_for_david_laurienti.htm.

Rubino, Joe, and Mitchell Byars. "Avalanche Victim David Laurienti Remembered
as Dedicated Father, Avid Outdoorsman." *Daily Camera*, Boulder, Colorado,
March 19, 2013. Accessed June 24, 2019. www.dailycamera.com/2013/03/19/
avalanche-victim-david-laurienti-remembered-as-dedicated-father-avid
-outdoorsman.

"Snow Eases but Chill Remains; Slide Might Have Killed Two." *Colorado Springs
Gazette Telegraph*, November 4, 1992, p. B5. Accessed June 24, 2019. https://
newspaperarchive.com/colorado-springs-gazette-telegraph-nov-04-1992-p-17.

"Two Killed While Climbing near Estes Park." *Fort Collins Coloradoan*, October 15,
1973, p. 2. Accessed June 24, 2019. www.newspapers.com/image/225557209/
?terms=%22David%2BEmerick%22.

United Press International. "2 Climbers Killed." *Citizens' Voice*, Wilkes-Barre, Pennsylvania, February 7, 1983, p. 6. Accessed June 24, 2019. www.newspapers.com/
image/438177552/?terms=Mark%2BFrevert.

CHAPTER 6

Associated Press. "Lightning Kills Girl near Estes." *Greeley Daily Tribune*, July 2, 1974,
p. 3. Accessed June 25, 2019. www.newspapers.com/image/27293099/?terms=
Barbara%2BGully.

———. "Lightning Kills Ohioan in Colorado." *Lima News*, Ohio, July 14, 2014,
p. 9. Accessed June 25, 2019. https://newspaperarchive.com/lima-news-jul-14
-2014-p-9.

———. "Missouri Woman Killed When Lightning Hits near Estes Park, Colo." *Maryville Daily Forum*, Missouri, August 7, 1964, p. 7. Accessed June 25, 2019. www.newspapers.com/image/87042715/?terms=Leola%2BSwain.

———. "Mountain Climber Killed by Lightning." *Austin American-Statesman*, Texas, August 2, 1922, p. 1. Accessed June 25, 2019. www.newspapers.com/image/359109956/?terms=Jesse%2BKitts.

"Brother of Mrs. Potter Is Victim of Lightning." *Sedalia Capital*, Missouri, August 4, 1922, p. 2. Accessed June 25, 2019. https://newspaperarchive.com/sedalia-capital-aug-04-1922-p-2.

Detterline, Jim, and Mark Magnuson. "Lightning, Poor Position—Late Afternoon, Colorado, Rocky Mountain National Park, Longs Peak." American Alpine Club Accident Report, 2001. Accessed June 25, 2019. http://publications.americanalpineclub.org/articles/13200106303/Lightning-Poor-PositionLate-Afternoon-Colorado-Rocky-Mountain-National-Park-Longs-Peak.

Emery, Erin. "Lightning Kills Hiker on Pikes Peak." *Denver Post*, July 26, 2000. Accessed June 25, 2019. http://extras.denverpost.com/news/news0726a.htm.

"Killed by Lightning Bolt." *Boston Globe*, August 27, 1914, p. 11. Accessed June 25, 2019. www.newspapers.com/image/430849275/?terms=Dillingham%2Blightning%2Bdeath.

"Lightning." Rocky Mountain National Park, accessed June 25, 2019. www.nps.gov/romo/planyourvisit/upload/lightning_2009.pdf.

"Lightning Kills Ex-Appleton Man." *Post-Crescent*, Appleton, Wisconsin, August 11, 1999, p. 19. Accessed June 25, 2019. www.newspapers.com/image/290813368/?terms=Michael%2BHines%20%20%.

"Lightning Kills Girl on Trail Ridge Road." *Fort Collins Coloradoan*, July 2, 1974, p. 10. Accessed June 25, 2019. https://coloradoan.newspapers.com/image/227208745/?terms=Barbara%2BGully.

Linsley, Brennan, and Dan Elliott. "Lightning Deaths Concern Park Visitors." Associated Press, located in *Clearfield Progress*, Pennsylvania, July 15, 2014, p. 14. Accessed June 25, 2019. https://newspaperarchive.com/clearfield-progress-jul-15-2014-p-14.

Medina, Jennifer. "Storms Delay Recovery of Climber's Body." *Denver Post*, July 14, 2000. Accessed June 25, 2019. http://extras.denverpost.com/news/news0714l.htm.

"Name of Victim from Saturday Lightning Incident Released." National Park Service news release, July 13, 2014. Accessed June 25, 2019. www.nps.gov/romo/learn/news/victims_name_released.htm.

". . . Prospecting above Timberline . . ." *Denver Republican*, June 22, 1896, found in Freudenburg, Betty D., *Facing the Frontier: The Story of the MacGregor Ranch*. Estes Park, CO: Rocky Mountain Nature Association, 2005, p. 91.

Rothenberg, Jackie. "Lightning Kills B'klyn Man in Colorado." *New York Post*, July 23, 1999. Accessed June 25, 2019. https://nypost.com/1999/07/23/lightning-kills-bklyn-man-in-colorado.

"Second Lightning Fatality in Two Days at Rocky Mountain National Park; Further Information and Identity of Friday Victim Released." National Park Service news

release, July 12, 2014. Accessed June 25, 2019. www.nps.gov/romo/learn/news/
pr_second_lightning_fatality_in_two_days_at_rocky_mountain_national_park
_further_information_and_identity_of_friday_victim_released.htm.
"Severe Weather 101—Lightning." National Severe Storm Laboratory, accessed June
25, 2019. www.nssl.noaa.gov/education/svrwx101/lightning/faq.
United Press International. "Lightning Victim, 17, 'Very Poor.'" *South Bend Tribune*,
Indiana, July 2, 1974, p. 7. Accessed June 25, 2019. www.newspapers.com/image/
515873227/?terms=Barbara%2BGully.
———. "Teenager Killed by Lightning." *Brownsville Herald*, Texas, July 4, 1974, p. 31.
Accessed June 25, 2019. www.newspapers.com/image/23496212/?terms=Barbara
%2BGully.

CHAPTER 7

Associated Press. "Boy Found Drowned in St. Vrain Creek." *Fort Collins Coloradoan*, August 3, 1972, p. 13. Accessed June 26, 2019. www.newspapers.com/
image/225540991/?terms=Danny%2BSaucier.
———. "Girl Found Still Alive in River." *St. Cloud Times*, Minnesota, July 14, 1986,
p. 2. Accessed June 26, 2019. www.newspapers.com/image/223135655/?terms
=Ellen%2BMarx.
———. "Honor Student Dies as Leap Falls Short in National Park." *Colorado Springs
Gazette Telegraph*, July 5, 1993, p. 10. Accessed June 26, 2019. https://newspaper
archive.com/colorado-springs-gazette-telegraph-jul-05-1993-p-10.
———. "Picture Brings Death to Estes Vacationer." *Albuquerque Journal*, July 18, 1947,
p. 9. Accessed June 26, 2019. www.newspapers.com/image/156343876/?terms=
%22Robert%2BEarl%2BBriggs%22.
———. "7-Year-Old Dies in Park." *Hattiesburg American*, Mississippi, July 5, 1987,
p. 10. Accessed June 26, 2019. www.newspapers.com/image/278161406/?terms
=Rey%2BDermody.
———. "Teen-Age Girl Dies after River Accident." *Argus-Leader*, Sioux Falls, South
Dakota, July 17, 1986, p. 26. Accessed June 26, 2019. www.newspapers.com/
image/239927274/?terms=Ellen%2BMarx.
———. "Texas Boy Drowns in St. Vrain Creek." *Fort Collins Coloradoan*, July 8, 1973,
p. 32. Accessed June 26, 2019. https://coloradoan.newspapers.com/image/
225546633/?terms=Kurt%2BPrimosch.
"Body of Local Man Recovered in Colorado." *Corpus Christi Caller-Times*, Texas,
June 20, 1964, p. 8. Accessed June 26, 2019. www.newspapers.com/image/
27737609/?terms=James%2BKeller.
Brandt, Steve. "Minneapolis Girl Critical after Hour in Mountain River." *Minneapolis
Star-Tribune*, July 14, 1986, p. 13. Accessed June 26, 2019. www.newspapers.com/
image/191428408/?terms=Ellen%2BMarx.
Healy, Jane. "Orland Girls' Dream Trip Cut Short by Tragic Drowning." *Orlando
Sentinel*, May 30, 1973, p. 145. Accessed June 26, 2019. www.newspapers.com/
image/304449290/?terms=Lois%2BMatthews.

International News Service. "Swift Current Is Blamed for Drowning Boy." *Courier-Gazette*, McKinney, Texas, July 18, 1947, p. 8. Accessed June 26, 2019. www.newspapers.com/image/56082181/?terms=drowning%2BRocky%2BMountain%2BNational%2BPark.

"River Victim's Funeral Pending." *Austin American-Statesman*, June 29, 1973, p. 6. Accessed June 26, 2019. www.newspapers.com/image/359265862/?terms=Sherran%2BJoy%2BHaley.

"13-Year-Old Dies." *Crowley Post Signal*, Louisiana, July 17, 1986, p. 2. Accessed June 26, 2019. www.newspapers.com/image/469602657/?terms=Ellen%2BMarx.

United Press International. "Body Recovered in Swollen River." *Waco News-Tribune*, Texas, June 29, 1973, p. 5. Accessed June 26, 2019. www.newspapers.com/image/65639718/?terms=Sherran%2BJoy%2BHaley.

"Woman Drowns in Swollen Canyon River." *Fort Collins Coloradoan*, June 28, 1973, p. 1. Accessed June 26, 2019. https://coloradoan.newspapers.com/image/225570191/?terms=Sherran%2BHaley.

"Youth, 6, Drowns in Thompson." *Fort Collins Coloradoan*, May 15, 1978, p. 3. Accessed June 26, 2019. https://coloradoan.newspapers.com/image/226850663/?terms=Christopher%2BErmijo.

CHAPTER 8

Associated Press. "Couple's Remains Recovered from Peak." *Daily Sentinel*, Grand Junction, Colorado, May 7, 2000, p. 20. Accessed April 25, 2019. www.newspapers.com/image/537241592/?terms=Comanche%2BPeak.

———. "Crash Kills 2." *Daily Sentinel*, Grand Junction, Colorado, August 17, 1977, p. 2. Accessed April 24, 2019. www.newspapers.com/image/537609900/?terms=plane%2Bcrash%2B%22Rocky%2BMountain%2BNational%2BPark%22.

———. "Denver Man Killed in Airplane Crash." *Daily Sentinel*, Grand Junction, Colorado, August 28, 1948. Accessed April 22, 2019. www.newspapers.com/image/536329527/?terms=Cranston%2Bdodd.

———. "East Slope Storm Blocks Route to Plane Crash Site." *Daily Sentinel*, Grand Junction, Colorado, April 14, 1967, p. 9. Accessed April 23, 2019. www.newspapers.com/image/537246378/?terms=plane%2Bcrash.

———. "Father, Daughters Survive Air Crash." *Daily Sentinel*, Grand Junction, Colorado, December 27, 1979, p. 3. Accessed April 25, 2019. www.newspapers.com/image/537710459/?terms=Virginia%2BKrieger.

———. "Father, Daughters Survive Frigid Two Days after Crash." *Daily Sentinel*, Grand Junction, Colorado, December 26, 1979, p. 3. Accessed April 25, 2019. www.newspapers.com/image/537710159/?terms=Virginia%2BKrieger.

———. "News in Brief." *Daily Sentinel*, Grand Junction, Colorado, April 20, 1967, p. 1. Accessed April 23, 2019. www.newspapers.com/image/537248573/?terms=plane%2Bcrash%2BSouth%2BSignal%2BMountain.

———. "Plane Crashes during Search." *Daily Sentinel*, Grand Junction, Colorado, April 13, 1989, p. 14. Accessed April 25, 2019. www.newspapers.com/image/539312360/?terms=Cessna.

———. "Plane Occupants Uninjured in Crash." *Garden City Telegram*, Kansas, April 13, 1989, p. 12. Accessed April 25, 2019. https://newspaperarchive.com/garden-city -telegram-apr-13-1989-p-12.

———. "Search Called Off for Steamboat Springs Pilot." *Daily Sentinel*, Grand Junction, Colorado, April 24, 1989, p. 10. Accessed April 25, 2019. www.newspapers .com/image/539324571/?terms=Cessna.

———. "Three of Six Survive Mountain Plane Crash." *Daily Sentinel*, Grand Junction, Colorado, April 13, 1967, p. 12. Accessed April 23, 2019. www.newspapers.com/ image/537245944/?terms=plane%2Bcrash.

———. "2 Die as Plane Crashes, Burns near Estes Park." *Colorado Springs Gazette Telegraph*, August 17, 1977, p. 6. Accessed April 24, 2019. www.newspapers.com/ image/65749803/?terms=plane%2Bcrash%2B%22Rocky%2BMountain%2B National%2BPark%22.

———. "Two Planes Crash in Hunt for 6 Missing Coloradans." *Daily Sentinel*, Grand Junction, Colorado, April 11, 1967, p. 9. Accessed April 23, 2019. www .newspapers.com/image/537245452/?terms=plane%2Bcrash%20%20%20https:// www.newspapers.com/image/537245944/?terms=plane%2Bcrash.

———. "Winds Impede Air Search for Missing Plane." *Colorado Springs Gazette Telegraph*, April 8, 1989, p. 17. Accessed April 25, 2019. https://newspaper archive.com/colorado-springs-gazette-telegraph-apr-08-1989-p-17.

"Estes Park, CO, Accident Number DEN00FA086." National Transportation Safety Board Aviation Accident Data Summary, April 30, 2000, accessed April 25, 2019. https://app.ntsb.gov/pdfgenerator/ReportGeneratorFile.ashx?EventID= 20001212X20795&AKey=1&RType=Summary&IType=FA.

"Estes Park, CO, Accident Number FTW96FA145." National Transportation Safety Board Aviation Accident Data Summary, January 31, 1996, accessed April 25, 2019. https://app.ntsb.gov/pdfgenerator/ReportGeneratorFile.ashx?EventID =20001208X05130&AKey=1&RType=Summary&IType=FA.

"Estes Park Plane Crash under Probe." International News Service, located in *Lincoln Journal Star*, Nebraska, August 28, 1948, p. 2. Accessed April 22, 2019. www .newspapers.com/image/310503696/?terms=Cranston%2BDodd.

"Fatal Crashes." *Steamboat Pilot & Today*, August 16, 2003. Accessed April 25, 2019. www.steamboatpilot.com/news/fatal-crashes.

"FG-1D Corsair." National Naval Aviation Museum. Accessed April 22, 2019. www .navalaviationmuseum.org/aircraft/fg-1d-corsair.

"Fires Postpone Recovery of Airplane Wreckage." *Colorado Springs Gazette Telegraph*, July 20, 1996, p. 16. Accessed April 25, 2019. https://newspaperarchive.com/ colorado-springs-gazette-telegraph-jul-20-1996-p-16.

"NTSB Identification: DEN67A0063, 14CFR Part 91 General Aviation, Aircraft: PIPER PA-32, Registration: N3511W." National Transportation Safety Board Accident Report, 4/18/67. Accessed 4/22/2019. www.ntsb.gov/_layouts/ntsb .aviation/brief.aspx?ev_id=19693&key=0.

"NTSB Identification: DEN77FA053, 14 CFR Part 91 General Aviation, Aircraft: MAULE M4, Registration: N4132C." National Transportation Safety Board

Accident Report. Accessed April 24, 2019. www.ntsb.gov/_Layouts/ntsb.aviation/brief.aspx?ev_id=45994&key=0.

"NTSB Identification: DEN80FA014, 14 CFR Part 91 General Aviation, Aircraft: PIPER PA-23, Registration: N2013P." National Transportation Safety Board Accident Report. Accessed April 25, 2019. www.ntsb.gov/_layouts/ntsb.aviation/brief.aspx?ev_id=32868&key=0.

"Remains of Pilot Found." *Colorado Springs Gazette Telegraph*, July 2, 1989, p. 26. Accessed April 25, 2019. https://newspaperarchive.com/colorado-springs-gazette-telegraph-jul-02-1989-p-26.

"Steamboat Sprg., CO, Accident Number DEN89FA149." National Transportation Safety Board Aviation Accident Data Summary, April 5, 1989. Accessed April 25, 2019. https://app.ntsb.gov/pdfgenerator/ReportGeneratorFile.ashx?EventID=20001213X28073&AKey=1&RType=Summary&IType=FA.

"27 August 1948, 1201, DODD, Cranston Harvey, Ist. Lt." Aircraft Accident Card, US Marine Corps, August 27, 1948. Accessed via AAIR Aviation Archaeological Investigation & Research, April 5, 2019. 480827 FG-1D 92255.pdf.

United Press International. "2 Crash Victims Identified," located in *Valley News*, Van Nuys, California, August 18, 1977, p. 12. Accessed April 24, 2019. www.newspapers.com/image/30384950/?terms=plane%2Bcrash%2B%22Rocky%2BMountain%2BNational%2BPark%22.

CHAPTER 9

Associated Press. "At Least 3 Missing in Estes Park Flood." *Daily Sentinel*, Grand Junction, Colorado, July 15, 1982, p. 1. Accessed May 14, 2019. www.newspapers.com/image/537707972/?terms=Lawn%2BLake%2Bflood.

———. "Body of Second Flood Victim Recovered near Estes Park." *Daily Sentinel*, Grand Junction, Colorado, July 21, 1982, p. 3. Accessed May 14, 2019. www.newspapers.com/image/537710714/?terms=Lawn%2BLake%2Bflood.

———. "Four Believed Dead in Estes." *Daily Sentinel*, Grand Junction, Colorado, July 16, 1982. Accessed May 14, 2019. www.newspapers.com/image/537708297/?terms=Lawn%2BLake%2Bflood.

———. "Park Service Must Pay $480,000 to Dead Camper's Family." *AP News*, February 21, 1985. Accessed May 14, 2019. www.apnews.com/50025311526c8ef605cb91321938f036.

———. "Search Narrowed for Victims of Flood." *Daily Sentinel*, Grand Junction, Colorado, July 18, 1982, p. 1. Accessed May 14, 2019. www.newspapers .com/image/537709077/?terms=Lawn%2BLake%2Bflood.

———. "Second Estes Park Lawsuit Seeks $2.5 Million Damages." *Daily Sentinel*, Grand Junction, Colorado, July 28, 1982, p. 2. Accessed July 1, 2019. www.newspapers.com/image/537714124/?terms=Lawn%2BLake%2Bflood.

"Body of Third Estes Park Victim Found." *Daily Sentinel*, Grand Junction, Colorado, August 16, 1982, p. 3. Accessed May 14, 2019. www.newspapers.com/image/537722214/?terms=Lawn%2BLake%2Bflood.

Cordsen, John. "1982 Flood Changed Downtown Estes Park." *Reporter-Herald*, Loveland, Colorado, July 13, 2012. Accessed May 14, 2019. www.reporterherald.com/2012/07/13/1982-flood-changed-downtown-estes-park.

"Dam Safety." *Daily Sentinel*, Grand Junction, Colorado, July 19, 1982, p. 4. Accessed May 14, 2019. www.newspapers.com/image/537710096/?terms=Lawn%2BLake%2Bflood.

Farrell, John A., and Bill McBean. "Colorado Dam Bursts; 4 Missing." *Denver Post*, located in *Capital Times*, Madison, Wisconsin, July 16, 1982, pp. 1 and 6. Accessed May 13, 2019. www.newspapers.com/image/521375316/?terms=%22Glen%2BKaye%22.

"Gutsy Estes Park Wastes No Time Rebuilding." *Daily Sentinel*, Grand Junction, Colorado, August 15, 1982, p. 12. Accessed July 1, 2019. www.newspapers.com/image/537721819/?terms=Lawn%2BLake%2Bflood.

Krizman, Steve. "Flood Creates Extended Stay for Rocky Mountain Campers." *Daily Sentinel*, Grand Junction, Colorado, July 17, 1982, p. 3. Accessed May 14, 2019. www.newspapers.com/image/537708859.

"Lawn Lake—12.5 Miles." ProTrails. Accessed May 13, 2019. www.protrails.com/trail/62/rocky-mountain-national-park-lawn-lake.

McMillan, Steve. "Estes Park Residents Begin Task of Digging Out from Mud." *Daily Sentinel*, Grand Junction, Colorado, July 17, 1982, p. 5. Accessed May 14, 2019. www.newspapers.com/image/537708870.

———. "Father Still Hoping Missing Son Is Alive." *Daily Sentinel*, Grand Junction, Colorado, July 16, 1982. Accessed May 14, 2019. www.newspapers.com/image/537708297.

———. "Husband of Camper: 'I'm Alive, She's Dead.'" *Daily Sentinel*, Grand Junction, Colorado, July 17, 1982, pp. 1 and 5. Accessed May 14, 2019. www.newspapers.com/image/537708842.

Moss, Michael. "Engineer Says Cuts Reduced Inspections at Collapsed Dam." *Daily Sentinel*, Grand Junction, Colorado, July 17, 1982. Accessed May 14, 2019. www.newspapers.com/image/537708842.

CHAPTER 10

Associated Press. "Aged Recluse Hanged by Two Money Seekers Despite Pleas." *Albuquerque Journal*, August 17, 1926, pp. 1 and 7. Accessed June 19, 2019. www.newspapers.com/image/156587614/?terms=Fred%2BSelak.

———. "Five Held for Disappearance of Fred Selak." *Daily Sentinel*, Grand Junction, Colorado, August 12, 1926, p. 3. Accessed June 19, 2019. www.newspapers.com/image/537268173/?terms=Fred%2BSelak.

———. "Pointer Solves Mystery Which Has Baffled Colorado Police for Weeks." *Baltimore Sun*, August 18, 1926, p. 1. Accessed June 19, 2019. www.newspapers.com/image/373427923.

———. "Ranger Testifies Diamond Ring Missing after Fatal Fall." *Colorado Springs Gazette*, September 10, 2015, p. B3. Accessed June 20, 2019. https://newspaperarchive.com/colorado-springs-gazette-sep-10-2015-p-15.

———. "Reward Offered to Locate Missing Man." *Arizona Daily Star*, July 30, 1926, p. 1. Accessed June 19, 2019. www.newspapers.com/image/163049152/?terms=Fred%2BSelak.

Gurman, Sadie. "Man Guilty of Pushing Wife off Colorado Cliff to Her Death." Associated Press, located in *Galveston Daily News*, Texas, September 22, 2015. Accessed June 20, 2019. https://newspaperarchive.com/galveston-county-daily-news-sep-22-2015-p-6.

———. "Prosecutor; Man Staged Deaths of 2 Wives." Associated Press, located in *Fort Collins Coloradoan*, September 9, 2015, p. A2. Accessed June 20, 2019. www.newspapers.com/image/127241783/?terms=death%2BRocky%2BMountain%2BNational%2BPark.

International News Service. "Robbed of $500,000—Hermit Believed to Have Been Killed and Contents of Cache Stolen." *The Times*, Munster, Indiana, July 26, 1926, p. 1. Accessed June 19, 2019. www.newspapers.com/image/306426510/?terms=Fred%2BSelak.

"The Murder of Fred Selak." *Daily Sentinel*, Grand Junction, Colorado, August 19, 1926, p. 4. Accessed June 19, 2019. www.newspapers.com/image/537271178/?terms=Fred%2BSelak.

"Neighbors Plan Hunt for Slain 'Hermit of Grand Lake.'" *Indiana Evening Gazette*, April 6, 1927, found at FindAGrave.com. Accessed June 19, 2019. www.findagrave.com/memorial/19477584/frederick-n_-selak.

Perry, Phyllis J. *It Happened in Rocky Mountain National Park: Stories of Events and People That Shaped a National Park*. Guilford, CT: TwoDot, 2018, pp. 79–80.

Udell, Erin. "Man Arrested in RMNP Death." *Fort Collins Coloradoan*, November 7, 2014, p. A4. Accessed June 20, 2019. www.newspapers.com/image/113865709/?terms=death%2BRocky%2BMountain%2BNational%2BPark.

United Press. "Two Are Hanged in Colorado Early This Morning for Murder." *Evening Journal*, Washington, Iowa, March 30, 1928, p. 1. Accessed June 19, 2019. https://newspaperarchive.com/washington-evening-journal-mar-30-1928-p-1.

CHAPTER 11

Associated Press. "CCC Hunt for Missing Denver Boy Is Ended." *Billings Gazette*, Montana, July 13, 1938, p. 12. Accessed June 26, 2019. www.newspapers.com/image/409731208/?terms=Alfred%2BBeilhartz.

———. "Denver Hiker May Have Seen Missing Child." *Greeley Daily Tribune*, July 8, 1938, p. 1. Accessed June 26, 2019. www.newspapers.com/image/24980826/?terms=Alfred%2BBeilhartz.

———. "Diverting River in Hunt for Body." *Evening Sun*, Baltimore, Maryland, July 5, 1938, p. 23. Accessed June 26, 2019. www.newspapers.com/image/369633930/?terms=Alfred%2BBeilhartz.

———. "Fresh Hunters Search Devil's Nest for Child." *Greeley Daily Tribune*, July 9, 1938, p. 1. Accessed June 26, 2019. www.newspapers.com/image/24981115/?terms=Alfred%2BBeilhartz.

———. "Hope Is Abandoned for Lost Climber." *Reno Gazette-Journal*, Nevada, August 21, 1933, p. 1. Accessed June 26, 2019. www.newspapers.com/image/148494635/ ?terms=Joseph%2BHalpern.

———. "Hounds Trail Boy, 4, Lost in Colorado Park." *San Francisco Examiner*, July 5, 1938, p. 11. Accessed June 26, 2019. www.newspapers.com/image/458085025/ ?terms=Alfred%2BBeilhartz.

———. "Hunt Abandoned for Miami Student Lost in Colorado Rockies." *Miami Silver Belt*, Arizona, October 20, 1949, p. 8. Accessed June 27, 2019. https:// newspaperarchive.com/miami-arizona-silver-belt-oct-20-1949-p-8.

———. "Hunt Wisconsin Youth Missing in Rocky Mountains." *The Courier*, Waterloo, Iowa, August 20, 1933, p. 1. Accessed June 26, 2019. www.newspapers.com/ image/356543993/?terms=Joseph%2BHalpern.

———. "Missing Boy." *El Paso Times*, July 12, 1938, p. 3. Accessed June 26, 2019. www.newspapers.com/image/429363838/?terms=Alfred%2BBeilhartz.

———. "Never Found." *Farmington Daily Times*, New Mexico, January 1, 1995, p. 32. Accessed June 27, 2019. https://newspaperarchive.com/farmington-daily-times -jan-01-1995-p-32.

———. "No Trace of Boy in Drained Stream." *Greeley Daily Tribune*, July 6, 1938, p. 1. Accessed June 26, 2019. www.newspapers.com/image/24980354/?terms =Alfred%2BBeilhartz.

———. "No Trace of Missing Boy." *Nebraska State Journal*, July 6, 1938, p. 1. Accessed June 26, 2019. www.newspapers.com/image/334578776/?terms=Alfred%2B Beilhartz.

———. "Searchers Fail to Find Lost Students." *Montana Standard*, Butte, Montana, October 14, 1949, p. 13. Accessed June 27, 2019. www.newspapers.com/image/ 349917148/?terms=Dale%2BDevitt%2BBruce%2BGerling.

———. "Searchers Seek Lost Students." *Montana Standard*, Butte, Montana, October 13, 1949, p. 10. Accessed June 27, 2019. https://newspaperarchive.com/butte -montana-standard-oct-13-1949-p-10.

———. "Search for Lost Students Pushed." *Austin American*, October 12, 1949, p. 31. Accessed June 27, 2019. https://newspaperarchive.com/austin-american-oct-12 -1949-p-31.

———. "Search Group for Baby Climb to Devils Nest." *Greeley Daily Tribune*, July 9, 1938, p. 10. Accessed June 26, 2019. www.newspapers.com/image/24981336/ ?terms=Alfred%2BBeilhartz.

———. "Snowdrifts Hide Lost Pair's Fate." *Reno Gazette-Journal*, October 13, 1949, p. 32. Accessed June 27, 2019. www.newspapers.com/image/147119908/ ?terms=Dale%2BDevitt%2BBruce%2BGerling.

———. "Unsuccessful Skier Search Suspended." *Daily Sentinel*, Grand Junction, Colorado, February 24, 1983, p. 3. Accessed June 27, 2019. www.newspapers.com/ image/538240962/?terms=Rudi%2BModer.

"Broad-Scale Efforts for James Pruitt Suspended." National Park Service news release, March 15, 2019. Accessed June 27, 2019. www.nps.gov/romo/learn/news/broad -scale-search-efforts-for-james-pruitt-suspended.htm.

"Day Four of Search Efforts for James Pruitt in Glacier Gorge Area." National Park Service news release, March 6, 2019. Accessed June 27, 2019. www.nps.gov/romo/learn/news/day-four-of-search-efforts-for-james-pruitt-in-glacier-gorge-area.htm.

"Extortionist Demands Ransom for Return of Denver Boy Who Disappeared in National Bank [*sic*]." *Greeley Daily Tribune*, November 29, 1938, p. 1. Accessed June 26, 2019. www.newspapers.com/image/25008158/?terms=Alfred%2BBeilhartz.

"German Skier Believed Dead." *Colorado Springs Gazette Telegraph*, February 24, 1983, p. 12. Accessed June 27, 2019. https://newspaperarchive.com/colorado-springs-gazette-telegraph-feb-24-1983-p-12.

"History." ProTrails Forum, June 9–21, 2011. Accessed June 27, 2019. http://forums.protrails.com/forums/topic/22328-history.

"Hunters Turn to Land for Beilhartz Boy." *Greeley Daily Tribune*, July 7, 1938, p. 1. Accessed June 26, 2019. www.newspapers.com/image/24980536/?terms=Alfred%2BBeilhartz.

International News Service. "Abandon Search." *Greensburg Daily News*, Indiana, October 17, 1949, p. 6. Accessed June 27, 2019. www.newspapers.com/image/15063821/?terms=Dale%2BDevitt%2BBruce%2BGerling.

———. "Father of Missing Lad Advances Kidnap Theory." *The Dispatch*, Moline, Illinois, July 8, 1938, p. 7. Accessed June 26, 2019. www.newspapers.com/image/341701628/?terms=Alfred%2BBeilhartz.

Logan, Charlie. "Climbing Alone, Inadequate Equipment, Heavy Snowfall, Colorado, Rocky Mountain National Park." American Alpine Club Accident Report, 1984. Accessed June 27, 2019. http://publications.americanalpineclub.org/articles/13198403400/Climbing-Alone-Inadequate-Equipment-Heavy-Snowfall-Colorado-Rocky-Mountain-National-Park.

"NamUs #MP2797, Joseph Laurence Halpern, Male, White/Caucasian." National Missing and Unidentified Persons System (NamUs). Accessed June 26, 2019. www.namus.gov/MissingPersons/Case#/2797.

Pialet, Tyler. "Search Efforts Suspended for Missing Man in RMNP." *Estes Park Trail-Gazette*, March 15, 2019. Accessed June 27, 2019. www.eptrail.com/2019/03/15/search-efforts-suspended-for-missing-man-in-rmnp.

"Recent Search Activities for Micah Tice." National Park Service news release, December 13, 2018. Accessed June 27, 2019. www.nps.gov/romo/learn/news/recent-search-activities-for-micah-tice.htm.

"Search Efforts Continued Monday for James Pruitt in Glacier Gorge Area." National Park Service news release, March 4, 2019. Accessed June 27, 2019. www.nps.gov/romo/learn/news/search-efforts-continued-monday-for-james-pruitt-in-glacier-gorge-area.htm.

"Search Efforts for Micah Tice Suspended." National Park Service news release, December 4, 2018. Accessed June 27, 2019. www.nps.gov/romo/learn/news/search-efforts-for-micah-tice-suspended.htm.

"Search Efforts Today for Man in the Glacier Gorge Area." National Park Service news release, March 3, 2019. Accessed June 27, 2019. www.nps.gov/romo/learn/news/search-efforts-today-for-man-in-the-glacier-gorge-area.htm.

Swanson, Sady. "Air Force Cadet Candidate Missing." *Fort Collins Coloradoan*, November 28, 2018, pp. 1 and 5. Accessed June 27, 2019. https://coloradoan.newspapers.com/image/509253948.

———. "RMNP: Visitors Spoke to Missing Hiker Saturday Morning." *Fort Collins Coloradoan*, December 1, 2018, pp. A1–A4. Accessed June 27, 2019. https://coloradoan.newspapers.com/image/509595919.

Udell, Erin. "Inside RMNP's 1933 Missing Hiker Mystery." *Windsor Beacon*, Colorado, August 19, 2018, pp. W1–W3. Accessed June 26, 2019. www.newspapers.com/image/477760391.

United Press. "Today Tragic Anniversary for Couple in Denver." *Austin American-Statesman*, July 4, 1939, p. 5. Accessed June 26, 2019. www.newspapers.com/image/366688958/?terms=Alfred%2BBeilhartz.

———. "Two Students Feared Lost in Mountains." *Bonham Daily Favorite*, Texas, October 12, 1949, p. 1. Accessed June 27, 2019. https://newspaperarchive.com/bonham-daily-favorite-oct-12-1949-p-1.

———. "Wisconsin Mountain Climber Still Missing." *Green Bay Press-Gazette*, Wisconsin, August 21, 1933, p. 7. Accessed June 26, 2019. www.newspapers.com/image/187539166/?terms=Joseph%2BHalpern.

"West: Fort Collins, Colo." *Fort Lauderdale Sun-Sentinel*, February 24, 1983, p. 3. Accessed June 27, 2019. www.newspapers.com/image/230529393/?terms=Rudi%2BModer.

Chapter 12

"Albert William Furch." *Chicago Tribune*, July 19, 1945, p. 16. Accessed June 28, 2019. www.newspapers.com/image/370085591/?terms=Albert%2BFurch.

Associated Press. "Boy Attacked by Lion Died of Asphyxiation." *Anderson Herald Bulletin*, Indiana, July 21, 1997, p. 14. Accessed June 28, 2019. https://newspaperarchive.com/anderson-herald-bulletin-jul-21-1997-p-14.

———. "Boy Killed in Rare Mountain Lion Attack." *New Mexican*, July 19, 1997, p 16. Accessed June 28, 2019. https://newspaperarchive.com/santa-fe-new-mexican-jul-19-1997-p-16.

———. "Missouri Woman Dies after Horse Throws Her in National Park." *Greeley Daily Tribune*, July 29, 1938, p. 1. Accessed June 28, 2019. www.newspapers.com/image/24985014/?terms=car%2Baccident%2BRocky%2BMountain%2BNational%2BPark.

———. "Mountain Lion Kills Boy, 10." *Anderson Herald Bulletin*, Indiana, July 19, 1997, p. 21. Accessed June 28, 2019. https://newspaperarchive.com/anderson-herald-bulletin-jul-19-1997-p-21.

———. "Mountain Lions Not Afraid of Humans." *Colorado Springs Gazette*, July 20, 1997, p. 28. Accessed June 28, 2019. https://newspaperarchive.com/colorado-springs-gazette-jul-20-1997-p-28.

———. "Toboggan Ride Proves Fatal to Denver Girl." *Billings Gazette*, Montana, June 27, 1927, p. 1. Accessed June 28, 2019. www.newspapers.com/image/413306381/?terms=Flora%2BNapier.

———. "Train, Auto and Plane Accidents Sunday Kill Seven; 8 Others Drowned." *Chillicothe Constitution-Tribune*, Missouri, June 28, 1927, p. 19. Accessed June 28, 2019. www.newspapers.com/image/19742545/?terms=Flora%2BNapier.

Cordsen, John. "Skier Dies in RMNP." *ClimbingLife*, October 3, 2008. Accessed June 28, 2019. http://climbinglife.com/skier-dies-in-rmnp.

"Former Ottumwan Dies in Colorado." *Ottumwa Courier*, Iowa, January 27, 1988, p. 3. Accessed June 28, 2019. https://newspaperarchive.com/ottumwa-courier-jan-27-1988-p-3.

Hughes, Trevor. "Hiker Killed by Falling Tree ID'd." *Fort Collins Coloradoan*, November 29, 2007, p. 3. Accessed June 28, 2019. https://coloradoan.newspapers.com/image/227180523/?terms=death%2BRocky%2BMountain%2BNational%2BPark.

Lingle, Courtney, and Kevin Duggan. "Teen's Death Brings Sadness, Insight to Rocky Students." *Fort Collins Coloradoan*, March 8, 2005, pp. 9 and 12. Accessed June 28, 2019. www.newspapers.com/image/227121613/?terms=Omar%2BMehdawi.

Nelson, Christina. "Seniors Say 'So Long!'" *Fort Collins Coloradoan*, May 23, 2005, p. 7. Accessed June 28, 2019. www.newspapers.com/image/227031365.

Sentinel Wire Service. "Iowa Man Dies in Skiing Accident." *Daily Sentinel*, Grand Junction, Colorado, February 4, 1985, p. 3. Accessed June 28, 2019. www.newspapers.com/image/538191153/?terms=Scott%2BAnderson.

"Services Slated Tuesday in Estes for Hebert Kuhn." *Greeley Daily Tribune*, July 26, 1969, p. 6. Accessed June 28, 2019. www.newspapers.com/image/25076615/?terms=Herbert%2BKuhn.

"A Terrible Experience." *Wichita Daily Eagle*, Kansas, September 1, 1889, p. 1. Accessed June 28, 2019. www.newspapers.com/image/145245020/?terms=Frank%2BStryker%20%20%20%20%20.

INDEX

kidnapping, 235
Kiener, Walter, 17, 65, 91–98
Kiener's Route, 19, 40, 65, 91, 103, 104, 107, 164, 165
Kirk, Edward J., 56–57
Kitts, Jesse, 175–76
Kitts, Lew, 24
Koczanski, Gregory J., 69
Kopetsky, Peter, 65–66
Kor, Layton, 111
Krieger family, 198–201
Krizman, Steve, 209
Kuhn, Herbert, 248

L
Ladue, Richard, 142
Lady Washington, Mount, 148
Lake Estes, 211, 213
Lake Helene, 171
Lamb, Carlyle, 3–7, 249, 250
Lamb, Elkanah, 2–3, 6–7
Lambs Slide, 3, 41, 77, 88, 90, 103, 104, 105, 106, 107, 108, 116, 165
Landgraf, Amel, 140
Larimer County Search and Rescue, 76, 81, 88, 154, 161, 163, 169, 245
Larson, Paul, 226
Laurienti, David, 157–63
Lavato, Charles, 67
Lawn Lake, 122, 150
Lawn Lake Flood, xi, 206–19
Lawn Lake Trail, 150–51, 157, 162, 233
Layne, Debra, 43
Lazar, Scott, 113
Ledges, the, 67–83, 84
Left Book, 143
Levings, Louis, 119–21
Lewis, Bob, 18, 19
Lewis, Lindsey, 76
lightning strikes, xi, 11, 55, 121, 140, 173–81, 267
  along Trail Ridge Road, 177–81
  on Longs Peak, 175–77
Lilly Lake, 26
limits, knowing, 264
Lingle, Courtney, 256
Little Matterhorn, 133

Loch Vale drainage, 245, 248
Loft, the, 62, 73–74, 75, 82, 84, 85
Loft Route, 85, 86–89, 154
Long Lake Trailhead, 207
Longs Peak, 55–57, 164. *See also* East Face; Keyhole Route; Ledges, the
  consequences of bad decisions, 57–62
  deaths on, xi, 2–7, 16–19, 37–39, 40–42, 45–89, 98–102, 249–50
  East Face (*See* East Face)
  as fourteener mountain, x, 16, 47
  hypothermia deaths on, 2–7, 16–21, 37–39, 40–43, 62
  last mile of, 53
  lightning strikes on, 175–77
  popularity of, 52, 90
  routes to the top, 84–86
  safety on, 266–69
  world record for female ascents, 163
Longs Peak Inn, 47, 49, 93, 96, 97, 120
Longs Peak Ranger Station, ix, 40, 105, 109, 267
Lost Lake, 150
Lovett, Norman, 123
Lower East Face, 112
Lower Roaring Fork River Valley, 33
Lumpy Ridge, 143–44, 146, 149

M
Mabon, Corbin, 59–60
MacGregor, Alexander, 174–75
Mack, Jim, 165, 168
Magnificent Mountain Women, The (Robertson), 91
Magnuson, Mark, 112, 228
Magnuson, Ruth, 35–37
Mainburg, John, 12–13
Marshall, Todd, 145–46
Martin, Todd, 167–70
Marx, Ellen, 184–85
Massari, Joe, 164–67
Matthews, Lois Lee, 185–86
May, Everett "Granny," 25
McClannan, Kent, 110–11, 113
McClintock, Brent, 147–48
McConnell, Jack and Thomas, 143–44
McCormick, Wayne, 57–58

ABOUT THE AUTHOR

Randi Minetor is the author of more than sixty books, including *Historic Rocky Mountain National Park*, *Historic Glacier National Park*, and five other books in the "Death in the Parks" series: *Death in Glacier National Park*, *Death in Zion National Park*, *Death on Mount Washington*, *Death on Katahdin*, and *Death in Acadia*. She has also written eight hiking guides to New York State, and she collaborates with her husband, photographer Nic Minetor, on books in FalconGuides' "Birding Field Guides" and "Best Easy Bird Guides" series. The Minetors live in upstate New York.